How to Get Published in the Best Management Journals

'To Penny, my Minerva' (Timothy Clark)

'To the memory of Alison Heaton (née Wright)' (Mike Wright)

'To my mentors and protégés' (David J. Ketchen, Jr.)

How to Get Published in the Best Management Journals

Edited by

Timothy Clark

Professor of Organizational Behaviour, Durham University Business School, UK

Mike Wright

Professor of Entrepreneurship, Imperial College Business School London, UK and University of Ghent, Belgium

David J. Ketchen, Jr.

Lowder Eminent Scholar, Raymond J. Harbert College of Business, Auburn University, USA

Cheltenham, UK • Northampton, MA, USA

Published by
Edward Elgar Publishing Limited
The Lypiatts
15 Lansdown Road
Cheltenham
Glos GL50 2JA
UK

Edward Elgar Publishing, Inc.
William Pratt House
9 Dewey Court
Northampton
Massachusetts 01060
USA

A catalogue record for this book
is available from the British Library

Library of Congress Control Number: 2016931775

This book is available electronically in the **Elgar**online
Business subject collection
DOI 10.4337/9781784714680

ISBN 978 1 78471 467 3 (cased)
ISBN 978 1 78471 468 0 (eBook)

Typeset by Columns Design XML Ltd, Reading
Printed and bound by CPI Group (UK) Ltd, Croydon, CR0 4YY

Contents

Figures

Tables

Contributors

Petra Andries is Assistant Professor of Entrepreneurship and Strategy at Ghent University. She conducts research in the field of entrepreneurship and innovation management. Petra has published in international journals (e.g. *Strategic Entrepreneurship Journal, Journal of Product Innovation Management*, and *Small Business Economics*), on topics including business model development, knowledge management, collaboration, and IP appropriability. She has also provided companies and policy makers with advice in these domains.

Yehuda Baruch is Professor of Management and Research Director at the Management School, University of Southampton. His research focuses on careers and global HRM. He has written 120 refereed papers, over 45 books and book chapters. He is an Associate Editor of *Human Resource Management* (US) and former Editor of *Group and Organization Management* and *Career Development International*.

Donald D. Bergh (Ph.D. Colorado-Boulder) serves as a member of the editorial review boards of *Academy of Management Journal, Strategic Management Journal*, and *Organizational Science* and as an Associate Editor of *Academy of Management Journal, Organizational Research Methods*, and *Journal of Management Studies*. He has written on corporate strategy and research methods topics. He co-edits a research methods book series with David J. Ketchen, Jr.

Sumon Kumar Bhaumik is a Professor of Finance at the Management School of the University of Sheffield and a Research Fellow at IZA (Institute for the Study of Labor), Bonn. He has published in leading journals in economics, management/international business, and finance.

Brian K. Boyd is Head and Chair Professor of Management at the City University of Hong Kong School of Business. He has served multiple terms as Associate and Guest Editor at several journals, and has also received awards for outstanding service to the editorial boards of *Academy of Management Journal* and *Strategic Management Journal*.

M. Ronald Buckley is the JC Penney Company Chair of Business Leadership and a Professor of Management and a Professor of Psychology in the Michael F. Price College of Business at the University of Oklahoma. He took his Ph.D. at Auburn University, mentored by many wonderful, caring, and thoughtful professors who are mentioned in his chapter. To them he owes a great debt! War Damn Eagle!

Pawan Budhwar is Professor of International Human Resource Management at Aston Business School. He has authored/edited 14 books and over 100 refereed journal articles. He is the Co-editor-in-Chief of *British Journal of Management*. He is the Co-founder and First Past President of the Indian Academy of Management. He is a Fellow of the British Academy of Management, the Higher Education Academy, and the Academy of Social Sciences.

Timothy Clark is Professor of Organizational Behaviour at Durham University Business School, UK. He is a former Associate Editor of *Human Relations* and former General Editor of *Journal of Management Studies*. He has served on numerous editorial boards and has been Chair of the Publications Committee of the British Academy of Management.

James G. Combs is the Dr. Phillips Chair of American Private Enterprise at the University of Central Florida. Jim's research interests include franchising, family business, and executive compensation. He has served as Associate Editor at the *Academy of Management Journal*, and is an Editor at *Entrepreneurship Theory and Practice*.

Douglas Cumming, J.D., Ph.D., CFA, is a Professor of Finance and Entrepreneurship and the Ontario Research Chair at the Schulich School of Business, York University. Douglas has published over a dozen books and 125 articles in journals such as the *Academy of Management Journal*, *Journal of Financial Economics*, *Review of Financial Studies*, and *Journal of International Business Studies*.

Saul Estrin is a Professor of Management and was the founding Head of the Department of Management at the London School of Economics. He was formerly a Professor of Economics, and Faculty Dean, at London Business School, where he also served in 2001 as Acting Dean. He held the Adecco Professorship of Business and Society at London Business School.

Gerald R. Ferris is the Francis Eppes Professor of Management, Professor of Psychology, and Professor of Sport Management at Florida State University. He received a Ph.D. in Business Administration from the University of Illinois at Urbana-Champaign. Ferris has research interests in the areas of social influence and effectiveness processes in organizations.

Denny Gioia is the Klein Professor of Management in the Smeal College of Business at Penn State. Previously he worked for Boeing Aerospace at Cape Kennedy during the Apollo program and for Ford as corporate recall coordinator. Current theory/research focuses on the ways in which identity and image relate to sensemaking, sensegiving, and organizational change.

Bill Harley is Professor of Management at the University of Melbourne. His research has been published in journals including *Journal of Management Studies*, the *British Journal of Industrial Relations*, and *Work Employment and Society*. From 2010 to 2015 Bill was Associate Editor/ General Editor of *Journal of Management Studies*.

Michael A. Hitt is a University Distinguished Professor Emeritus at Texas A&M University and a Distinguished Research Fellow at Texas Christian University. He is a former Editor of the *Academy of Management Journal* and *Strategic Entrepreneurship Journal*. He is a Fellow in the Academy of Management and Strategic Management Society and a former President of both organizations.

Gerard P. Hodgkinson is Professor of Strategic Management and Behavioural Science at Warwick Business School, University of Warwick. From 1999 to 2006 he was the Editor-in-Chief of the *British Journal of Management*, and from 2005 to 2016 he co-edited the *International Review of Industrial and Organizational Psychology* (now incorporated as an Annual Review Issue in the *Journal of Organizational Behavior*). He is currently an Associate Editor of the *Journal of Management* and serves on the editorial boards of the *Academy of Management Review* and *Strategic Management Journal*.

R. Duane Ireland is a University Distinguished Professor and holds the Conn Chair in New Ventures Leadership at Texas A&M University. He is a former Editor of the *Academy of Management Journal*, a former President of the Academy of Management, and a Fellow of the Academy of Management and of the Strategic Management Society.

Franz W. Kellermanns is the Addison H. & Gertrude C. Reese Endowed Chair and Professor of Management in the Belk College of Business at the University of North Carolina–Charlotte. He holds a joint appointment with the Center for Family Business at the WHU–Otto Beisheim School of Management (Germany).

David J. Ketchen, Jr. currently serves as Lowder Eminent Scholar and Research Director of the Lowder Center for Family Business and Entrepreneurship at Auburn University. He has served as an Associate Editor for seven scholarly journals and has served as an editorial board member for fourteen journals.

Bruce T. Lamont (Ph.D. University of North Carolina) is the Thomas L. Williams Eminent Scholar in Strategy and Entrepreneurship in the College of Business at Florida State University. His current research addresses the effective management of acquisition integration processes, knowledge investments, and novel applications of theory to the African context.

Aija Leiponen is an Associate Professor with the Dyson School of Applied Economics and Management at Cornell University and with Imperial College Business School (London, UK). Her research in the field of strategy focuses on the impact of inter-organizational cooperation on innovation in digital industries. She is a Co-editor for media innovations of the Strategic Management Society.

Ben R. Martin is Professor of Science and Technology Policy Studies at SPRU, where he was formerly Director. He has carried out research for over 30 years on science policy, establishing techniques for evaluating scientific research and pioneering 'technology foresight'. Since 2004, he has been Editor of *Research Policy*.

Will Mitchell is the Anthony S. Fell Chair in New Technologies and Commercialization at the Rotman School of Management of the University of Toronto. He publishes actively in the strategy field, with an emphasis on business dynamics in developed and emerging markets, and teaches courses on related strategy topics in degree and executive programs. He is a Co-editor for on-line media of the Strategic Management Society.

Torben Pedersen is a Professor at Bocconi University, Italy. His research interests are mainly on globalization, organizational design, offshoring/outsourcing, knowledge management, and subsidiary strategies. He has published more than 100 journal articles and books on these topics and is Co-editor of the *Global Strategy Journal.*

Pamela L. Perrewé is the Haywood and Betty Taylor Eminent Scholar of Business Administration and Distinguished Research Professor at Florida State University. Her research interests are in job stress, political skill, self-regulation, and personality. She is the Lead Editor of *Research in Occupational Stress and Well Being* by Emerald Publishing.

Annette L. Ranft (B.S., Appalachian State University; M.S., Georgia Tech; Ph.D., UNC-Chapel Hill) is the Stephen P. Zelnak Dean and Professor of Management in the Poole College of Management at North Carolina State University. She has served as an Associate Editor of the *Journal of Management* and on numerous editorial boards of top journals.

Philip L. Roth is a Professor of Management at Clemson University (Ph.D., University of Houston). Phil's interests involve employee selection and meta-analysis. He is a Fellow of SIOP. He served as Chair of the Research Methods Division and representative for the Human Resources Division of the Academy of Management.

Anne D. Smith (B.S., McIntire School of Commerce, University of Virginia; MBA, Ph.D., UNC-Chapel Hill) is the Department Head, Professor of Management, and the Flaskerud Professor in Business at the Haslam College of Business, University of Tennessee, Knoxville. She is currently an Associate Editor at *Organizational Research Methods*, primarily handling qualitative submissions.

Charles C. Snow is Professor Emeritus of Strategy and Organization at The Pennsylvania State University. He is a Fellow of the Academy of Management, a Founding Member of the Organizational Design Community, and the Founding Co-editor of the *Journal of Organization Design*.

William H. Starbuck is a Visiting Professor at University of Oregon and Professor Emeritus at New York University. He edited *Administrative Science Quarterly*, chaired the screening committee for the Fulbright awards in business management, and was President of the Academy of Management. His research interests include research methodology, innovation, and societal trends.

Wayne H. Stewart, Jr. is Professor of Management at Clemson University (Ph.D., University of North Texas). His research interests entail themes of uncertainty and change, including individual and team issues in entrepreneurship, and managing flexibility and adaptability for organizational rejuvenation, particularly in transition contexts.

Stephen Tallman is the E. Claiborne Robins Distinguished Professor of Business at the University of Richmond in the United States. He is the founder and Co-editor of *Global Strategy Journal*. His research interests include global strategies, international alliances and joint ventures, industry clusters, and knowledge management in the multinational firm.

Steven Toms is Professor of Accounting at Leeds University Business School. His research interests cover accounting, accountability, performance measurement, and corporate governance from a historical perspective. He specializes in cotton and textile history from the industrial revolution to the present day. He was Editor of *Business History*, 2007–2013.

Rolf van Dick is Professor of Social Psychology at Goethe University. After his Ph.D. at Marburg University, he worked at Aston Business School. He was Visiting Professor in the US, Greece, and Nepal and served as Editor of the *British Journal of Management* and the *Journal of Personnel Psychology*.

Geoffrey Wood is Dean and Professor of International Business at Essex Business School. He has authored/co-authored/edited 12 books, and over 120 articles in peer-reviewed journals. He is Editor-in-Chief of the *British Journal of Management* and also serves on the BAM Council. He is also Editor of the ABS Journal Ranking List.

Mike Wright is Professor of Entrepreneurship, Director of the Centre for Management Buyout Research at Imperial College Business School, and Visiting Professor at the University of Ghent. He is Co-editor of *Strategic Entrepreneurship Journal* and of *Academy of Management Perspectives* and was formerly a General Editor of *Journal of Management Studies*.

Daphne W. Yiu is an Associate Professor at the Chinese University of Hong Kong. Her research interests lie in strategies and governance in emerging markets and Asia. She served as the President of Asia Academy of Management, and is a Senior Editor at *Asia Pacific Journal of Management* and *Journal of World Business*.

1. Publishing in management – exhilaration, bafflement and frustration

Timothy Clark, Mike Wright and David J. Ketchen, Jr.

This book offers a series of chapters intended to help demystify the journal publishing process. The chapters provide practical advice on a wide range of important topics. A quick look at the table of contents reveals that our author list contains leading academics in the management discipline. You may wonder why these very busy and experienced people have taken the time to share their thoughts on the publication process. Simply put, because advancing knowledge by publishing in leading journals is at the heart of the academic enterprise. Promotion systems for academics in management in universities around the world stress the significance of an individual scholar's contribution based on her/his published work, primarily in journals. Thus, career advancement, scholarly reputation and pay are intimately tied to being able to publish in journals.

Scholars find the journal publishing process exhilarating, baffling and frustrating in equal measure. The professional joy and excitement of receiving an acceptance letter following a long-drawn-out process in which you have diligently responded to successive rounds of reviewers' comments is probably only matched by a letter awarding a research grant. Contrast this to the sense of dejection and distress that accompanies a rejection letter. This is further exacerbated if the reviewers' comments and decision appear to be harsh and make little sense. It is even more disappointing if the paper appears to have been progressing through different rounds of reviewing only to be rejected late in the process. One has to start all over again. Whether we realize it or not, academics are not too dissimilar to actors in that they constantly have to audition their work in journals or to research funders. Learning to live with rejection is a key part of the role. We cannot be successful with every submission.

Even though the chances of acceptance are reducing to well below 10 per cent in many leading journals in the discipline, there is increasing pressure on academics to publish in journals, and in what are considered to be the 'right' journals in particular. While individual departments and schools have had internal 'private' journals lists for many years to aid colleagues' decisions when submitting work and to aid assessments of quality at the point of recruitment or promotion, a number of 'public' national and international journals lists have gained prominence in recent years. These have increasingly replaced the Business and Management journal rankings produced by services such as the Web of Science™.

In the United Kingdom, the Chartered Association of Business Schools created the 'Academic Journal Guide' in 2015 building on the 'The ABS Guide 2010'. This ranked 1,401 journals across five categories ranging from 4* (journals of 'distinction') to 1 (journals of 'modest standard'). Since 2007, the Australian Business Deans Council has produced successive iterations of its 'Journal Quality List'. The latest version encompassed 2,767 journals and rated them A* to C. In France, Centre National de la Recherche Scientifique (CNRS) has produced a 'Journal Ranking in Economics and Management' since 2004. This ranks journals from 1 ('distinguished') to 4 ('low selectivity'). In 2008, the European Science Foundation developed an 'initial' journal list for humanities – the European Reference Index for the Humanities (ERIH). Now run by the Norwegian Social Science Data Services (NSD), this was relaunched in 2014 as ERIH PLUS and has been extended to include the social sciences. Although not an evaluative ranking service, journals are included in accordance with published criteria. The main aims of this initiative are to 'enhance the global visibility of high-quality research in the humanities and social sciences across Europe, and to facilitate access to research journals published in all European languages'. Finally, several trade publishers have produced journal lists as part of the intellectual capital or research scores in their MBA rankings. The most prominent are the lists used by *Bloomberg Businessweek* and the *Financial Times*.

Given that several of these lists contribute to the rankings of business schools, they have a significant influence on the perceptions of reputations of schools and so impact on the scholars whose published work in these journals undergirds their rankings. As two of the editors of this volume noted in an editorial for the *Journal of Management Studies* (Clark and Wright, 2007, p. 613),

Whereas the ranking of journals in which people publish has always had implications for personal reputation, peer recognition and career advancement, increasingly it is impacting much more directly on institutional reputations and department rankings and in turn on access to resources and potential recruitment of staff and students. Individual publication choices and success are therefore assuming ever greater institutional significance.

To manage institutional reputations, individual business schools are increasingly abandoning their own lists and adopting those mentioned above. As a consequence, scholars in different business schools are being encouraged to submit only to those journals which are more highly ranked on these lists. It comes as no surprise that submission rates, desk rejection rates (i.e., rejection by the editors prior to seeking reviewer comments) and overall rejection rates in 'top tier' journals have increased (Judge, Cable, Colbert and Rynes, 2007, p. 501; Monastersky, 2005). Indeed, we have experienced such trends during our tenures as editors of different journals with submission rates increasing significantly, desk rejection rates creeping to over 50 per cent and general acceptance rates dropping to well below 10 per cent (see, for example, Clark and Wright, 2007).

Although we lack the hard data needed to draw a firm conclusion, our observation when acting as journal editors over the past couple of decades is that landing reviewers who are bona fide experts on a journal submission's topic has become increasingly difficult across time. Leading journals are attracting more and more submissions every year while the pool of available expert reviewers appears to be increasing only slightly, if at all. This has created a basic supply–demand imbalance that does not work in authors' favour. One potential result is that any given submission may not be receiving the same calibre of expert vetting as it would have in years past. Relative to ten or twenty years ago, a paper that you submit today may be assigned to reviewers who are much less experienced and who know far less about your specific topic.

Beyond this systemic macro trend, a quick immersion into the voluminous literature on the peer-review process indicates that there are a number of failings that either individually or in combination may prevent or forestall innovative material from being published in highly regarded journals. In a seminal study on peer review, Peters and Ceci (1982) resubmitted 12 articles to the psychology journals in which they had already been refereed and published 18 to 32 months earlier. To disguise the papers a number of 'cosmetic' alterations were made to the titles, abstracts and opening paragraphs in the introduction, but their 'meaning was not changed'. In addition, 'fictitious' names for authors and institutional affiliations were used. Nine of the manuscripts were sent out for review (three were detected). Only two of the eighteen reviewers recommended that the papers be accepted. Hence, only one article was accepted with the consequence that one journal made an identical evaluation over the two periods of time. This article generated a voluminous response (over 70 commentaries in the same issue) and provoked heated discussion across different disciplines as to the ability of the review process to determine the level of quality, interestingness, contribution and likely impact of an article under consideration (see, for example, Bedeian, 2003; Campanario, 1998; Miller, 2006; Osterloh and Frey, 2015; Starbuck, 2003, 2005). Given the critical weaknesses in the review process, it has been questioned by a range of commentators whether superior quality work is published in journals as a consequence of reviewers' comments and therefore whether the most able scholars are being hired and promoted on the basis of such published work. This literature highlights three general flaws in the journal review process.

First, reviewers are often accused of being overly harsh in their judgements. They approach manuscripts assiduously looking to expose weaknesses rather than balancing these with an equivalent appreciation of the merits. In a system where the work of others is evaluated anonymously, the incentives to be constructive and polite may lessen. People may communicate more bluntly than they would face-to-face.

Furthermore, reviews are solicited from people who are invariably busy and have simply added a further task to their already over-committed diaries. In these circumstances, reviewers may adopt a shorthand approach in which they prioritize the finding of faults and weaknesses rather engaging positively with the ideas, arguments and evidence in the paper from the author's point of view. In addition, as Starbuck (2003) suggests, this approach may in part arise from reviewers seeing themselves as superior to the authors (in their role as reviewers). He comments: 'Occasionally reviewers seem arrogant, disrespectful, even nasty' (p. 344). They believe they know better than the authors and could write a better article. They therefore often see their role as telling the author to write the paper they would write. This can lead to a situation where authors feel their ideas are unappreciated, undervalued and ignored.

Managing reviewers is a key task that falls to editors. In our experience, there are three basic approaches that editors take to this task. 'Posties' (or, in US terminology, 'mail carriers') simply collect the reviews, add little independent thought or synthesis of reviewers' ideas, pass along reviews to the authors and accept a paper only if the reviewers say to do so. Editors abdicating their authority in this way can be very harmful to authors. For example, authors may feel that they are being forced to write the paper the reviewers want them to write or responding to points that are superficial, misguided or just wrong. In these circumstances, reviewers may become uninvited ghost-writers and/or veto wielders.

In a recent baffling case, a revision of a conceptual paper was rejected without all of the reviews being received. One reviewer recommended acceptance with no further revisions, a second reviewer vehemently opposed the paper, and the third reviewer was not sent the revision due to an administrative glitch. The action editor based his decision on the fact that the negative reviewer 'was extremely forceful' in his/her comments. After it became known that the third reviewer was not given the opportunity to participate, the action editor refused the authors' request to collect the third review and then revisit his decision. Worse, in the first round of review, the decision letter had been written based on the first two reviews and the third review was sent to the authors about a week later with no effort to reconcile important discrepancies between it and the other reviews. Sure enough, some of the very negative reviewer's key concerns about the revision revolved around material that was added to the paper in order to respond to the third reviewer. Although most 'postie editors' are not as callow and impotent as this one, the anecdote illustrates the danger of allowing reviewers to dominate decision making in the review process.

A much different approach is adopted by 'emperors'. These editors downplay or even disregard the reviews; only their opinions matters, even if they know little about the subject matter. Luckily, these people are few and far between. Like the emperor in Hans Christian Andersen's legendary fable, however, they resist being told that they have 'no clothes'.

Lastly, 'judges' live by the mantra that reviewers review and editors decide. They gather relevant evidence by reading the paper and studying the reviews, analyse the evidence, and make informed decisions. When revision opportunities are granted, judges synthesize reviewers' input in their decision letters in order to give authors the best opportunity to succeed. Importantly, judges are not afraid to contradict a reviewer within the effort to advance the state of research knowledge. Some editors of this type emphasize that reviewers must 'step into the framework of the authors when evaluating a paper, rather than imposing their preferred framework or perspective on those authors (and thereby asking the authors to write the reviewer's preferred paper)' (Miller and Van de Ven, 2015, p. 118; see also Clair, 2015).

Second,[1] as Peters and Ceci (1982) suggest, a number of factors have been found to bias reviewer judgements (see Campanario [1998] for a full review). Where authors' identities are known, their institutional affiliations and social networks may influence judgements. However, these factors are reduced when a blind review process is used, although not eradicated because with the Internet and electronic dissemination of manuscripts an author's identity is very difficult to hide (see Hillman and Rynes, 2007). Here issues such as the apparent complexity of language, use of citations, appropriate jargon, sophisticated statistical procedures, and presentation of positive and significant results that do not merely replicate previous findings have all been found to influence or bias decisions.

Third, and perhaps the area which has received greatest empirical attention, studies in a range of disciplines have consistently reported low overall inter-referee agreement (see Hendrick, 1977; Gottfredson, 1978; Scott, 1974; Cicchetti, 1980, 1991; Scar and Weber, 1978). Evidence within management studies is more scant. Starbuck (2003) reports a study he undertook while editor of *Administrative Science Quarterly*. An examination of 500 pairs of reviews revealed a correlation of 0.12. He concluded that 'It was so low that knowing what one reviewer had said about a manuscript would tell me almost nothing about what a second reviewer had said or would say' (p. 346).

Given this context, authors need to take every step they can within the confines of professionalism and ethics to maximize their submission's chance of success. Accordingly, this book's chapters are intended to provide actionable advice that authors can leverage. Lest our thoughts in this brief introduction be taken as overly pessimistic, we want to stress that we have found the research process to be personally and professionally fulfilling, as have the authors who have contributed to this book. Our hope is that each reader will find one or more tips in the chapters that follow that resonate, will act on these tips, and will be better able to place research papers in our discipline's leading journals.

We have structured the book in three parts. The book can, of course, be read in its entirety, but many readers may prefer to dip into various topics to suit their particular needs. Part I contains general contributions on important aspects of the publishing process. We start in Chapter 2 with an in-depth case study of a paper travelling through the review process which includes the perspectives of the authors, the editor and the reviewers. This chapter sets the scene for the remainder of the book and is followed by a chapter that examines the range of issues arising at different stages in the journal submission and review processes (Chapter 3). Ethics and integrity in academic research has always been important, but it has taken on particular significance in recent years. Accordingly, we devote Chapter 4 specifically to this topic. As academic careers are not just about getting that first job and then achieving tenure but are also about sustaining publications in the long run, Chapter 5 outlines some strategies for achieving this. Increasingly, the focus of attention is on publishing in leading international journals, which are oftentimes US based. However, as Chapter 6 shows, using the example of Asia, other contexts can provide opportunities to publish quality research. This chapter discusses the similarities and differences in publishing Asian research in Asia management journals as compared to those in North America. The final chapter in Part I presents insights into the deficiencies of the review process and how authors should consider and approach feedback from reviewers.

Part II contains short contributions on specific topics essential to resolving practical key issues in undertaking good research and the preparation of publishable manuscripts. We have organized this part into four sections relating to Becoming a Scholar (Chapters 8–12), Getting Your Methods Right (Chapters 13–15), Navigating the Review Process (Chapters 16–18) and Understanding the Journals (Chapters 19–25). In soliciting these chapters, we encouraged authors to draw on their considerable experience as authors, editors and reviewers to share candid confidences that readers might not pick up anywhere else. They fully embraced this charge and we have picked up some great 'behind the curtain' tips while editing their chapters.

Part III (Chapters 26–32) contains contributions that address publishing across disciplinary boundaries. This part delves into the challenges of publishing in journals for scholars from other related disciplines including business history, economics, finance, human resource management, international business and psychology, and also for management scholars seeking to publish their work in journals in these areas. Each author presents insights regarding key issues of difference in the positioning of papers, use and development of theory, data and methods, analysis and discussion of findings, and contribution. The authors also identify differences in the review process between management journals and these other areas and provide specific examples from their own experience.

Finally, we thank all our contributors for the fascinating insights they have provided on publishing in management journals.

NOTE

1. This and the next paragraph are replicated with permission from Clark and Wright (2007).

REFERENCES

Bedeian, A.C. (2003). 'The manuscript review process: The proper role of authors, referees, and editors', *Journal of Management Inquiry*, **12**, 331–338.

Campanario, J. (1998). 'Peer review for journals as it stands today – Part 1', *Science Communication*, **19**, 181–211.

Cicchetti, D. (1980). 'Reliability of reviews for the *American Psychologist*: A biostatistical assessment of the data', *American Psychologist*, **35**, 300–303.

Cicchetti, D. (1991). 'The reliability of peer review for manuscript and grant submission: A cross-disciplinary investigation', *Behavioral and Brain Sciences*, **14**, 119–186.

Clair, J.A. (2015). 'Toward a Bill of Rights for manuscript submitters', *Academy of Management Learning and Education*, **14** (1), 111–131.

Clark, T. and M. Wright (2007). 'Reviewing journal rankings and revisiting peer reviews: Editorial perspectives', *Journal of Management Studies*, **44**, 612–621.

Gottfredson, S. (1978). 'Evaluating psychological research reports: Dimensions, reliability and correlates of quality judgements', *American Psychologist*, **33**, 920–934.

Hendrick, C. (1977). 'Editorial comment', *Personality and Social Psychology Bulletin*, **3**, 1–2.

Hillman, A. and S. Rynes (2007). 'The future of double-blind review in management', *Journal of Management Studies*, **44**, 622–627.

Judge, T.A., D.M. Cable, A.E Colbert and S.L. Rynes (2007). 'What causes a management article to be cited: Article, author, or journal?', *Academy of Management Journal*, **50**, 491–506.

Miller, C.C. (2006). 'Peer review in the organizational and management sciences: Prevalence and effects of reviewer hostility, bias and dissensus', *Academy of Management Journal*, **49**, 425–431.

Miller, C.C. and A.H. Van de Ven (2015). 'Peer review, root canals, and other amazing life events', *Academy of Management Discoveries*, **1** (2), 117–123.

Monastersky, R. (2005). 'The number that's devouring science', *Chronicle of Higher Education*, **52** (8), A12, http://chronicle.com/free/v52/i08/08a01201.htm (accessed 2 December 2015).

Osterloh, M. and B.S. Frey (2015). 'Ranking games', *Evaluation Review*, **39** (1), 102–129.

Peters, D. and S. Ceci (1982). 'Peer-review practices of psychological journals: The fate of published articles, submitted again', *Behavioral and Brain Sciences*, **5**, 187–255.

Scar, S. and B. Weber (1978). 'The reliability of reviews for the *American Psychologist*', *American Psychologist*, **33**, 935.

Scott, W. (1974). 'Interreferee agreement on some characteristics of manuscripts submitted to the *Journal of Personality and Social Psychology*', *American Psychologist*, **29**, 698–792.

Starbuck, W. (2003). 'Turning lemons into lemonade: Where is the value in peer review?', *Journal of Management Inquiry*, **12**, 344–351.

Starbuck, W.H. (2005). 'How much better are the most prestigious journals? The statistics of academic publication', *Organization Science*, **16**, 180–200.

PART I

The publishing process

2. The publishing process: a case study

Petra Andries and Mike Wright

INTRODUCTION

As we have seen in Chapter 1, the review process can be quite lengthy and involve major changes to all aspects of a paper. As authors, Reviewers and editors on a paper we tend to only see our side of the process, or at best have a partial view of the other parties' perspective through decision letters and authors' responses. In this chapter we use a case study of a paper passing through the review process to interweave these different perspectives. One of us, Petra, was lead author on the paper, while the other, Mike, was the action editor. We present the process in the form of a first person dialogue between us, interspersed with the comments from the Reviewers. We conclude with some general reflections for the publishing process.

BACKGROUND TO THE PAPER

Petra: As a new doctoral student, I interviewed several founders of technology-based ventures. I asked them what decisions were keeping them awake at night. Besides the question of whether and when to go global, another important issue emerged, namely the majority of these entrepreneurs were not sure how to develop their technologies into viable business models. They were faced with not only significant levels of technological uncertainty, but also with major market uncertainties. Overall, they stated that they did not have any insights or guidelines on how to create, deliver and capture value from their technologies. Studying the literature, I found out that two possible approaches to business model development under such uncertainty were advanced, namely focused commitment and sequential experimentation, but that little empirical evidence was available on how to implement these approaches, or on their usefulness. Given this gap in the literature, and the clear need of practitioners for more insights, I decided to dedicate my doctorate to the topic of business model development in highly uncertain contexts.

THE INITIAL SUBMISSION

Petra: In December 2009, together with co-authors Koenraad Debackere and Bart van Looy, we submitted the paper to *Strategic Entrepreneurship Journal* (SEJ). Although the journal was fairly new, it clearly had the aspiration and potential to become a top journal in the field of entrepreneurship, and we believed that both contentwise and methodologically our paper could fit in this outlet. The paper, which was at that point in time titled 'Simultaneous experimentation as an entrepreneurial strategy for emergent markets: transcending the trade-off between flexibility and funding?', started from the observation that defining a viable business model in emerging, uncertain industries is difficult and that the approaches advanced in the available literature have their limitations. On the one hand, a dedicated focus on one specific business model allows for attracting resources and realizing first mover advantages, but hinders flexibility. On the other hand, sequential experimentation financed through bootstrapping allows for flexible business model adaptation but imposes resource constraints. As new ventures would benefit from both resources and flexibility, the main purpose of the paper was to investigate whether and how ventures in emerging industries characterized by uncertainty could balance the attainment of financial resources with flexibility when developing their business models.

The paper combined two different methods in order to research this issue. In the first part of the paper, we used six in-depth case studies, identifying two approaches to business model development and mapping the rationale and consequences of both approaches in terms of flexibility and resource acquisitions. The main contribution of the initial submission was in the identification of 'simultaneous experimentation' as an approach to business model development (see also the abstract of the initial paper in the Appendix). This approach had not been previously identified in the literature and had the potential to enable both resource acquisition and flexibility. The second part of the paper consisted of an analytical model comparing the expected profits of different approaches, suggesting that in emerging industries characterized by uncertainty, simultaneous experimentation is more appropriate than focused commitment.

Mike: At the time I was an associate editor of SEJ. When the co-editors assigned me the role of action editor for the paper, I realized that I needed Reviewers that could evaluate both the qualitative and the analytical part of the paper. SEJ's policy is to have two Reviewers. I decided to contact one case study expert (Reviewer 1), as well as one expert in analytical modelling who had at the same time an open mind to alternative research methods (Reviewer 2). I selected the particular Reviewers based on my tacit knowledge, built up over time as both an editor and a researcher, of who was active in these areas and likely to prove a good Reviewer.

ROUND ONE

Mike: When the reviews came back in March 2010, I immediately noticed that the Reviewers differed in their appreciation and commenting of the paper. Reviewer 1 was encouraging about the paper's potential in terms of topic and qualitative approach but questioned if the authors could deliver. A first main concern regarded the coding of the business model changes, where the Reviewer pointed to a disconnect between the conceptual framework used and the actual coding. Secondly, s/he truly disliked the analytical part of the paper, arguing that this type of modelling is in general uninteresting and lacks managerial relevance.

> **Reviewer 1:** I don't mean to be impertinent, but such an approach epitomizes what's wrong with management research. No manager would ever take this seriously – there is no face validity to the analysis, nor is there relevance to the framework. These attempts – and yours is just the one in front of me – reflect a physics envy that has led to the irrelevance of management science anywhere outside our little academy.

Mike: Reviewer 2 on the other hand found the mixed methods interesting, but thought the analytical model was flawed and needed better justification.

> **Reviewer 2:** The manuscript is well written. The topic is interesting. I especially appreciate the use of a multi-method approach. My main concern is regarding the limitations of the analytical framework (and hence its contributions and implications).

Mike: Despite the criticisms, the Reviewer was very constructive in his/her feedback, providing several suggestions for improving the analytical model. In his/her review of the analytical model, the Reviewer also questioned the logic of the paper, and more precisely the relevance of the 'resource acquisition' concept for the development of the paper as a whole:

Reviewer 2: The front end of the paper offers the notion of 'acquiring financial resources' (and related concepts of flexibility and commitment towards investors) when arguing about the type of business model approach (focused versus unfocused). However, the analytical development appears disconnected from the acquisition of financial resources. [...] Again, the discussion on funding acquisition seems to be a distraction. As far as I can tell, this work is about two types of business model development, and that is it.

Mike: Authors perhaps do not realize, but Reviewers frequently disagree in their comments on papers. The Reviewers on this paper had particularly notable differing views on some aspects. In particular, as the Reviewers took different positions with respect to the analytical model, I provided guidance in my correspondence with the authors. I supported the suggestion of Reviewer 1 to drop the analytical model from the paper. My reasoning here was based on the disconnect between the analytical model and the front end of the paper, as identified by Reviewer 2. It seemed to me that to pursue the development of the model along the lines of Reviewer 2 would take the paper in a different direction away from the novelty of the fieldwork.

Petra: The fact that the editor clearly took a position was of course of great help to us as we were confronted with two opposing reviews. We decided to drop the analytical model completely and explain in our reply to Reviewer 2 that this decision was following suggestions by Reviewer 1 and by the editor. However, two important issues remained. Firstly, we decided to completely redo the coding of the business model changes, following closely the conceptual framework used in the paper. The analyses based on this new coding did not lead to different results. Secondly, a decision had to be made regarding the notion of 'resource acquisition' and, as a consequence, also regarding the notion of 'flexibility'. A first option was to abstain from discussing these notions in the introduction section and to no longer use them for demonstrating the disadvantages of focused commitment and sequential experimentation. The main research question would then simply be what kinds of approaches to business model development existed. Afraid that this would significantly reduce the contribution of the paper, we instead decided to rewrite the introduction section explaining in greater detail that the resource acquisition problem related to experimentation called for further research. It took us several months to implement these changes, and we resubmitted the paper in July 2010.

ROUND TWO

Mike: I sent the revised paper back to the same Reviewers. When I received their reports, I was confronted with even more diverging reviews, which were emphasized in their confidential comments to me. Reviewer 1 was very positive while Reviewer 2, on the other hand, was disappointed with the turn the paper had taken.

> **Reviewer 1:** The paper has potential to be outstanding with some editing. They are very close. […] I would be willing to let this go without seeing it again. […] So few longitudinal papers of this magnitude ever make it through the review process, and this one holds important insights into entrepreneurial organizing and methods.

> **Reviewer 2:** In the first version I especially appreciated the use of a multi-method approach. Now that it is no longer the case (i.e. the analytical model has been removed), the work is not as rigorous.

Mike: In comments to the authors, Reviewer 2 repeated that s/he still saw a disconnection between the external financing discussions and the approaches to business model development, and raised doubts about the appropriateness of one specific case study. My view was that the authors were making progress and that they should be encouraged in the direction they were taking. It did not seem to me that reintroducing the analytical model would add novelty to the paper's contribution. Reviewer 1 raised a number of smaller issues that were easy to deal with, and that pertained mostly to the way the literature section was organized and to the presentation of the results in figures and tables. In addition to these comments, in my decision letter giving the authors the opportunity for a further major revise and resubmit, I asked them to bring out their contribution more clearly, stating:

> **Editor:** From my own reading of the paper, I think you need to do the following to bring this out. First, you need to strengthen the research gap and your contribution to addressing it in the Introduction. For example, a short paragraph in the Introduction would help to sharpen this. Second, it would help to encapsulate your theoretical contribution if you were to develop some testable propositions. At present, it is a bit too general. Third, in the Concluding section, you should again stress your contribution.

Petra: In our reaction to this second round of reviews, which we received in October 2010, we made several changes to the paper. Firstly, we made another attempt at better explaining the research gap and contribution by expanding the introduction section. Secondly, we again added more information on the case study selection and on the period documented for each case. Thirdly, we provided much more textual information and tables on different steps of the analyses. All these changes significantly increased the length of the paper. Finally, we debated among ourselves on the development of testable propositions. We found it difficult to develop testable propositions that logically resulted from the qualitative analysis, and as a support for one of the five propositions we developed, we reintroduced the analytical model in an appendix and resubmitted the paper in June 2011.

ROUND THREE

Mike: I again sent the paper back to the same Reviewers. When the Reviewers read this second revision of the paper, they reacted very differently. Reviewer 1 expressed his/her appreciation of the work that had been put into the revisions and wrote in the confidential comments to me that s/he 'loved' the paper and that s/he would accept it without any further changes. Reviewer 2, however, was still very negative about the paper, but admitted at the same time that s/he was not an expert in qualitative research:

> **Reviewer 2:** I am afraid I cannot upgrade from the previous two rounds of reviews. Please note, however, that I am not an expert on case study analysis, which I now view as this manuscript's main research approach (the formal model has become a distraction that can be removed).

Mike: At this point, it was clear to me that, if I gave the authors another chance, there was no use in going back to the Reviewers given these comments. I prioritized Reviewer 1's assessment over Reviewer 2's. The paper was now more squarely in Reviewer 1's domain of expertise while this was not the case for Reviewer 2. Instead, I would have to guide the authors myself. Based on my own reading, I therefore communicated to the authors my own main concerns about the paper. Firstly, I asked for additional clarification on the case study selection:

> **Editor:** You also need to say more about [...] why you only looked at emergent industries and not a 'control' group of non-emergent industries/ firms, why six was an appropriate number of firms – while you go for maximum variation, why is this more appropriate for the approach you are adopting than looking for 'extreme cases' (Eisenhardt)? You say very little about your interviews – with whom? When? How many? How long? How many times? Etc.

Secondly, I again urged the authors to drop the analytical model and to rephrase the propositions so they could be tested empirically. I also requested them to demonstrate more clearly how the propositions were derived from the case study evidence and how they fit together. This is a very important issue in helping to make a coherent conceptual contribution in qualitative papers; at this point the propositions were rather ad hoc. I stressed that a clear conceptual framework could help in this respect, and this would also allow the contribution of the paper to be brought out. I suggested that the effectuation literature could be an option. Finally, I asked for more information on the coding of business model changes. Whereas the paper at that time coded business model changes, the coding did not distinguish between tweaks to the initial business model or the development of a completely new one.

Petra: Overall, this new round of reviews was quite a disappointment for us as authors. It was September 2011, we had now been in the review process for almost two years, and had in this period recoded all the data and rewritten practically every single part of the paper. Nevertheless, the same comments kept coming back. As a result, the momentum was a bit lost at this point, resulting in rather fruitless discussions among us as authors on how to revise the paper.

As I had no more ideas left on how to deal with the comments that had been raised before, I decided to tackle the one new issue that the editor had raised, namely the distinction between incremental and radical business model changes. I added an additional layer of coding to the cases, which resulted in new and very interesting insights. It turned out that the ventures using simultaneous experimentation developed a portfolio of experiments, in which each experiment was closely related to another experiment in the portfolio. However, by developing a portfolio of such related experiments, they actually generated a highly diverse set of business model experiments. This finding was novel and conceptually important, since it went against the common assumption in the organizational learning literature that only distant search (i.e. experimentation with unrelated business models) would generate variety. This was a key turning point in the development of the paper. Not only did it solve the editor's rather practical concern about the coding, it also made it clear to us that the right way forward was to position the paper in the organizational learning literature rather than the effectuation literature that the editor had initially suggested. The funny thing was that the organizational learning literature stream had a central role in my doctoral dissertation, but that we had failed to see its relevance for this particular paper. It was as if all the pieces were finally falling in place.

By adding this additional layer of analysis, the paper made a much larger contribution. Also, from the analyses, it became much easier to develop interesting and testable propositions. And the use of organizational learning theory as a conceptual framework suddenly made writing it all up and bringing out the contribution more simple. We did not need the resource acquisition notion any more, and neither did we need the analytical model. The case study analyses, with this new layer, findings and conceptual framework, could stand on its own. We re-submitted the new version in March 2012.

ROUNDS FOUR AND FIVE TO THE FINISHING LINE

Petra: Once we had made the above turn, we had little difficulty encompassing the remaining comments that followed in the final two review rounds, and that related mainly to the presentation of the data and analyses and to the drastic shortening of the paper. In line with the editor's suggestion, the propositions were once more rephrased in a more symmetric way, with comparable propositions formulated for both identified approaches to business model development.

Mike: Although the authors had introduced the propositions, I felt that I needed to push them a bit more in these last rounds to polish the elegance of the propositions so that the novelty of the conceptual contribution would be much clearer and more coherent. This can take more than one iteration to achieve, but it is worth doing as the paper is more likely to get cited. The other issue, again very common as a paper goes through multiple rounds, is the need to reduce its length. This could be, and was, achieved without loss of content by dropping superfluous references, tables and figures, as well as wordsmithing the paper.

The paper was accepted in July 2012, 31 months after submission, and was eventually published as Petra Andries, Koenraad Debackere and Bart van Looy (2013), 'Simultaneous experimentation as a learning strategy: business model development under uncertainty', *Strategic Entrepreneurship Journal*, 7(4): 288–310. The abstract of the final paper can be found in the Appendix.

LOOKING BACK: REFLECTIONS FOR THE PUBLISHING PROCESS

Some summary reflections on the insights we gained from the review process are shown in Table 2.1.

Table 2.1   Summary insights from the review process

	Editor's perspective	Author's perspective
For authors	Persistence and tenacity is important.	Don't be afraid to write the paper as it really evolved. If some concepts emerged from the analyses, then it is fine to show that.
	Need to let go of cherished material.	Think thoroughly about case study selection. It is a crucial decision that is difficult to change afterwards.
	Spend time pre-submission on focusing and framing the paper.	Need to manage author tensions on how to revise the paper. Undertake concrete actions to move forward instead of having fruitless discussions.
	Take especial care in addressing both Reviewers when they are split, and to avoid losing the more positive one in dealing with negative ones.	Take each Reviewer comment seriously. Acknowledge the shortcomings of the paper.
	There is a need to show significant improvements across review rounds.	Follow editors' and Reviewers' suggestions for improvement, unless you are convinced that there are better ways of solving the problem.
For editors	As there are not many great papers out there, editors need to be aware of diamonds in the rough and work with authors.	Pointing out the flaws in a paper is important, but providing constructive suggestions for improving it is even more valuable.
	Editors need to provide clear guidance to authors in case of split Reviewers. This guidance may well go beyond Reviewer comments.	Try to work with Reviewers that remain polite. Even authors of lower quality papers have most probably gone through a great deal of effort to develop them and deserve a minimal level of courtesy and respect.

Mike: Looking back on this lengthy submission and review process, it seemed to me that the paper was a diamond in the rough that took some time to bring out. In my view, it is not unusual for it to take some time to demonstrate convincingly how novel propositions arise from the data. Despite the Reviewers' comments it seemed to take some time for the authors to drop their model and the quantitative material. This may have been because of their search for the way forward but usually I'd expect authors to follow a recommendation and let go. The material on the case selection also took a little time to polish and I would suggest that it is important for qualitative researchers to pay particular attention to this issue at the outset. The good thing, and the reason why I continued through so many revision rounds, is that the authors showed significant progress in every round. As an editor, I really like to work with others and help them move their paper forward.

Petra: I've learned a lot from this review process. Firstly, I think we made the process unnecessarily difficult for ourselves by explicitly positioning the paper with respect to resource constraints and flexibility. We were afraid that simply asking what kinds of approaches to business model development existed would be insufficient for capturing the reader's interest. Therefore, we had added the discussion on resource acquisition and flexibility to the front end of the paper, although these concepts actually emerged from the case study analyses. I learned that it is not necessary to write up a qualitative paper as if all the central constructs were known beforehand. It is fine to show how the insights really emerged, with some constructs coming from the literature, and others emerging from the case study analyses. Also, the multiple comments and questions on the cases we selected have made me much more aware of the importance of a well-thought-out approach to case study selection.

As for working with co-authors, this lengthy revision process taught me that, in times of tension over how to revise the paper, it is better to focus on concrete actions, such as additional analyses requested by the Reviewers. Tackling the practical issues first can provide new insights that allow you to move forward with other comments without getting stuck in fruitless discussion among co-authors.

Furthermore, I have learned a lot about the willingness of some Reviewers and editors to help anonymous colleagues in improving their work. In review processes of other papers, I was at times shocked by the impoliteness and negativity of certain Reviewers. In the case of this particular paper, however, I was truly impressed with the two Reviewers' and the editor's constructive critiques and suggestions for improvement, without which the paper would not have made the contribution it does now. Seeing how much effort these colleagues devoted to the reviews was a real inspiration, and I try to be equally constructive when serving as a Reviewer myself.

Finally, this review process is a good illustration of how – as an author – you can accommodate the comments of the editor and the Reviewers while staying loyal to what you think is the core message and strength of the paper. While it is important to acknowledge the shortcomings of your paper as pointed out by the editor and the Reviewers, it is not always necessary to exactly follow their proposals on how to resolve these issues. Since, as an author, you are well aware of the field and of your data, it is possible to come up with different, but even better solutions.

APPENDIX

Abstract of the Initial Submission

The unpredictable nature of emergent markets implies that ventures entering such markets are confronted with technological and commercial uncertainty. Defining a viable business model under such circumstances is a complex and precarious endeavour. Previous research has either advanced the idea of focus – in order to attract resources and realize first mover advantages – or sequential experimentation financed through bootstrapping, implying limited resources during initial phases of the venture. As such, a trade-off between flexibility and resource acquisition has been introduced. Within this contribution we explore how ventures starting up in emergent industries can balance the attainment of financial resources with flexibility and business model adaptation. Based on a sequence analysis of six case studies, we identify two distinctive approaches to business development in emergent industries: focused commitment versus simultaneous experimentation. Our findings reveal that focused commitment is instrumental for acquiring resources but at the same time impedes flexibility, while simultaneous experimentation allows to attract resources while maintaining manoeuvring space for business model adaptation. An analytical comparison of both approaches suggests that simultaneous experimentation is indeed a more viable strategy when entering emergent industries.

Abstract of the Published Paper

Ventures operating under uncertainty face challenges defining a sustainable value proposition. Six longitudinal case studies reveal two approaches to business model development: focused commitment and simultaneous experimentation. While focused commitment positively affects initial growth, this commitment and lack of variety jeopardize long-term survival. Simultaneous experimentation implies lower initial growth levels, but facilitates long-term survival by enacting variety in a resource-effective manner. This paper enriches organizational learning

theory by demonstrating that not only distant search but also simultaneous experimentation results in variety. Moreover, simultaneous
experimentation implies effectual behaviour and reconciles the apparent
juxtaposition between 'action' and 'planning.'

3. Getting published: an editorial and journal ranker's perspective

Geoffrey Wood and Pawan Budhwar

INTRODUCTION

The opportunity to share one's ideas with a wider audience is one of the most rewarding parts of being an academic. Finding one's work side by side with leading scholars in the field, and being part of a wider debate, is very much part of this. However, whilst getting published is considerably easier than coming up with genuinely new ideas, the task brings with it its own challenges. Most quality journals reject the overwhelming majority of submissions. Hence, publishing in leading journals has become increasingly competitive. This short review seeks to provide some insights to maximize your chances of success.

HOW TO CHOOSE A JOURNAL, AND HOW DO JOURNAL RANKINGS FIT IN?

Level of Work

The journal eco-system is a very diverse and rich one, and there is a huge range of journals to choose from. In the case of the United Kingdom, many universities require staff to produce work of at least 3* level[1] (in some instances, higher) on the ABS (Association of Business School) Guide to be included in the Research Excellence Framework (an exercise carried out every 5–6 years to assess and rank the research quality of higher education institutions in the United Kingdom); if one is guided by this logic, then the list of options immediately becomes much narrower. Three key issues are worth considering here. The first is that one has to be realistic; some work, owing to limitations in data, method or theoretical underpinnings will never get published in a journal that is highly respectable (e.g., ranked 3* or 4* using the ABS Guide). Getting such work published in lower ranked journals means one's ideas might not initially reach as wide an audience as would otherwise be the case; also too many articles published in modestly ranked journals may create the impression of excessive 'noise' on one's CV unless there is a clear upward trajectory. However, a note of caution is due here. Most top journals started off from quite modest beginnings, and some articles in quite modestly ranked journals have ended up being widely cited (see Chapter 7 in this volume). It is also worth considering that more modestly ranked journals are often more open to very innovative and unusual work; some (but not all) of the most highly ranked journals are quite conservative in terms of what they take. However, the best-regarded journals are likely to find it a great deal easier to find reviewers, and this means that they are likely (but not always) to get better reviews quicker.

Right Fit

Most journals clearly highlight the kinds of areas (e.g., general management, organization studies, work psychology) and the nature (e.g., empirical versus review or academic versus practitioner oriented) of manuscripts they will publish. In order to ensure the right fit exists between a given manuscript ready for submission and the chosen journal it would be sensible to do a thorough analysis of the kinds of manuscripts the journal has been publishing. It would also be helpful if you can find debates and discussions taking place in the journal which are related to your own research and the contents of your manuscript. It is also worth scrutinizing editorials, as they often summarize what the editors are looking for. And, if you are not citing anything from the journal, this may indicate a poor fit.

Avoiding Desk Rejection

Most top journals desk reject a high number of papers (typically 50 per cent or more of submissions). There are four issues to consider here. First, you need to ensure the basic fundamentals of the research on which the manuscript is based are in place (i.e., the 'why', 'what' and 'how' questions are adequately addressed). This will include clear and timely aims/research questions, an up-to-date literature analysis (highlighting gaps worth filling), appropriate theoretical underpinning for the research (less valid for practitioner journals), relevant and robust methodology, suitable data analysis in the case of empirical papers, useful discussion highlighting the rationale for the main findings, and key implications/ contributions of the research. Depending on the nature of the research investigation/analysis, other elements such as theoretically driven hypotheses, proposed linkages between independent and dependent variables, and recommendations for future research should also be included.

It is also important to ensure that the writing in the manuscript is of quality (e.g., error-free, jargon-free, reader-friendly, as per the submission guidelines of the journal). This can be challenging for inexperienced authors and (in the case of Anglophone journals) those whose first language is not English and who lack proficiency in it. Steps should be taken to ensure quality (e.g., via peer reviews or getting the help of a professional copy editor). Also, take the necessary care in preparing the submission, such as making sure it adheres to journal style (not that of the journal's closest rival, as this makes it obvious that the paper has already been rejected at least once), and make reference to previous work published in the journal (checking carefully that one is not essentially duplicating work already published). Equally important, where possible, link your work with the published work in the journal. Second, look closely at one's data; does it really bring new information to the table? For example, there are vast bodies of work out there based on the studies of students, for the simple reason that it is easy. However, no matter what you call them ('future business leaders', 'emerging entrepreneurs') they are simply one's students, with the inevitable power imbalances between them and academic staff (see Chapter 28 in this volume). Third, as pointed out above, one should make sure the literature review is up to date, and at least indicates some awareness of the target journal; a lack of attention to this is a sure sign of a zombie paper that has been subject to multiple rejections but simply will not go away. Zombies can certainly be safely interred somewhere, but it is harder if everybody can see what they are. Finally, be cautious in using esoteric statistical tests (as opposed to novel approaches that may take a field forward) that nobody knows much about; this is sometimes a sign that an author has run wild on one of the many commercial software statistical analysis and modelling packages but does not really know what s/he is doing. There is then a need to understand what the given journal considers to be appropriate statistical tests and levels of analysis.

The success rate of publishing in leading journals has got a great deal tougher as a large number of scholars from emerging markets have raised their skills and aspirations to publish in such journals. Consequently, journals are increasingly becoming overloaded. Again, better PhD training has made recent graduates very much aware of journal hierarchies and ways of enhancing one's success in getting published. And, of course, if you are reading this chapter, there are many others also reading it, and taking its lessons to heart! Editors of established journals cannot carry more than a limited number of submissions and tend to look for obvious faults; one should not make it easy for them! Positive features that editors look for are clarity (i.e., can one tell what the paper is about by reading it), balanced structure (devoting appropriate space to each part of the paper – from introduction to conclusion), an interesting and timely research problem, a convincing theoretical underpinning (for academic oriented journals), novelty (without being freaky; in reality, this is a difficult balance), being interesting (in other words, giving readers good reasons to carry on reading and citing the paper) and clear implications.

DEALING WITH REVIEWERS

How Are Reviewers Selected?

There are four broad ways in which reviewers are selected. First, they are chosen from among the editor's list of personal contacts. Second, they are thrown up by a keyword search of the journal's electronic database of existing reviewers and those who have submitted papers. Third, they are nominated by the author her/himself. And fourth, some editors look at the references used in the manuscript to identify potential reviewers. The first group are likely to be experienced reviewers (as the editor will probably have used them before), but may not be very narrow subject experts with highly specialized expertise on the topic of the paper. This is not a bad thing, as they are likely to mirror the typical reader, and if one cannot clearly explain what one is doing, it is highly likely that one is talking rubbish. As they are personal contacts of the editor, they may reflect her/his interests. The second are likely to know a great deal of the topic, but may not always be that experienced (depending on how the database is compiled; e.g., some include unsuccessful paper authors). The third are the most dangerous; our experience is that quite often nominated reviewers will either reject the paper or simply refuse to review it at all. Regrettably, in business and management studies, 'friends' do not always seem to be 'friends' under the cloak of anonymity. The fourth should be able to do a good review job, as they are aware of research developments in the field.

Dealing with Reviewer Comments

There are a number of different grades of revise and resubmit. A minor changes verdict (quite unusual on the first round these days) normally means that as long as you faithfully take on board the reviewers' comments, you are likely to get published. If you think a reviewer is wrong, it is not wise to engage in trench warfare, but rather attempt to promote a compromise revision that will satisfy her/him, whilst tactfully pointing out what may not be accomplished. A major revise and resubmit (often with the 'high risk' proviso added) is a much less secure business. Here it is wise not only to seek to take the changes on board, but invest a great deal of time in the response to the reviewer and get the opinions of friendly experts as to whether or not you have done enough (see Chapters 16–18 in this volume). Most people do not like bad news; many authors will try and bluff themselves that the reviewers are wrong, and try and wear them down with obfuscation and half measures, inevitably leading to a rejection. A reject and resubmit normally follows a limited review by the editor; s/he clearly believes the paper has merits, but is unlikely to survive the review process unless some obvious faults are carefully attended to. Cynics have suggested that this is a way of relieving the hassles of finding reviewers and of scaring away authors when the journal is overloaded, as invariably some authors will be so disheartened so as to go quietly into the night, empty-handed.

Resubmission and Responding

Upon receiving a revise and resubmit decision, it is critical to do a thorough revision job. How you respond to the reviewers' comments both in your revised manuscript and in your response letter is equally important. Meeting the given time target to resubmit is important and practical not only for your manuscript but also to aid the original reviewers in remembering the detail of your manuscript. It is crucial that all the points raised by the reviewers are systematically addressed and a convincing response is provided in the response letter. Of course, if you disagree with certain points brought up by the reviewers then you should raise them in your response letter to the editor with a solid rationale and evidence for the same. A good response letter will not only address each and every point raised by both the action editor and the reviewers but will also provide an acknowledgement of the useful comments made by the reviewers, a clear logic for all the responses and details of the amendments carried out (where, why and how). Thanking the reviewers for their insights is always welcome as long as authors do not go over the top in this matter. Any document submitted should be error-free. This is quite a challenge for non-native speakers of English, who should seek relevant help to ensure this.

Yourself as a Reviewer

It may seem perfectly rational to deluge journals with your own work whilst refusing to review other authors' papers, as this will free up time to whack out yet more papers. This is clearly unethical. However, selfish scholars who are undeterred by appeals to their conscience need to carefully consider two points. The first is that reviewing lots of papers gives you a much clearer idea as to the quality of competing work, what types of papers are sent out to review (as adverse to desk rejected) by a particular journal and what is the present state of the literature. The second is most journals and publishers keep electronic records of reviewers, including how many papers they have refused and the quality of their reports. If you repeatedly refuse to review papers or give poor quality reviews then this greatly reduces your chances of ever being invited onto an editorial board or to guest edit a journal special issue. Also, if a paper is a close call and the author has consistently refused to review, the close call might turn into a rejection. If you are community minded you probably need to write two reviews for every paper you submit.

CONCLUSION

By avoiding some obvious mistakes, and taking a little care to understand the journal and what its reviewers might expect, one has a much greater chance of not being desk rejected. Whilst revise and resubmits can themselves be daunting, this verdict indicates interest from the journal in your work and that there is indeed some merit in your paper.

NOTE

1. 4* = they publish 'most original and best executed research', 3* = they publish 'original and well executed research'.

4. Ethics and integrity in publishing

Ben R. Martin

INTRODUCTION

Academic researchers operate in an increasingly competitive environment. They compete for research funds (with success rates for grant applications now often below 20 per cent), tenure and promotion. Their institutions compete in research assessment exercises or in international university rankings. Academics are subject to ever more intrusive forms of evaluation, often heavily dependent on performance indicators linked to success in publishing – in particular, numbers of publications, numbers of citations, numbers of articles in 'top' journals (frequently linked with journal impact factors) and one's h-index.

For most of its history, the academic community has operated within fairly loose norms and conventions with regard to what constitutes 'research integrity' and the ethics of publishing (Schminke, 2009, p. 586). That was sufficient until quite recently. Academics constituted a 'Republic of Science', in which a combination of the values instilled in young researchers and 'self-policing' through peer review ensured the great majority did indeed carry out their research with integrity (Anderson et al., 2013, pp. 220–222; Martin, 2013, p. 1005). Research misconduct was infrequent and generally low-level, with the penalties for transgressing (loss of reputation, funding or position) strong enough to deter all but a few (Martin, 2012, p. 97).

However, over the last 20–30 years, evaluations and performance indicators have become more pervasive, and the level of competition (both individual and institutional) more pronounced. Freeman et al. (2001, p. 2293) liken the situation today to a 'tournament' which offers 'players' a chance of a major prize (tenure, a chair, scientific reputation), but which 'fosters intense competition by amplifying small differences in productivity into large differences in recognition and reward … Because the differences in rewards exceed the differences in output, there is a disproportionate incentive to "win".' Hence, it is perhaps not surprising that more researchers are being tempted to 'cut corners' (Anderson et al.,

2013, pp. 237–238; Bedeian et al., 2010, pp. 720–721). As Mumford et al. (2007, p. 362) note in their study of environmental influences on ethical decision-making: 'excessive competitive pressure may lead to the acquisition of beliefs likely to engender the potential for unethical decisions throughout an individual's career'.[1] Similarly, Necker (2014, p. 1747) found that 'perceived pressure is … positively related to the admission of being involved in several unaccepted research practices … consistent with the notion that the "publish or perish" culture motivates researchers to violate research norms'.

Unethical behaviour may take various forms – 'borrowing' ideas or material from others without acknowledgement, 'slicing' research results into ever slimmer 'salami' papers, recycling already published material without bringing this to the reader's attention or 'tidying up' data to increase the apparent statistical significance of the findings (thus enhancing the chances of publication). Often the 'boundary' between acceptable and unacceptable research behaviour is ill-defined, with little by way of universally accepted rules. Inevitably some have sought to take advantage of this, trying to unilaterally shift the boundary between what constitutes acceptable and unacceptable research behaviour in their favour.

The aim of this chapter is to set out as clearly as possible 'the rules of the game', and to explain how these are interpreted by academic 'gate-keepers' such as journal editors. This includes offering advice on how to avoid ending up in a situation where your integrity as a researcher might come under question.[2]

The structure of the remainder of the chapter is as follows: in the next section we consider the nature and extent of the problem. This is followed by sections on research misconduct and on inappropriate or dubious research conduct. The penultimate section discusses misbehaviour by editors. The chapter ends with a summary of the main conclusions.

NATURE AND EXTENT OF THE PROBLEM

First, we need to consider what is meant by 'integrity' with respect to research. The primary aim of scientific research is to produce 'reliable knowledge' (Ziman, 1978). As Anderson et al. (2013, p. 218) state:

> integrity is a matter of trustworthiness … Research findings have integrity if they can be trusted … The integrity of research findings is, in turn, dependent on the integrity of the research process that produced them, including data,

methods of analysis, and presentation and interpretation in publications. Here, integrity is a matter of careful and precise work that meets the standards of the scientific method and best practice in the relevant field(s), as well as transparency in the presentation of all results and appropriately justified interpretations of all findings.

Over the last 10–15 years, problems with research integrity have escalated rapidly. To take one measure, the number of retractions by journals of articles found to be flawed has risen more than ten-fold in just ten years (van Noorden, 2011, p. 26). And that's just for the most serious cases where a full retraction of the paper is deemed necessary; for each of these there are many others that are subject to some form of 'corrigendum' (ibid.).

While problems with research integrity initially centred around biomedical research, they are now widespread throughout research.[3] In management studies, Honig and Bedi (2012) found that 13 per cent of papers selected (after peer review) for presentation at the Academy of Management contained 'significant plagiarism' (i.e. more than 5 per cent of plagiarised text) while a further 12 per cent contained at least 'some amount of plagiarism'. As we shall see later, plagiarism is universally regarded as a serious form of research misconduct, but there are various, less serious misdemeanours which are far more common. In a survey of economists, Necker (2014, p. 1747) found that no less than 'Ninety-four percent report having engaged in at least one unaccepted research practice.'

Journal editors are faced with a growing number and range of cases not just of research misconduct but also other forms of inappropriate or dubious behaviour (Schminke and Ambrose, 2011, p. 399). They are struggling to keep such problems in check, as numerous editorials lay testimony.[4]

RESEARCH MISCONDUCT

Research misconduct is conventionally defined as 'fabrication, falsification, or plagiarism in proposing, performing, or reviewing research, or in reporting research results'.[5] This is the definition adopted by the US National Institutes of Health (the world's largest research funding agency) and widely used by others. The American Psychological Association, for instance, uses a similar definition.[6]

In social sciences, a number of cases of data fabrication (defined as 'Making up data or results and recording or reporting them'[7]) have come to light. For example, the social psychologist, Diederik Stapel, 'perpetrated an audacious academic fraud by making up studies that told the world what it wanted to hear about human nature'.[8] While the number of *detected* cases of data fabrication is quite low, the actual incidence is undoubtedly much higher. For example, a survey of business school faculty by Bedeian et al. (2010) revealed that 'one out of four respondents (26.8%) reported knowledge of instances where faculty have fabricated results'. Moreover, this only covers cases *known* to colleagues, so the actual incidence may be considerably higher.

Rather more common are instances of data falsification, which is defined as 'Manipulating research materials, equipment, or processes, or changing or omitting data or results such that the research is not accurately represented in the research record.'[9] There is growing evidence of researchers engaging in dubious practices to inflate the apparent statistical significance of their empirical findings, in particular to generate exaggerated p-values. As social scientists have developed more sophisticated statistical techniques, such sharp practices are not always immediately apparent to referees or editors. Concern over the inflation of statistical significance first emerged in the biomedical area, with Ioannidis (2005) concluding that 'most discovered true associations are inflated'. However, the problem is certainly not confined to biomedical research. For example, Bakker and Wicherts (2011, p. 666) found that 'around 18% of statistical results in the psychological literature are incorrectly reported'. An analysis of three leading accountancy journals by Basu and Park (2014, p. 1) showed that 'the frequencies of p-values just below conventional significance levels are higher than frequencies just above these levels',[10] a finding that 'likely derive[s] from selective reporting of statistically significant results or searching across research designs for p-values for Test variables below conventional significance levels'. (We return later to the issue of retrospectively fitting hypotheses to data in order to arrive at supposedly significant findings.)

Bedeian et al. (2010) focused specifically on misconduct in the field of management research. In a survey of faculty at over 100 leading US business schools, they found that 'Close to 80% of survey respondents reported knowledge of faculty who either have "withheld methodological details or results" or "have selected only those data that support a hypothesis and withheld the rest" (i.e., "cooking" data)' (ibid., p. 718). In addition, 'some 60% of respondents reported knowledge of faculty who have "dropped observations or data points from analyses based on a gut feeling that they were inaccurate," what many would consider an example of "data trimming"' (ibid., p. 719).[11] The latter is a particularly 'grey' area, since 'winsorisation' (the assigning of lesser weight to what appears to be a spurious outlier or modifying its value so it is closer to other sample values) is a fairly common statistical technique (see e.g. Ghosh and Vogt, 2012). The boundary between acceptable 'winsorisation' (i.e. modifying outliers) and unacceptable 'data-trimming' (i.e. completely dropping outliers) is a fine one, hence the onus is very much on authors to be completely open with their readers so that the latter can make their own judgement as to whether the specific methodology employed is acceptable in the circumstances or not.

Plagiarism, the third main form of research misconduct, can be defined as 'The appropriation of another person's ideas, processes, results, or words without giving appropriate credit.'[12] This also now seems to be widespread. In their survey of business schools, Bedeian et al. (2010, p. 718) found that 'Over 70% [of faculty] reported being aware of colleagues who have engaged in plagiarism, or stated more formally, have "used another's ideas without permission or giving due credit".'

There are a number of instances of blatant plagiarism where whole sections or even entire papers are lifted from other sources and presented as the author's 'own' work. A prominent example is Hans Werner Gottinger, who on a dozen or more occasions was caught misappropriating the work of others and presenting it as his own (Abbott, 2007; Martin et al., 2007; Martin, 2012). Journal editors occasionally come across such cases. Fortunately, they often involve 'authors blessed with a singular degree of stupidity or laziness, who are either unaware that merely substituting their name at the top of an existing paper is unlikely to fool anyone, or unwilling to put in the effort needed to camouflage their plagiarism in a more sophisticated manner' (Martin, 2013, p. 1007).

Much more common, however, are papers where there are repeated instances of a few sentences being lifted from other sources without this being apparent to the reader. The rules on plagiarism make it clear that an author has just two choices: either to place such material in quotation marks (or indent it for longer quotations) or to paraphrase it – that is, to rewrite it *entirely in the author's own words*. There is no 'third way'. Many authors assume that citing the source at the end of the lifted material is somehow sufficient to avoid a charge of plagiarism. However, the rules here are clear; this, too, is a form of plagiarism. The instructions given to students by universities on plagiarism and how to avoid it are typically very explicit on such matters.[13] If your paper falls foul of your own university's rules for students on plagiarism, then clearly an editor is unlikely to believe your claim that you were unaware that failure either to place lifted material in quotation marks or to paraphrase it constitutes plagiarism.

INAPPROPRIATE AND DUBIOUS RESEARCH CONDUCT

Besides research misconduct, there are certain forms of behaviour that are widely judged to be 'inappropriate', while other activities are less clear-cut and are often grouped together under a heading such as 'dubious' research conduct.[14] The former category covers activities where there are some conventions or guidelines but perhaps not universal consensus on what constitutes 'the rules of the game'. The latter includes activities that, while not necessarily explicitly ruled out, nevertheless would be considered by most reasonable researchers as antithetical to the spirit of the research enterprise. Let us consider some common examples.

Salami Publishing, Redundant Publication and Self-Plagiarism[15]

In recent years, there have been growing numbers of cases involving 'self-plagiarism' and the related phenomena of 'salami publishing' and 'redundant publication'. Of these, salami publishing is perhaps the least serious and the one where the rules are least clear. It can be defined as

> the deliberate attempt by an author or team of authors to inappropriately inflate the total of publications yielded by a particular research study ... through a process of subdividing the published output into a number of thin 'slices' or 'least publishable units', thereby either generating a greater number of separate publications than is merited by the overall contribution to knowledge offered by that study, or creating a situation where the research community would instead be better served by the results being combined in a single or a smaller number of publications. (Martin, 2013, p. 1008)

Salami publishing can often result in 'redundant' (or 'duplicate') publication, which may be defined as 'a paper where the existence of one or more prior (or contemporaneous) papers by the same author(s) means that the new paper offers insufficient of an original contribution to knowledge to merit publication in its own right' (ibid.).[16] In some cases, redundant publication can involve the more serious offence of self-plagiarism.

> 'Self-plagiarism' can be defined as the practice by an author (or co-authors) of reproducing text, ideas, data, findings or other material from one or more earlier (or contemporaneous) papers by the same author(s) *without explicitly citing or otherwise acknowledging those other papers*, thereby misleading the reader (and in particular referees and editors) as to the level of originality of that paper. Such an attempt to present one's own previously published work as

though it were original is a form of deception (in contrast to plagiarism, which is a form of theft). (ibid., emphasis added)

A prominent case of self-plagiarism in management studies came to light in 2012. In just half a dozen years, the individual concerned had gone from PhD student to full professor at a leading German university, publishing more than 60 journal articles including over a dozen in top journals. When suspicions were aroused, many were found to be very closely related, with most being based on just two studies. Not only had the author failed to cite other closely related papers (thereby misleading editors about the originality of his work), he had also camouflaged the similarities by giving the same variable different names in different papers. A couple of years earlier, the individual had been feted as 'the undisputed shooting star of business science in Germany'.[17] In terms of journal publications, he came top in the 'under 40' category of the *Handelsblatt* research ranking of German-speaking business school faculty, and second overall. However, once the offences came to light,[18] over a dozen of his articles were retracted by journals, and he was subsequently forced to resign from his chair.[19]

In cases of alleged self-plagiarism, the debate frequently hinges on what constitutes 'prior publication'. In the past (i.e. the pre-digital age), editors were often more relaxed about this. Authors would sometimes argue that they were free to publish essentially the same study in different journals if those journals were aimed at different audiences. That argument may have had some merit in former times when researchers had to go to libraries to access publications and could only keep up with a small number of selected journals in their field. Now in the digital age, however, most journals are accessible through university libraries and a simple key-word search is likely to find any relevant article, whatever journal it was published in.[20] Consequently, many editors now take a tougher line. A recent casualty was Bruno Frey, who with colleagues published papers in four journals on the same study (of who survived the sinking of the Titanic). Each article failed to cite the others, thus deceiving readers about the level of that paper's originality. On learning of the deception, the editor of one journal wrote a public letter to Frey and colleagues, stating that their 'publication of this substantive material in multiple journals simultaneously' represented 'a violation of the spirit of the editorial agreement' that they signed when submitting the paper and claiming it was 'original work' (Autor, 2011, p. 239).

By convention, there are still a few, specific exemptions with regard to what constitutes 'prior publication'. In particular, doctoral theses do not count.[21] Likewise, working papers and conference presentations have traditionally been seen as 'pre-prints' rather than 'publications'. In the past, the difference was easier to spot since the former frequently took the form of typescript 'mimeos'. However, in the electronic age, with papers typeset so that they resemble the format of published articles, and with those papers widely circulated in digital form, the boundary between a 'pre-print' and a 'publication' is much more blurred. Electronic working papers may be widely circulated for some period of time, during which they may earn numerous citations.[22] Conference papers, which in the past might be circulated only to conference attendees on a CD-ROM, are now often made publicly available through the conference website and to this extent might be considered a form of 'publication'. As a result of this blurring of the boundaries, editors may take different views as to where one draws the line between 'pre-publication' and 'publication'.

My own view (one shared by many journal editors but not all) is that working papers and conference papers are circulated to elicit critical feedback and are thus an essential part of the quality control and improvement process essential in research. A particular problem can arise, however, when conference papers are published as part of the conference proceedings. If a fairly full version of a paper appears in such proceedings, for many editors that constitutes 'prior publication'.[23] If, however, only a short version (e.g. a quarter the length) appears in the proceedings, an editor may take the view that the full paper still contains sufficient originality to merit publication in a journal. Where an author is in any doubt as to what constitutes 'prior publication', the rule is simple: inform the editor of the full facts and ask for a ruling. Editors much prefer to be told in advance about such complications rather than finding out later at third hand. When thus approached by an author, they are likely to be sympathetic and offer a way round the potential problem, for example, by suitably differentiating the new paper from the earlier version.[24]

Retrofitting Hypotheses to Empirical Results (or HARKing)

As the use of increasingly sophisticated statistical methods has grown, and as journals have come to place a premium on methodological rigour, so the temptation has grown among researchers to engage in a process of retrofitting hypotheses to empirical results in order to increase the apparent statistical significance of the findings. This phenomenon has been termed HARKing (Hypothesizing After the Results are Known) by Kerr (1998), who identified various forms as well as the driving forces. As Leung (2011, p. 471) notes: 'The pure form of this practice is likely to breach research ethics and impede theoretical development by suppressing the falsification process.' In particular, 'when such hypotheses are data driven, they are inherently susceptible to capitalization on chance and are nothing more than a disguised form of data dredging' (Bedeian, 2004, p. 207).

Evidence of just how widespread such research behaviour now is comes from the survey by Bedeian et al. (2010, p. 719) of US business school faculty, over 90 per cent of whom reported knowledge of such practices. This very high figure may be partly because HARKing is not always easy to detect, especially if the authors have been adept in covering their tracks (e.g. by revising the literature review and modifying the paper's motivation). However, probably a more important reason is that such practices are often encouraged by referees, who may call for certain hypotheses to be recast or dropped, particularly those yielding null results, and for new ones to be added (Bedeian, 2004, p. 207). Further evidence that the practice is now very common comes from O'Boyle et al. (2014), who compared the empirical findings from PhD theses with those from subsequent journal articles based on the same doctoral studies. They found that 'from dissertation to journal article, the ratio of supported to unsupported hypotheses more than doubled ... The rise in predictive accuracy resulted from the dropping of statistically non-significant hypotheses, the addition of statistically significant hypotheses, the reversing of predicted direction of hypotheses, and alterations to data.' They describe this form of publication bias[25] in which 'ugly initial results metamorphosize into beautiful articles' as 'the Chrysalis Effect' (ibid., p. 1). While some researchers may take a different view, arguing perhaps that they were encouraged down this route by reviewers, many editors would nevertheless see this as inappropriate research behaviour. Although difficult to spot, once one has been caught, editors and others may subsequently treat all one's papers as suspect, since the charge is equally hard to disprove. One's reputation in the research community will therefore suffer accordingly.

Gift Authorship

Being listed as one of the authors of a paper means taking full responsibility for the content and not just accepting credit for the contribution. However, as the pressures to publish have grown, there has been a tendency for authors to be added who have made no substantial contribution, perhaps in return for a reciprocal favour with another paper. In their survey of business school faculty, Bedeian et al. (2010, p. 720) found that 'Nearly eight of ten (78.9%) respondents reported knowledge of instances where faculty have "inappropriately accepted or assigned authorship credit".' The effect is to artificially inflate the reputation of the 'honorary' authors. The rules of the Academy of Management Code of Ethics are clear: authorship should be 'based on the scientific or professional contributions of the individuals involved'. Researchers should take authorship credit 'only for work they have actually performed or to which they have contributed'.[26]

Some Specific Examples of Inappropriate or Dubious Research Conduct

To guide the reader through these rules and conventions and help them see exactly where the boundary lies, let us consider some common examples of inappropriate or questionable research conduct.[27] One involves repeated instances of phrases or sentences lifted from other sources, especially in the literature review section. As noted above, the author must *either* place the lifted text in quotation marks *or* they must rewrite it entirely in their own words. Listing the source is not sufficient, although omitting it makes the offence worse, since it suggests a premeditated intention to deceive the reader. Editors may be prepared to overlook one or two cases of this in a paper as an 'honest error', but not if persistently repeated.

Similar comments refer to the case of an author who makes use of an idea, concept, methodological approach or whatever from another source without proper attribution. Scientific knowledge is the product of a collective endeavour, where each generation 'stands on the shoulders' of those who have gone before, giving them full and explicit credit for each of the intellectual 'building blocks' used in one's study. An occasional oversight may be forgivable but repeated failure to adhere to this convention again risks being interpreted as a deliberate attempt to exaggerate the originality of one's own research by downplaying the contributions of others. Such 'carelessness' is likely to be spotted by referees. Moreover, once an individual acquires a reputation for such intellectual self-aggrandisement, it takes years to overcome.

The next example of inappropriate behaviour focuses not so much on 'prior publication' but on what might be termed 'parallel publication'. When a paper is submitted to a journal, it is judged primarily on whether it represents a substantial original contribution to knowledge. Most journals require the submitting author to confirm the paper has not been *previously* published in whole or part. Many authors duly tick this box but often fail to divulge that one or more closely related papers have been submitted to, or are about to be submitted to, other journals. Only after the paper in question has been accepted does the editor find out that a significant part of its supposed contribution has also been made in parallel papers. If the existence of those parallel papers had been disclosed at the start so that the editor was able to check its specific contribution compared with the parallel papers, then that paper may have been rejected. To this extent, editors are likely to feel that they have been deliberately misled.

This form of behaviour is quite common and becoming more so as pressure mounts on researchers to publish more articles. Authors challenged about this come up with various excuses. One is that the journals are aimed at different audiences so they are justified in preparing two articles with overlapping contributions. As noted above, this explanation might have had some validity in the pre-digital age but much less so now. Furthermore, the explicit consent of the editors of both the journals concerned must be obtained by the author beforehand.

A second excuse that authors come up with is that they failed to disclose the existence of the parallel paper(s) in order to ensure a 'double-blind' review process. This is disingenuous because most journals require both a 'full' and a 'blinded' version of the paper, with the former (seen only by the editor) citing all relevant sources.[28]

A third and even more specious 'explanation' is that 'My supervisor told me not to include self-citations in my papers.' This is simply incorrect; authors are expected to cite all material that pertains to the claimed originality of the paper in question. If a reference is not appropriate, then a mention in the acknowledgements section of the parallel paper(s) is another option. Failing that, the existence of any parallel papers (whatever stage of preparation they are at) should be declared in the covering letter to the journal editor at the time of submission so the editor can form a judgement about the submitted paper's originality.

Lastly, some authors, when challenged about their failure to divulge other parallel papers, try to hide behind the letter of the law, saying that they were asked only to confirm that the submitted paper had not been *previously* published in whole or in part. Such a response suggests premeditated intent to hide from the editor related papers which, if declared, would lead to the editor taking a different view on the submitted paper's originality. The rule here, as elsewhere, is simple: if in any doubt, tell the editor at the start about the circumstances. Editors thus approached tend to be more sympathetic and to work with the author to find an acceptable way forward.[29]

UNSCRUPULOUS EDITORS, JIF-BOOSTING RUSES AND COERCIVE CITATIONS[30]

Lest this chapter be seen as implying that only authors and relatively junior researchers are guilty of misconduct, let me stress that senior academics including editors sometimes overstep the mark.[31] Editors, too, are under pressure from growing competition between journals and the ill-considered use of performance indicators. Journals are increasingly judged by a single metric – the journal impact factor (JIF). When first introduced, this may have been a reasonable indicator of journal standing, although much less so for social sciences where the two-year 'citation window' is far too short. However, over recent years, this indicator has been subject to a growing range of 'game-playing' activities, some perhaps just 'within the rules', others certainly not. At the more 'innocent' end of the spectrum is the publication of various forms of 'non-research articles' (e.g. regular editorials, frequent discussion papers) which, because of the idiosyncratic way in which JIF is calculated, can add to a journal's citation total without counting in the denominator of the equation used to calculate the average number of citations per paper on which the JIF figure is based. Rather more egregious is the publication of apparently 'helpful' editorials advising prospective authors on what sort of papers the journal accepts, which then go on to list most articles published over the previous two years (i.e. the period used to calculate the JIF). One such editorial can singlehandedly raise a journal's JIF by 50 per cent or more.

An ingenious ruse employed by certain journals (often high-ranking ones, at least in terms of JIF) is to make numerous articles available on-line but to delay publishing them for one or two years or even longer. During that wait, on-line papers accrue citations for the journal while not counting in the denominator of the JIF calculation. Thus, if the number of papers waiting in the on-line 'queue' is similar to the number of articles published every two years, one can double the number of papers earning citations without affecting the denominator and hence potentially double a journal's JIF.[32] However, that is only the first of several 'benefits' for the journal's JIF. A second comes when a paper that has waited in the on-line queue is finally published in a journal issue. It then gets a further two years to contribute to that journal's JIF (i.e. a form of 'double-dipping'), again markedly inflating the JIF. A third benefit derives from the fact that, by that stage, papers that have already existed in on-line form for one or two years are likely to be accruing citations at a far faster rate (perhaps up to double) than in their first couple of years, further inflating the JIF. Yet the JIF benefits do not stop there! A fourth benefit can be derived if an astute editor 'cherry-picks' from among the on-line papers those now earning most citations and ensures these are published next,[33] while uncited papers are left to continue languishing in the on-line 'queue', thereby preventing them from 'diluting' the JIF. All very ingenious! And since no rules have apparently been broken, this is unlikely to be viewed as research 'misconduct'. However, such disingenuous manipulation of the JIF figure by editors would surely be seen by most as inappropriate or dubious behaviour,[34] not least by the hundreds of frustrated authors of papers held in the on-line queue for a couple of years who run the risk of their papers being 'scooped'.

Another troubling aspect of JIF-related behaviour is the pressure imposed by editors on authors to cite more articles published in the journal to which a paper has been submitted. There are concerns that certain journals will no longer consider papers that contain fewer than x citations to articles in that journal.[35] My own view as editor of a leading journal is that this is inappropriate. Work on a particular topic is inevitably published in a range of related journals, and no single journal can pretend that it has some monopoly position with regard to previous relevant research. However, editors can reasonably expect authors to relate their paper to literature that the journal's readers are familiar with, some of which may have been published in the journal but much of which will almost certainly have been published elsewhere.

Where editors do understandably get irritated is when a paper has been rejected by another journal and then is submitted to their journal without the authors having made any effort to reorient the topic to the interests of readers of that new journal. (This is often apparent from an unnaturally high percentage of references to one particular journal.) Failure to do even the most basic 'homework' in reorienting the paper before re-submission to the second journal is likely to result in immediate desk rejection.

The most insidious form of misconduct by editors involves 'coercive citation'. At a certain point in the editorial process, the journal editor asks (or 'advises') the author to include more references to the journal. Often this occurs towards the end of the process, with a message to the effect that the paper is close to being accepted, subject to the author adding some references to articles published in the journal *over the last two years*. This emphasis on recent articles is a clue to the game being played – namely, trying to inflate the journal's JIF. The fact that it often occurs towards the end of the editing process is deliberate, since authors are then at their most vulnerable to such pressure. It constitutes a blatant abuse of power by editors, particularly over junior researchers (who are more likely to accede).

The phenomenon of 'coercive citation' was exposed in a survey of several thousand social scientists conducted by Wilhite and Fong (2012). They showed that this misconduct was not confined to lesser journals (as one might have expected); top journals, leading publishers, the most eminent professional associations were all involved.[36] My advice to authors confronted with such editorial pressure is clear – stand firm and resist. If the editor repeats the threat, make it clear you intend to take the matter up with members of the advisory board for the journal or the publisher, or COPE (the international and widely respected Committee on Publication Ethics).

CONCLUSIONS

This chapter has considered not only outright misconduct but also various forms of inappropriate or dubious conduct. All of these seem to be on the increase, not least because of ever more pervasive pressures associated with evaluation and performance indicators. You, as an individual researcher, will certainly be subject to those pressures, and may even be tempted to 'cut corners'. However, you should bear in mind that reputation is all important to your future and career prospects. Once damaged, that reputation can never be fully regained.

For research misconduct, the rules on data fabrication or falsification and on plagiarism are clear and universally agreed. They are set out by professional associations such as the Academy of Management (summarised in Schminke, 2009) and by journals and publishers. In addition, further guidance on the rules can be obtained from the website of COPE.[37]

With regard to inappropriate or dubious research behaviour, the rules are often less clear. However, this should not be taken to mean that there are no rules or that they can be ignored. There are a number of simple guidelines or questions one should address. These include:

1. If this was a piece of work by one of my students, would it pass the university rules (e.g. with regard to plagiarism)?
2. Is there something in (or about) this paper which, if the full facts became known to my colleagues, would result in me being embarrassed?
3. Would I object if the journal editor revealed to the wider research community exactly what I had done in this study or paper?

If the answer to any of these is 'yes' or even 'perhaps', that should give pause for thought. If in doubt about something, raise it with the editor[38] for advice on how best to proceed. Honesty and transparency will bring sympathy and help with how best to overcome the potential problem. Failure to disclose, in contrast, runs the risk of being construed as a deliberate premeditated attempt to deceive.

Let me end with a plea. With the growing prevalence of research misconduct or inappropriate behaviour, the problem cannot be left to editors alone to sort out. If you spot clear evidence of misconduct or of inappropriate or dubious behaviour (whether by a colleague or the author of a paper you have been asked to review, or by an editor or whoever), report it to the appropriate authority. Don't 'cross to the other side of the road', leaving it to 'someone else' to deal with. This merely makes the situation worse for everyone, resulting over time in a 'tragedy of the commons' (Hardin, 1968; Martin, 2007, p. 66). In certain respects, unethical behaviour is 'contagious' in that misconduct by some can negatively affect the behaviour of others (Gino et al., 2009). Conversely, in a community where it is widely known that not only do most practitioners abide by the rules but they also cooperate in seeing the rules are adhered to and enforced, fewer will be tempted to transgress.[39]

ACKNOWLEDGEMENTS

The author acknowledges the support of SPRU (Science Policy Research Unit) and the University of Sussex. *Research Policy* editors along with numerous referees have played a major role in helping investigate the cases drawn upon here. He is also grateful to the editors of this volume for very helpful comments on an earlier draft. However, responsibility for the views expressed here and for any remaining errors lies with the author alone.

NOTES

1. This phenomenon is certainly not confined to academia. In the financial sector, for example, excessive competition and the resulting anxiety associated with fear of failure 'disrupts people's capacity to make good decisions, often leading them to behave less ethically' (PWC, 2015, p. 3).
2. Roig (2011) provides a very useful guide on how to avoid plagiarism, self-plagiarism and other questionable research practices. Other helpful resources are listed at http://ori.hhs.gov/research-misconduct-0 (accessed on 9 July 2015).
3. For a systematic review and meta-analysis of the extent of research misconduct, see Fanelli (2009).

4. For a recent example in management studies, see Harley et al. (2014). Further examples are cited in Martin (2013).
5. See http://grants.nih.gov/grants/research_integrity/research_misconduct.htm (accessed on 3 June 2015). Anderson et al. (2013) provide an extensive review of the literature on research misconduct, including definitions, prominent cases, evidence on prevalence, factors encouraging misconduct, and how best to deal with it.
6. See https://apa.org/research/responsible/misconduct/index.aspx (accessed on 3 June 2015).
7. See http://grants.nih.gov/grants/research_integrity/research_misconduct.htm (accessed on 5 June 2015).
8. See http://www.nytimes.com/2013/04/28/magazine/diederik-stapels-audacious-academic-fraud.html?pagewanted=all (accessed on 11 June 2015).
9. See http://grants.nih.gov/grants/research_integrity/research_misconduct.htm (accessed on 5 June 2015).
10. A similar finding was obtained by Masicampo and Lalande (2012) in an analysis of three top psychology journals, and by Ridley et al. (2007, p. 1082) who analysed three leading biology journals and found 'a remarkable excess of probability values being cited on, or just below, each threshold relative to the smoothed theoretical distributions'.
11. See also the discussion in Sterba (2006, p. 315) about 'unethical data manipulations aimed at clipping and preening a sample to move a finding of $p = .06$ ... into the golden area of $p < .05$'.
12. See http://grants.nih.gov/grants/research_integrity/research_misconduct.htm (accessed on 5 June 2015).
13. Useful tutorials can be found at https://www.indiana.edu/~istd/ (accessed on 5 June 2015) while other examples are given at the end of Roig (2011).
14. Sometimes termed 'questionable research practices', these include 'taking undeserved credit for intellectual contributions or discoveries; either accepting or awarding "honorary" or "gift" authorship of publications; using university equipment, funds, or facilities for private benefit; duplicate publication of data; piecemeal publishing (i.e., deliberately splitting research results into the "smallest publishable units" to increase the number of one's publications); and keeping sloppy or incomplete research records' (Bedeian et al., 2010, p. 717).
15. This section draws extensively on Martin (2013).
16. The practice is again quite widespread, with 86 per cent of U.S. business school faculty reporting 'knowledge of faculty who have "published the same data or results in two or more publications"' (Bedeian et al., 2010, p. 719).
17. See http://www.handelsblatt.com/politik/konjunktur/oekonomie/nachrichten/ulrich-lichten thaler-der-junge-der-alles-richtig-macht/3200312.html and http://olafstorbeck.blogstrasse2. de/?p=1634 (accessed on 11 June 2015).
18. Besides self-plagiarism, these included (deliberate) omitted variable bias and misreporting exaggerated p-values (see *Research Policy*, 2012).
19. See http://retractionwatch.com/2014/10/10/after-16-retractions-management-professor-lichtenthaler-resigns-post/ (accessed on 9 July 2015).
20. This is reflected in the reference section of this chapter, which includes journals far from the author's own field.
21. See e.g. http://www.nature.com/authors/policies/duplicate.html (accessed on 20 June 2015).
22. NBER papers often fall into this category (see https://ideas.repec.org/top/top.series.hindex 10.html – accessed on 9 July 2015).
23. Hence, if an author is offered the opportunity for a relatively full version of their paper to be published in the conference proceedings, the most sensible response may be to decline since there is a considerable potential cost and little potential gain (the status of such conference publications is generally low).
24. This is one situation where the well-known saying 'It's easier to ask forgiveness than it is to get permission' (generally attributed to Rear Admiral Grace Hopper) is actually reversed. (I am grateful to one of the editors for this observation.)

25. A study of publication bias in strategic management research can be found in Harrison et al. (2014, p. 1), who conclude that 'publication bias affects many, but not all, topics in strategic management research'.
26. See http://aom.org/uploadedFiles/About_AOM/Governance/AOM_Code_of_Ethics.pdf (accessed on 11 June 2015). Note that this wording does not mean that an 'author' has to have contributed to the actual writing of the text (he or she may lack the skills or experience required for this), but merely that they should have contributed substantially to the research on which the eventual publication is based.
27. Other examples can be found in Chen (2011), Schminke (2009) and Schminke and Ambrose (2011). (The last of these provides an introduction to a Special Editors Forum in *Management and Organization Review*, in which several of the papers are relevant here.) In an ironic twist, it was later discovered that Schminke and Ambrose (2011) contained significant elements of self-plagiarism of Schminke (2009) so it was retracted (see Tsui et al., 2014).
28. Even where a journal asks only for a 'blinded' version, this should contain all relevant self-citations in a form such as 'identifying self-citation temporarily suppressed'. This then means that the editor and reviewers are aware there is a closely related paper, even though its identity is suppressed, and the editor can specifically ask to see it if this is necessary to judge the level of originality of the paper under consideration.
29. A more detailed analysis of how to deal with the issue of multiple papers from the same dataset can be found in Kirkman and Chen (2011). They, too, conclude with the advice that authors should 'always err on the side of transparency by alerting the editor to the existence of each paper and by proactively sharing their own uniqueness analysis to assist the editor in making an informed decision about the papers' (ibid., pp. 444–445).
30. Since writing this chapter, the author has prepared a more extensive editorial on the JIF-boosting stratagems employed by journal editors (see Martin, 2016).
31. Elsewhere, I noted that 'many cases of misconduct are perpetrated by quite senior researchers, often full professors. Their misdeeds tend to involve less obvious encroachments across the boundary between acceptable and unacceptable behaviour. Indeed, often they seem to have convinced themselves that they have not been guilty of any such encroachment – that the boundary is simply in a different location than academic convention would suggest. Moreover, being more experienced, they may be more adept in attempting to cover their tracks' (Martin, 2013, p. 1011). Moreover, senior researchers, when confronted with evidence of misconduct, have an unsavoury habit of blaming this on a junior colleague, ignoring the fact that authorship brings with it full responsibility for all aspects of the paper (Schminke, 2009, p. 588).
32. For an example of a journal with an unusually large backlog (going back three years and totalling well in excess of the number of articles published over the two previous years), see http://jom.sagepub.com/content/early/recent (accessed on 10 July 2015). Several other top management journals have a backlog of a year or more.
33. Thus, one of the most highly cited recent articles in the case of the journal mentioned in the previous footnote was published on-line in April 2010 but only appeared in print nearly three years later in February 2013.
34. The acid test is whether the editors involved would feel uncomfortable if they were publicly named. (The interested reader might like to check which high-ranking management journals currently have an on-line 'queue' of a year or more and hence are benefiting from this JIF-boosting stratagem.)
35. Specific examples are discussed in http://olafstorbeck.blogstrasse2.de/?p=1536 (accessed on 9 July 2015). However, after the phenomenon of 'coercive citation' was exposed by Wilhite and Fong (2012), the journals most guilty of this practice have become the target of some derision.
36. The Supplementary Online Material linked to Wilhite and Fong (2012) names the journals found guilty of such practice (see Table S12 in http://www.sciencemag.org/content/335/6068/542/suppl/DC1 – accessed on 10 July 2015).

37.   See   http://publicationethics.org/files/Internationalpercent20standards_authors_forpercent 20website_11_Nov_2011.pdf (accessed on 10 July 2015).
38.   Another option when in doubt is to discuss the situation or dilemma with one's mentor, peers or senior colleagues in order to obtain an outside and more objective perspective.
39.   'There is simply no better protection for the integrity of science than the careful and watchful commitment of researchers as they go about their everyday work ... This is the responsibility of all researchers as the guardians of research integrity' (Anderson et al., 2013, p. 253).

REFERENCES

Abbott, A. (2007). 'Academic accused of living on borrowed lines', *Nature*, **448**, 632–633.
Anderson, M.S., M.A. Shaw, N.H. Steneck, E. Konkle and T. Kamata (2013). 'Research integrity and misconduct in the academic profession', in M.B. Paulsen (ed.), *Higher Education: Handbook of Theory and Research* **28**, Dordrecht: Springer, pp. 217–261.
Autor, D.H. (2011). 'Letter to Professor Bruno Frey', *Journal of Economic Perspectives*, **25**, 239–240.
Bakker, M. and J.M. Wicherts (2011). 'The (mis)reporting of statistical results in psychology journals', *Behavior Research*, **43**, 666–678.
Basu, S. and H.-U. Park (2014), 'Publication bias in recent empirical accounting research' (downloaded on 11 June 2015 from SSRN at http://papers.ssrn.com/sol3/papers.cfm?abstract_id=2379889).
Bedeian, A.G. (2004). 'Peer review and the social construction of knowledge in the management discipline', *Academy of Management Learning and Education*, **3**, 198–216.
Bedeian, A.G., S.G. Taylor and A.N. Miller (2010). 'Management science on the credibility bubble: cardinal sins and various misdemeanours', *Academy of Management Learning and Education*, **9**, 715–725.
Chen, X.-P. (2011). 'Author ethical dilemmas in the research publication process', *Management and Organization Review*, **7**, 423–432.
Fanelli, D. (2009). 'How many scientists fabricate and falsify research? A systematic review and meta-analysis of survey data', *PLoS One*, **4** (5), e5738.
Freeman, R., E. Weinstein, E. Marincola, J. Rosenbaum and F. Solomon (2001). 'Competition and careers in biosciences', *Science*, **294**, 2293–2294.
Ghosh, D. and A. Vogt (2012). 'Outliers: an evaluation of methodologies', *Section on Survey Research Methods – JSM 2012*, 3455–3460 (downloaded on 9 July 2015 from www.amstat.org/sections/SRMS/Proceedings/y2012/Files/304068_72402.pdf).
Gino, F., S. Ayal and D. Ariely (2009). 'Contagion and differentiation in unethical behaviour: the effect of one bad apple on the barrel', *Psychological Science*, **20**, 393–398.
Hardin, G. (1968). 'The tragedy of the commons', *Science*, **162**, 1243–1248.
Harley, B., D. Faems and A. Corbett (2014). 'A few bad apples or the tip of an iceberg? Academic misconduct in publishing', *Journal of Management Studies*, **51**, 1361–1363.

Harrison, J.S., G.C. Banks, J.M. Pollack, E.H. O'Boyle and J. Short (2014). 'Publication bias in strategic management research', *Journal of Management* (available on-line as DOI: 10.1177/0149206314535438).

Honig, B. and A. Bedi (2012). 'The fox in the hen house: a critical examination of plagiarism among members of the Academy of Management', *Academy of Management Learning and Education*, **11**, 101–123.

Ioannidis, J.P.A. (2005). 'Why most discovered true associations are inflated', *Epidemiology*, **19**, 640–648.

Kerr, N.L. (1998). 'HARKing: hypothesizing after the results are known', *Personality and Social Psychology Review*, **2**, 196–217.

Kirkman, B.L. and G. Chen (2011). 'Maximizing your data or data slicing? Recommendations for managing multiple submissions from the same dataset', *Management and Organization Review*, **7**, 433–446.

Leung, K. (2011). 'Presenting post hoc hypotheses as a priori: ethical and theoretical issues', *Management and Organization Review*, **4**, 471–479.

Martin, B.R. (2007). 'Research misconduct – does self-policing work?', *Confluence 2007/2008* (Interdisciplinary Communications of the Centre for Advanced Study at the Norwegian Academy of Science and Letters), 59–69 (downloaded on 9 July 2015 from http://www.cas.uio.no/Publications/Seminar/Confluence.pdf#page=61).

Martin, B.R. (2012). 'Does peer review work as a self-policing mechanism in preventing misconduct: a case study of a serial plagiarist', in T. Mayer and N. Steneck (eds), *Promoting Research Integrity in a Global Environment*, London/Singapore: World Scientific Publishing/Imperial College Press, pp. 97–114.

Martin, B.R. (2013). 'Whither research integrity? Plagiarism, self-plagiarism and coercive citation in an age of research assessment', *Research Policy*, **42**, 1005–1014.

Martin, B.R. (2016). 'Editors' JIF-boosting stratagems – which are appropriate and which not?', *Research Policy*, **45**, 1–7.

Martin, B.R. et al. (2007). 'Keeping plagiarism at bay – a salutary tale', *Research Policy*, **36**, 905–911.

Masicampo, E.J. and D.R. Lalande (2012). 'A peculiar prevalence of p values just below .05', *Quarterly Journal of Experimental Psychology*, **65**, 2271–2279.

Mumford, M.D., S.T. Murphy, S. Connelly, J.H. Hill, A.L. Antes, R.P. Brown and L.D. Devenport (2007). 'Environmental influences on ethical decision making: climate and environmental predictors of research integrity', *Ethics and Behavior*, **17**, 337–366.

Necker, S. (2014). 'Scientific misbehavior in economics', *Research Policy*, **43**, 1747–1759.

O'Boyle, E.H., G.C. Banks and E. Gonzalez-Mulé (2014). 'The Chrysalis Effect: how ugly initial results metamorphosize into beautiful articles', *Journal of Management* (available on-line as DOI: 10.1177/0149206314527133).

PWC (2015). *Stand Out for the Right Reasons: Why You Don't Scare Bankers into Doing the Right Thing*, report by PWC and London Business School (downloaded on 9 July 2015 from http://pwc.blogs.com/files/why-you-cant-scare-bankers-into-doing-the-right-thing.pdf).

Research Policy (2012). 'Retraction notice to "The role of corporate technology strategy and patent portfolios in low-, medium- and high-technology firms" [Res. Policy 38 (2009) 559–569] and "Determinants of proactive and reactive technology licensing: A contingency perspective" [Res. Policy 39 (2010) 55–66]', *Research Policy*, **41**, 1499.

Ridley, J., N. Kolm, R.P. Freckelton and M.J.G. Gage (2007). 'An unexpected influence of widely used significance thresholds on the distribution of reported *P*-values', *Journal of Evolutionary Biology*, **20**, 1082–1089.

Roig, M. (2011). 'Avoiding plagiarism, self-plagiarism, and other questionable writing practices: a guide to ethical writing' (downloaded on 11 June 2015 from http://ori.hhs.gov/sites/default/files/plagiarism.pdf).

Schminke, M. (2009). 'Editor's comments: the better angels of our nature – ethics and integrity in the publishing process', *Academy of Management Review*, **34**, 586–591.

Schminke, M. and M.L. Ambrose (2011). 'Ethics and integrity in the publishing process: myths, facts, and a roadmap', *Management and Organization Review*, **7**, 397–406 [subsequently retracted for self-plagiarism – see Tsui et al., 2014].

Sterba, S.K. (2006). 'Misconduct in the analysis and reporting of data: bridging methodological and ethical agendas for change', *Ethics & Behavior*, **16**, 305–318.

Tsui, A.S., A.Y. Lewin, N. Schminke and M. Ambrose (2014). 'Retraction statement for "Ethics and integrity of the publishing process: myths, facts, and a roadmap" by Marshall Schminke and Maureen L. Ambrose', *Management and Organization Review*, **10**, 157–162.

Van Noorden, R. (2011). 'The trouble with retractions', *Nature*, **478**, 26–28.

Wilhite, A.W. and E.A. Fong (2012). 'Coercive citation in academic publishing', *Science*, **335**, 542–543.

Ziman, J. (1978). *Reliable Knowledge: An Exploration of the Grounds for Belief in Science*, Cambridge: Cambridge University Press.

5. Sustaining a publications career[*]

Mike Wright

INTRODUCTION

We live in a time of turbulence for academic researchers, perhaps especially so for those in management. Politicians question the benefits for business of encouraging management academics to publish in "obscure U.S. journals" (whether this means obscure European journals are acceptable or beyond the pale is left unsaid). Instead business school academics should offer more practical help to business. Pressures on internal resources from reductions in public funding and in income generated from executive education undermine budgets to support research. Sharply increased tuition fees for students shift the emphasis to delivering high quality teaching. At the same time, submissions to journals have been rising significantly in recent years as a result of a worldwide surge of research activity. With space in most journals remaining unchanged, acceptance rates have been falling sharply and now stand at around 5 percent for major management journals. Thresholds to get published have therefore increased, with reviewers and editors becoming more demanding (Clark et al., 2006, 2013). Publication in quality journals has, however, long been recognized to be highly skewed (e.g. Podsakoff et al., 2008); fewer scholars continue to publish in quality journals over a long period.

These trends may mean that publications careers become even more highly skewed. Even though scholars may have published successfully already, they face demands for new skills and need both to be able to identify new opportunities and exploit them more efficiently if they are to sustain a publications career. Accordingly, this chapter sets out to explore the challenges in sustaining a publications career in management and how these may be met.

This chapter unfolds as follows. In the following section I set out the pressure points concerning when scholars need to assess how they can sustain their publications. I then discuss why it is therefore important to develop a publications strategy that is maintained over a longer period. In the third section I analyze what scholars can do to develop a sustainable publications strategy by outlining the heterogeneity of publication outlets. The fourth section then addresses how scholars can realize such a strategy by adopting various routes including developing strategic entre-preneurial actions that involve exploring and subsequently exploiting new opportunities for research and accessing the human and social resources required. Throughout the chapter I draw on my career to illustrate one approach to sustaining publications, notably based on experience with the Center for Management Buyout Research (CMBOR), which was for-mally created in 1986 although the research opportunity had initially been identified in 1981 as management buyouts were seen as a new entrepreneurial phenomenon (Wright and Coyne, 1985). This experience, which covers a 30-year publications record, is summarized in Table 5.1. Finally, the chapter presents some conclusions.

WHEN?

There are a number of pressure points where scholars need to (re)assess how they are going to sustain a publications career.

After PhD

As doctoral students we invest considerable effort in a process of research training that involves the development of expertise in a particu-lar domain, theoretical area and methodological tools. This underpins a stream of publications leading up to and directly from the PhD. It may also prompt a number of follow-on publications that help establish an initial reputation. Indeed, evidence indicates that those who publish prior to receiving their doctorate (Park and Gordon, 1996) are more likely to continue publishing for up to ten years afterwards.

However, at some point the momentum from this initial topic area will likely begin to run out of steam. Having addressed major paradigm chan-ging questions, further publications likely involve more incremental contri-butions that themselves become harder to publish as it becomes more challenging to convince reviewers and editors that there is sufficient novelty in the original topic to warrant publication in a good journal. Further, it becomes increasingly difficult to exploit new angles from the dataset gathered during doctoral studies. This dataset too is likely to become outdated and at the very least require more recent observations to be added. New challenges are therefore introduced regarding how or whether a dataset can be extended or whether a new one needs to be created.

Table 5.1 An illustration of sustaining publication output

Year/Period	Topic/Research Questions	Theories	Team	Publications	Other spin-off and complementary publications
1981–1985	Review: general descriptive analysis Impact: employment and employee relations		Coyne Coyne, Lockley	Book, practitioner journals IRJ, RS	Management control, industrial relations, state enterprise efficiency auditing
1986–1989	Vendor source: divestment, trading relationships, financial structuring Vendor source: privatization U.K. Review: general impact	Transaction costs, agency theory, resource dependency theory Agency	Thompson, Robbie, Chiplin, Mulley, Chiplin, Robbie, Thompson Coyne, Robbie, Thompson	JMS, ABR, JES, BER, PE PMM, FS, APCE LRP, Omega, BAR, JACF	Divestment, marketing financial services and deregulation, regulation and efficiency of state enterprises
1990–1995	Private equity firms: market development Variety (MBOs, MBIs) Vendor source: Bankruptcy Vendor source: privatization U.K., CEE Impact: longevity Impact: employee relations Impact: performance	Agency Agency theory Life-cycle	Thompson, Robbie Robbie Robbie, Ennew Thompson, Robbie, Filatotchev, Buck, Petrin Thompson, Robbie, Romanet, Bruining, Herst Chiplin, Robbie Thompson, Robbie, Ennew	JBV, RS Omega, JMS Omega FAM, CES, EAWM, FS, SS, PAD, IBR, IJTE, JBE, OXRP SMJ, JBFA, ETP, SIJ IRJ BSR, SIPE, ISBJ, EJ	Trade credit, public sector auditing, privatization in general, corporate governance
1996–2000	Vendor source: privatization U.K., CEE Impact: longevity/failure Impact: performance Financial aspects Review articles	Agency theory, stakeholder agency theory, entrepreneurial cognition Agency Agency Contracting	Hoskisson, Filatotchev, Buck, Busenitz, Dial, Grosfeld, Wieser, Wilson, Pendleton Wilson, Robbie, Ennew Wilson, Robbie Citron, Robbie Robbie, Chiplin, Albrighton	AMR, CMR, JDS, JCE, AMP, JWB, EoT, JMS, LGS, APCE, BJIR, EoP, MDE, BSR, JESBF ABR, CGIR JBFA, BH	Corporate governance, VCs (monitoring, syndication, etc.), serial entrepreneurs, divestment and corporate refocusing, employee ownership, emerging economy strategies

Year/Period	Topic/Research Questions	Theories	Team	Publications	Other spin-off and complementary publications
2001–2005	Private equity firms: market development and firm behavior Vendor source: privatizations Vendor source: family firms Vendor source: stock market impact Impact: employee relations Impact: MBO firm performance Impact: longevity/failure Review article	Agency theory, entrepreneurial cognition Stewardship Agency Agency	Kitamura, Hoskisson, Bruining, Bonnet, Toms Hoskisson, Busenitz, Filatotchev, Buck, Dyomina Westhead, Howarth Weir Bacon, Dyomina, Bruining, Boselie Siegel, Harris Jelic, Saadouni, Citron, Robbie Filatotchev, Buck	JPE, LRP, MAR, BH AME, VC, JIBS JBV JBFA, AFE BJIR, IJHRM RES JBFA, EFM APCE	Serial entrepreneurs, VCs (syndication, internationalization), divestment and corporate restructuring, academic spin-offs and technology transfer, corporate governance, internationalization, emerging economies, RBV, entrepreneurial teams, journal reviewing and editing
2006–2010	Private equity firms: market development, behavior, partner select Vendor source: family firms Vendor source: stock market firms Impact: employee relations Impact: employment Impact: MBO firm performance Impact: longevity/failure Review articles	Agency, RBV, SE	Renneboog, Scholes, Simon, Meuleman, Manigart, Lockett, Frobisher, Jackson Scholes, Westhead, Bruining, Burrows Renneboog, Weir, Laing, Burrows Bacon, Meuleman, Wood, Bruining, Boselie, Dyomina Amess, Girma Amess, Meuleman, Scholes, Nikoskelainen Citron Siegel, Cumming, Gilligan, Amess, Wood, Weir, Girma	JACF, JMS, JBFA SBE JCF, CGIR, EFM, ABR HR, JIR IJEB JCF, ETP ABR JCF, VC, IJMR, BH, CGIR	Academic spin-offs and technology transfer, VCs, serial entrepreneurs, internationalization, IPOs, returnee entrepreneurs, HRM, RBV, journal editing and publishing, corporate entrepreneurship

2011–	Topic	Authors	Journals	Themes
	Private equity firm behavior/ internationalization/ negotiation	Meuleman, Kellermanns	JBV, in progress	Academic spin-offs and technology transfer, VCs, serial entrepreneurs, internationalization and international entrepreneurship, IPOs, returnee entrepreneurs, HRM, RBV, journal editing and publishing, corporate entrepreneurship, management teams, future of entrepreneurship research, family firms, emerging economies, corporate governance, entrepreneurial growth, directors of entrepreneurial firms
	IT			
	Agency	Jelic	EFM	
	Ethics	Scholes, Li	JBE	
	Vendor source: secondary buyouts	Scholes, Westhead, Chua, Chrisman, Lloyd	ISBJ, JFBS	
	Vendor source: privatization	Sudarsanam, Huang, Weir	CGIR, JMG	
	Vendor source: family firms	Bacon, Meuleman	AMP, IR	
	Vendor source: stock market firms	Wilson, Nikoskelainen, Maula, Bruining, Verwaal, Alperovych	JCF, JBF, SBE, EJOR	
	Impact: employee relations	Jelic	MDE	
	Impact: MBO firm performance	Amess, Girma	SBE	
	Impact: longevity	Siegel, Shawky, Wood	CGIR, JCF, CC	
	Impact: employment			
	Review articles			Social capital, microfinance

Notes:

Key to Journals: ABR = Accounting and Business Research; AME = Academy of Management Executive/Perspectives; AMR = Academy of Management Review; AFE = Applied Financial Economics; AMP = Academy of Management Executives; APCE = Annals of Public and Cooperative Economics; BAR = British Accounting Review; BER = Bulletin of Economic Research; BH = Business History; BJIR = British Journal of Industrial Relations; BSR = Business Strategy Review; CC= Competition and Change; CES = Comparative Economic Studies; CGIR = Corporate Governance – International Review; CMR = California Management Review; EAWM = Economic Analysis and Workers Management; EFM = European Financial Management; EJ = Economic Journal; ETP = Entrepreneurship Theory and Practice; EJOR = European Journal of Operations Research; EoP = Economics of Planning; EoT = Economics of Transition; FAM = Financial Accountability and Management; FS = Fiscal Studies; HR = Human Relations; IBR = International Business Review; IJEB = International Journal of Economics and Business; IJHRM = International Journal of Human Resource Management; IJMR = International Journal of Management Reviews; IJTE = International Journal of Transport Economics; IR = Industrial Relations; IRJ = Industrial Relations Journal; ISBJ = International Small Business Journal; JACF = Journal of Applied Corporate Finance; JBE = Journal of Business Ethics; JBF = Journal of Banking and Finance; JBFA = Journal of Business Finance and Accounting; JBV = Journal of Business Venturing; JCE = Journal of Comparative Economics; JCF = Journal of Corporate Finance; JDS = Journal of Development Studies; JES = Journal of Economic Studies; JESBF = Journal of Entrepreneurship and Small Business Finance; JFBS = Journal of Family Business Strategy; JIBS = Journal of International Business Studies; JIR = Journal of Industrial Relations; JMG = Journal of Management and Governance; JMS = Journal of Management Studies; JPE = Journal of Private Equity; JWB = Journal of World Business; LGS = Local Government Studies; LRP = Long Range Planning; MAR = Management Accounting Research; MDE = Managerial and Decision Economics; OXRP = Oxford Review of Economic Policy; PAD = Public Administration and Development; PE = Piccola Empresa; PMM = Public Money and Management; RS = Regional Studies; RES = Review of Economics and Statistics; SBE = Small Business Economics; SIJ = Services Industries Journal; SJPE = Scottish Journal of Political Economy; SMJ = Strategic Management Journal; SS = Soviet Studies (Europe-Asia Studies); VC = Venture Capital.

Other abbreviations: CEE = Central and Eastern Europe; HRM = human resource management; IPOs = initial public offerings; MBI = management buyin; MBO = management buyout; RBV = resource based view; SE = strategic entrepreneurship; VCs = venture capitalists.

After Tenure and Promotion

The huge effort required to achieve tenure may leave many scholars with little motivation or energy to maintain a publishing career. Studies tend to show a decline in research productivity post-tenure, although there are variations in the timing and extent of the decline. Harrison (2006) notes that those whose publications are in print when they get tenure are more likely to continue to publish afterwards. Estes and Polnick (2012) notably suggest that reductions in productivity post-tenure are due to reduced motivation as faculty do not value the outcomes from sustaining higher levels of productivity. During this period in their careers, some faculty may transition into a more mentoring role wherein they guide doctoral students and junior colleagues. However, in countries that have introduced national research assessment frameworks, such as the U.K. where tenure is absent, there is pressure and incentives to continue to publish at least four good papers every five years or so.

After Career Breaks

Career breaks that affect publishing can take several forms. Major managerial, editorial or other service jobs can place severe time constraints on one's ability to publish. Maternity leave likely has a major impact for the publishing careers of women faculty. Yet, at a time when academics are expected to make an impact along multiple dimensions, it becomes increasingly difficult to put a stop to a publishing career. The national research assessment and evaluation exercises just noted may still require those performing significant managerial roles to demonstrate a quality publications return (www.ref.ac.uk), although there is some allowance for maternity leave. Many managerial roles, such as head of department, may be for only a limited period of time, after which there is a need to return to normal scholarly activities. While traditionally academics in the hard sciences and engineering may have built up large teams of researchers, this is typically less so in the social sciences and in management in particular. Accordingly, scholars likely face major challenges associated with re-entering the publishing process, especially as the literature and key research questions as well as methods will have moved on.

WHY?

The reasons to maintain a strong publications record are influenced by individual and environmental level factors. Quite apart from personal interest and motivation, my view was that continuing to publish despite the demands of reviewers and editors was a great way to maintain one's sanity. Maybe dealing with referees is soul-destroying, but for me the opportunity cost seemed to be a life devoted to interminable faculty meetings.

There may be good reasons to maintain a publishing career even after securing tenure or promotion. Annual performance reviews likely take account of publications as one element in setting salary. Besides an absence of salary enhancement, a lack of publications may lead to compensatory increases in teaching, administration and service workloads. So, essentially, individuals need to make choices about how they see their career developing.

Environmental level factors can have a huge influence on the need to sustain a publications career. Schools frequently change deans, and deans come in with new aims and strategies. On the one hand, having sustained a publications record can provide for mobility if a change of direction by the new dean means that there ceases to be a good fit. On the other hand, a sustained publications record can mean a scholar is well-placed if the new dean's intention is to ramp up the research rating in an otherwise under-performing school. Continuing a publications record as a dean or head of department may bring a strong demonstration of leadership in such circumstances.

National research assessment exercises with their requirements to continue to produce at a specified volume and quality of output, say, every five to seven years, create demands to continue to publish. Some of these exercises are increasingly demanding different forms of output than publication in traditional academic journals. In particular, policymakers are looking for academic research to have a wider impact on society, such as through changing policy and firm behavior. The result of such exercises may be seen by some as pernicious as they can produce a focus on journal publications to the exclusion of other forms of scholarly output and endeavor. They have typically created a transfer market in academics with publications records that will be judged of high quality by review panels. This can serve to break through rigid salary structures in some contexts that do not fairly reflect performance. However, national evaluation exercises can contain idiosyncrasies and perverse incentives that have implications for sustaining a publications career. For example, in the U.K. constraints on authors in the same department reporting the same piece of co-authored work essentially means that there is an incentive to work with colleagues at another university, which would mean that an article could be reported twice. The alternative is that by remaining in the same department and continuing to co-author one may have to publish twice the level of output during the assessment period. A further inconsistency may arise with respect to a different aspect of the researcher's output. For example, in the U.K., while researchers moving to another institution can take their publications with them to be returned for the Research Excellence Framework by their new institution they are prevented from transferring the impact their research may have generated.

WHAT?

So, there are good reasons to sustain a publications career, but what do you need to do to achieve it?

Develop a Heterogeneous Portfolio for Momentum

Developing a heterogeneous portfolio in the types of publications can be an important means of facilitating a sustained career. Tenure committees focus on publications in a, usually, tightly drawn list of journals. Similarly, national research assessment exercises typically expect to see a specific number of publications per scholar in a set period and reserve their highest evaluation for publications in so-called top journals. Most weight seems likely to be given to rigorously reviewed theoretical and empirical papers; indeed in some cases to the exclusion of other types of paper, let alone other types of output. Yet we know that papers published in what may be regarded as lower level journals oftentimes have higher citation rates than papers published in top journals (Starbuck, 2005 and this volume). Neglecting second tier but still very good journal outlets may mean that opportunities to publish important contributions are forgone (Clark and Wright, 2009). Or, seen from another perspective, a focus solely on publishing in the very top journals will likely lead to a short publications career. It is sometimes thought that authors of highly cited works publish few papers. However, this is not necessarily the case. For example, while Nobel Prize winner Ronald Coase earned his reputation based on his work on transaction costs and the nature of the firm, and the problem of social cost (Coase, 1992), he published numerous other papers (http://www.coase.org/coasepublications.htm).

More general evidence supports this view. Citation classics, in general, appear to emerge as regular parts of a larger research programme rather than as one-off pieces divorced from a stream of published articles (Hollenbeck and Mannor, 2007). Hence, actively pursuing a sustained publications career likely brings the benefits of professional developmental experiences that enhance the overall impact of one's research.

Further Empirical/Theoretical Articles

Entering new areas can involve publishing on topics that are related to prior publications, which allows for building upon tacit knowledge and conceptual tools. Alternatively, entering unrelated areas likely requires a bigger investment and dealing with greater competition. Scholars studying a particular managerial phenomenon may enhance the longevity of their research agenda by seeking connections with wider literatures and developing collaborations with teams with expertise in those areas (see below).

For example, my research on management buyouts, while involving a new form of entrepreneurial organization, offered opportunities for new insights and contributions in the finance, strategy, economics and human resource management (HRM) literatures, as I explain in more detail below.

From Traditional Journal Articles to Position/Think Pieces

Although as scholars our focus from doctoral studies onwards is on learning how to publish traditional theoretical and empirical articles, having developed a reputation in a particular area can create space and open up opportunities for other kinds of journal articles. Position pieces, keynote articles and contributions to debates provide the opportunity to stand back and say things that are not feasible in a traditional journal article. Oftentimes such articles are invited, but some journals allocate space for authors to submit such articles or propose topics for debate. These articles are often in more lowly ranked journals, but not always. For example, when Tim Clark and I were General Editors at the *Journal of Management Studies* we introduced the "Point–CounterPoint Section" (PCP) to stimulate debates on emerging topics or to reinvigorate existing areas. The articles are typically subject to development review in order to ensure quality is maintained. They can become highly cited. For example, after I ceased being an editor, Igor Filatotchev and I put together a PCP on governance in multinational corporations in 2011. While the paper by

Peter Buckley and Roger Strange analyzed developments in internaliz-ation theory, a key theory in international business, the paper by Igor and I adopted an agency perspective on corporate governance in multinational corporations that challenges the prevailing perspective (Filatotchev and Wright, 2011).

As a doctoral student, publishing articles based on a review of the literature can be quite challenging. This is typically because a literature review article requires more than a summary of the literature. In particular, review articles in good journals that are open to this kind of contribution (such as the *Journal of Management, Journal of Manage-ment Studies* and *International Journal of Management Reviews*) require added value in terms of the development of an over-arching research framework which helps identify directions for further research. More experienced authors are likely to be able to undertake a review of a particular literature from a position of 'authority' and to be better placed to see the 'road ahead' and/or distil the literature into a framework for further research. Not to be ignored, they may also be better placed to convince journal editors to commission such an article.

Guest editing special issues is a further publication outlet where scholars can build on their experience as an author, but also as a reviewer, to convince regular editors of the journal to extend the opportunity to bring together articles on an interesting new area (see Chapter 23 in this volume). The role of special issues is usually to open up a new area rather than close down an old one, though the area does need to be sufficiently developed to generate a stream of articles of sufficient quality. Like review articles, writing the introductory article to a special issue provides the guest editor with the opportunity to set out a new research agenda rather than simply summarizing the articles in the special issue. Three special issue introductions that I have co-authored with guest co-editors have become highly cited (Hoskisson et al.'s (2000) introduction to the *Academy of Management Journal* special issue on "Strategies in emerging markets"; Barney et al.'s (2001) introduction to the *Journal of Management* special issue on the "Resource-based view of the firm"; Wright et al.'s (2005) introduction to the *Journal of Manage-ment Studies* special issue on " Strategies in emerging markets: Challeng-ing the conventional wisdom"). Note that the *Journal of Management Studies* special issue represents an important dimension of sustaining a publications career as it arose as a direct consequence of profile and collaborative links formed as a result of the *Academy of Management Journal* special issue.

Although in an audit culture or for tenure purposes books, particularly research monographs, may not count as much as journal articles, they offer scope to tackle 'big questions' and open up important new areas. These monographs provide an opportunity to bring together previous work and broaden the discussion and contribution. They can become very highly cited and should be seen as an important part of your portfolio of research output. As an example, my journal publications on academic entrepreneurship led co-authors and myself to synthesize and extend the insights gained in an initial book aimed at both a practitioner and research audience (Wright et al., 2007), which itself has become highly cited, and a subsequent book (Link et al., 2015) reflecting on the more mature state of academic entrepreneurship research.

A further aspect of sustaining a publications career is to gain impact through reaching a wider audience that includes practitioners and policy-makers (Aguinis et al., 2012; Bartunek et al., 2001). However, a tenure process and evaluation system that focuses on publishing in top tier academic journals likely downplays the incentive to publish articles in practitioner journals, even though some of these are high quality and articles within them may become highly cited. For example, practitioner journals like *Harvard Business Review* and *California Management Review* feature in the approved list of 45 journals that contribute to a school's ranking in the *Financial Times* Top 100 MBA programmes yet may well be absent from a school's tenure list. Quite apart from the inconsistency in a school's tenure policies and its aims to have its MBA ranked highly, not targeting practitioner journals can undermine efforts to sustain a publications career. Practitioner journals can be viewed as a means of product differentiation that helps extend the publication of research output beyond traditional academic papers. More experienced scholars may be better placed than less experienced co-authors to identify how academic insights can be presented to address the challenges faced by practitioners.

Besides publications in practitioner journals, engaging with practice through the publication of reports and white papers for industry, professional and governmental bodies may further help sustain a publications career in academic journals. Engagement through social media, while promoting existing research and insights, can also garner useful feedback. Such engagement can take scholars beyond the closed loop of the academic literature to observe puzzles that challenge existing theory and evidence, as well as the emergence of new phenomena that help identify the boundaries of existing theories. The key is to link such observations on the ground to the existing literature in order to develop novel insights. Sometimes this may lead, as Ronald Coase observed in commenting on his contribution during his Nobel Prize Lecture, to the inclusion in our analysis of features so obvious that they have tended to be overlooked, but which can become seminal (Coase, 1992).

The development of the rigor-relevance debate in the context of the policy debate about the contribution and impact of management research has brought to the fore the importance of interacting with practice (Clark et al., 2013). As a way of sustaining a publications career in a turbulent environment, such interactions need to be seen as complementary to rather than as substitutes for publishing in academic journals.

Throughout the life of CMBOR the strategy has been to publish quarterly reports of market trends in management buyouts and private equity in order to garner media coverage for research funders from the industry. This has led to interviews with and invitations to write commentary articles in national and international news media (e.g. an interview for a BBC Radio 4 File On Four program devoted to private equity). In turn, this profile has attracted further research funding for particular projects (e.g. several from the European, Dutch and British Private Equity and Venture Capital Associations). The deliberate strategy has been to approach these projects with a view to being able to subsequently generate further academic journal articles from the research.

Although there was a high level of media interest in reports of trends in the phenomenon, for many years this impact did not count for career enhancement purposes. The latest Research Excellence Framework in the U.K. (covering the period 2008–2013) belatedly did so, and the impact case I produced on CMBOR (available at http://results.ref.ac.uk/Submissions/Impact/1565) was rated as outstanding by the review panel, showing that academic journal publications and practice/policy impact can be highly complementary.

HOW?

The key remaining question concerns how can scholars develop and implement strategies to sustain their publications career?

Being Strategically Entrepreneurial

There may be a tendency to focus on individual papers or projects. Some new areas may garner a lot of interest and generate publications because they happen to be fashionable. But topics go out of fashion and there is a need to ride the waves of fashion. This may be difficult without adopting a more strategic entrepreneurial perspective that involves envisioning an over-arching research program. Developing a research program therefore means thinking about the "big questions" that need to be addressed in your area. In other words, the longevity of a publishing career will be influenced by the scope of the initial area the scholar starts with. Scholars therefore need to develop generalized non-tradable assets (Gedajlovic and Carney, 2010). These concern the conceptual tools they develop and the empirical contexts they study. But they also concern developing the capabilities for strategic entrepreneurship. Being entrepreneurial involves creating, recognizing and exploiting new opportunities (Alvarez and Barney, 2007). Strategic entrepreneurship involves connecting opportunities with the resources needed to deliver on them (Ireland et al., 2003).

We know from evidence on repeat entrepreneurs that the ability to create, identify and pursue new opportunities successfully may be influenced, positively or negatively, by cognitive biases (Ucbasaran et al., 2008, 2009). Repeat entrepreneurs may attempt to use the same "recipes" that worked well in prior ventures when current environmental conditions require a different approach and may be a new direction. Making a switch to a new area presents challenges. On the one hand, liabilities of newness suggest difficulties in getting up to speed to join an existing "conversation". On the other hand, there may be benefits of newness for experienced scholars to enter a new area. The subtlety of wisdom resulting from having learned how to identify, frame and execute opportunities may help reduce the barriers to entering a new area. But there is also the need to access the resources to realize these new opportunities, in which the development of social capital and teams has an important role to play.

A schematic development of a portfolio of research programs is shown in Figure 5.1. Doctoral research training provides the basis for an initial research program. This program may come to an end once a PhD dissertation is completed and publications achieved from it. However, it may also be possible to continue and develop this research program over many years. I have found that by making links between a current research program and other emerging areas it is possible to identify and exploit new research opportunities that can be developed into a parallel research program. This continual process of seeking out new research opportunities may lead to the development of new research programs over time. Some may turn out to be limited and wither away after a few papers. Others may provide a stepping-stone from a declining area and help trigger a resurgence of research activity. Just as you need to be open to new opportunities, you also need to curtail research programs when the well is running dry. Identifying, building up and sustaining these new research programs requires the development of resources and capabilities, to which we now turn.

Figure 5.1   Schematic sustaining of a publications career

Using the case of CMBOR, Figure 5.2 indicates how sustainability was developed from what appeared initially to be a very narrow and transitory phenomenon. The potential longevity of management buyouts as a research agenda was not initially evident. Indeed, as a then junior lecturer (i.e. assistant professor) I was told by my head of department that I was wasting my academic career as the phenomenon would disappear once the recession of the early 1980s ended! Fortunately, this was a pre-national research evaluation world. Had it not been it might well have meant that the research trajectory would not have been pursued. Still, promotion to reader (associate professor), although in the event six years away, would require the demonstration of a publications record in good journals. Over 35 years and multiple millions of dollars of research funding later this research is still yielding good journal publications.

As Table 5.1 and Figure 5.2 show, the focus of the research program evolved over time. Five broad themes were sustained over the period: private equity market and firm behavior; vendor sources of deals; impact of buyouts on employment and employee relations; impact of buyouts on performance and longevity; and review articles.

While exploiting the initial investment in the area, to sustain the research agenda and publications over time, it was necessary to explore for new opportunities associated with developments in the management buyout market and to connect to various general literatures and debates.

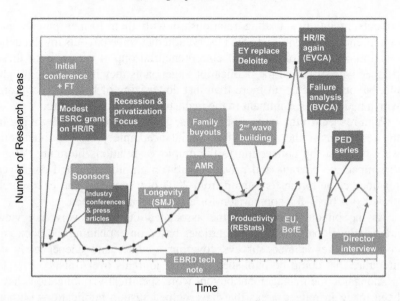

Notes: AMR = Academy of Management Review; BofE = Bank of England; BVCA = British Venture Capital Association; EBRD = European Bank for Reconstruction and Development; FT = Financial Times; HR/IR = Human Resource/Industrial Relations; PED = Private Equity Demystified; REStats = Review of Economics and Statistics; SMJ = Strategic Management Journal.

Figure 5.2   Thirty-five years of management buyouts and private equity research

The evolution of the management buyout phenomenon and related activities over time, notably through waves of activity in the 1980s and from the late 1990s to 2007, led to new research opportunities, even within the same broad topic areas, as the research and policy issues have differed over time. For example, the prominence of different vendor sources of buyouts over time generated new dimensions of the phenomenon which enabled links to different literatures to be made. Hence, while management buyouts themselves are quite narrow, the agenda has been sustained through identifying different dimensions that link to the literatures on entrepreneurship, finance, strategy, economics, employee relations/HR, international business, ethics, and so on.

These literatures also provided important links to different theoretical tools. In particular, although the finance literature has focused on agency theory, this is a narrow conceptual approach that limits insights on the buyout phenomenon. For example, transaction costs and resource dependency theories could be applied to the observation that some buyouts maintain a trading relationship with their former parent, and entrepreneurial cognition to the observation that some buyouts involved the recognition and exploitation of entrepreneurial opportunities. Both these perspectives sustained the publications agenda as they helped to highlight that buyouts were about more than just downsizing of listed corporations which had been predominant in the mainstream finance literature.

With respect to the impact of buyouts, given the focus on job saving in the recession of the early 1980s, initial academic journal publications were obtained by connecting to the employee relations literature. When the impact of buyouts and private equity on employment and employee relations came to the fore again from 2007 onwards, this earlier research provided a basis for comparison for a new research agenda.

As the buyout market and the associated literature evolved, review articles developed from general articles based on explaining the phenomenon to more detailed surveys covering a wider and deeper body of literature that could be published in better journals over time.

Alongside the management buyout work specifically, publications have been made in related areas that have helped sustain publications output. To some extent there has been a two-way flow of insights and identification of opportunities for projects and papers. Notably, the closeness of management buyouts and private equity to venture capital leant itself easily to the development of this area as a related core program. Studying the concept of an entity being transferred from being part of one organization to becoming an independently owned firm also meant that it was a relatively short step to recognizing the research opportunities of academic spin-offs from universities. Research in this area has developed into a further core program (Siegel and Wright, 2015).

Initially, my interest in management buyouts involved riskier exploration activity while at the time I was exploiting previous investments in work on management control systems (at the time I taught management accounting and was collaborating with an electrical engineering colleague) and, separately, efficiency and accountability in state owned enterprises (I had previously worked in a state owned firm and had written a Masters dissertation on inflation accounting and performance in the gas industry). These early core research areas declined as privatization took hold.

While these topics were at some distance from management buyouts there were subsequent opportunities to make connections that were not initially remotely envisaged. For example, the development of state enterprise privatizations in the U.K. from the mid-1980s and subsequently in former centrally planned economies after the fall of the Berlin Wall saw an important role for management and employee buyouts. This policy development and CMBOR's unique track record in buyouts opened up opportunities for policy and practical impact through advice that led to the publication of reports aimed at these audiences in addition to academic publications. A growing profile and reaching out from studying buyouts in emerging economies led to connections being made with other researchers interested in strategy in emerging economies and, subsequently, returnee entrepreneurs. This research led to the development of a new core area of research and the development of an extended team of researchers and collaborators (Buck, Filatotchev, Hoskisson, Liu, Lu, Honig, Drori, Peng, Pruthi), as summarized in Table 5.2.

Table 5.2   Emerging economies research

• 2000 AMJ Special Issue	➤ Broadening out of recognition
• 2005 JMS Special Issue	
• 2006: BA Funded survey	➤ Builds on EE program
• 2008: ETP SI University vs non-university location choice & asset complementarity	➤ Ground clearing survey of returnees only; cross-section, ltd measures
• 2009: JIBS Exporting & knowledge transfer	
• 2009: ETP SI Transnationals; SEJ SI IE	
• 2010: JIBS Knowledge spillovers	➤ Broaden agenda
• 2011: SEJ Networks & spillovers	➤ Archival database
• 2012: ResPol Knowledge spillovers and mobility	
• 2013: Book ch. Resources	
• 2013: SEJ SI SE in EE	➤ Recognition
• 2013: ISBE Returnees, transnationals & entry networks in India	➤ Broadening agenda
• 2013: IBR TMT and diversification	➤ Extending context & RQs
• 2014: JIBS Int experience & home/host institutions	➤ Returnees just one aspect of TMT human & social capital
• 2014: ISBJ Learning and returnees	
• 2014: JMS Classic Paper	

Notes: AMJ = Academy of Management Journal; BA = British Academy; EE = Emerging Economies; ETP SI = Entrepreneurship Theory and Practice Special Issue; ISBE = Institute for Small Business and Entrepreneurship; ISBJ = International Small Business Journal; IBR = International Business Review; JIBS = Journal of International Business Studies; JMS = Journal of Management Studies; ResPol = Research Policy; SE in EE = Strategic Entrepreneurship in Emerging Economies; SEJ = Strategic Entrepreneurship Journal; SEJ SI IE = Strategic Entrepreneurship Journal Special Issue on International Entrepreneurship; TMT = top management teams.

Social Capital

Developing your social capital can provide a basis for unlocking new opportunities and accessing complementary expertise. Social capital represents the resources associated with individuals' networks of relationships (Gedajlovic et al., 2013). Scholars build their social capital initially through working with supervisors, attending doctoral colloquia, presenting at conferences, and so on. But the paradox of embeddedness in existing social relationships is well-known (Uzzi, 1997; Meuleman et al., 2010). For example, family firms may benefit from the social capital of the founder but this may lead to inward looking behavior, missed opportunities for growth and ultimately a threat to the survival of the firm (Steier et al., 2009; Wilson et al., 2013). For family firms and scholars alike, new social capital may need to be built in order to break out of the straight jacket of existing trajectories.

How can you build new social capital? Social capital through collaboration with actual or potential team members can be built by delivering quality contributions on time. A reputation for delivery can mean team members will want to work with you again (see Chapter 12 in this volume). Providing timely, detailed and insightful informal comments on colleagues' working papers or on papers of scholars working in your area also builds social capital. Supervising doctoral students is a way to build social capital for the future as those students go on to become faculty members.

Some activities, while potentially being onerous or seen as purely altruistic, can generate significant benefits for sustaining a publications career. A willingness to contribute to learned societies by, for example, organizing and participating in doctoral and junior faculty colloquia such as those run by the divisions of the Academy of Management at the annual conference can both build social capital and provide exposure to emerging ideas.

Taking on editorial and reviewing roles and performing them effectively can help sustain a publishing career. For example, the social capital that is developed can make editors more predisposed to accept proposals for special issues as they know that scholars will be able to deliver a quality contribution that fits with that particular journal's expectations. Such activities also generate advance exposure to emerging ideas and methods that can help extend expertise and, without involving plagiarism, suggest new directions for existing research agendas.

Team Building

There is little doubt that building teams of collaborators is a key way to developing a sustained publications career. There is clear evidence that the mean number of authors per journal paper has been increasing over time. For example, analysis of trends in the *Journal of Management Studies* since it was founded in 1964 shows that in the first five years, over four fifths (81.3 percent) of articles published were single authored. In contrast, in 2005–2009 only a quarter (25.1 percent) of articles were single authored and the number of triple-authored papers also exceeded the number of single-authored papers, with the number of papers with four authors also noticeably increased (Clark et al., 2014). This trend is perhaps not too surprising given the demands for papers to show novel contributions, conceptual development and high quality data and analytical techniques.

Team working helps maintain momentum on projects and papers, particularly in the face of other demands on scholars' time that emerge as careers develop. A number of writers have stressed the importance of maintaining momentum in sustaining a publishing career, such as setting aside regular parts of each day to write, rather than waiting for some mythical ideal of a dedicated block of time (Boice, 1992). Moreover, even if a sabbatical period is secured, planning momentum ahead of time can help optimize the eventual output. If a co-author is unable to devote large blocks of time during a particular period, having team members who can push the work forward can be very useful. Even being able to work briefly on a paper before passing it on in a timely manner to co-authors can help maintain momentum.

Building a team also brings complementary expertise. Such complementarity is not just in relation to conceptual and empirical expertise. Complementarity can also extend to the different perspectives that team members bring to bear on a research question that can contribute to novel syntheses. Further, a team member who is able to position and frame a paper in relation to the literature, and who is able to draw out the contribution of a paper, possesses an important skill. While oftentimes under-recognized, such expertise can make the difference between whether a paper is published or not. Unless a paper's contribution to addressing an important research gap is clearly articulated in the Introduction, editors and reviewers may not be convinced (see Chapter 10 in this volume). More experienced team members may be better placed to perform this role and this too can enable them to extend their publishing career.

As scholars' research agendas develop, the nature of research teams may also evolve. The composition and dynamics of an initial team may change and new teams may be formed either instead or alongside. From my own experience, the development of new research avenues beyond the initial work on management buyouts involved building different teams of co-authors with knowledge and empirical skills in these new areas as well as with junior colleagues. At the same time colleagues in these other areas had the incentive to collaborate as the topic offered access to a novel dataset and research question that had not previously been addressed in their area. This approach included developing collaborative links with colleagues when I was at Nottingham as it was necessary to understand what was required to publish in journals in these areas. For example, research on employee relations aspects of buyouts involved the development of a collaborative team including Nick Bacon, at that time a professor of industrial relations, and Louise Scholes, at that time a researcher in CMBOR. Similarly, work on management and employee buyouts in Eastern Europe involved building a research team comprising Igor Filatotchev and Trevor Buck, who had expertise in former centrally planned economies and corporate governance.

Some team members have been co-authors of mine for some 20 years (Thompson, Filatotchev, Bruining, Wilson), while others are much shorter term or even one-off collaborators. Some team members' involvement has ebbed and flowed as the agenda has changed over the different waves of buyouts and private equity (Wilson). Some team members have continued the collaboration in other areas beyond management buyouts. For example, collaboration with Filatotchev on privatization buyouts in emerging economies has evolved into research on both initial public offerings (IPOs) and returnee entrepreneurs.

Various conflicts can arise which undermine the longevity of teams. Author order on papers can be especially contentious, especially for authors concerned about promotion or like me happen to have a family name towards the end of the alphabet! There are various ways to alleviate this problem that should be addressed at the outset. For example, authors may agree to include a note that authors are listed alphabetically but all contributed equally. For teams that work successfully together over a sustained period, one practical solution that enables each team member to be first author is to take the lead in turn in writing the first draft of a paper, even if it is only a rough draft, and to be responsible for driving a paper to completion. This was a strategy we adopted, for example, in the team with Buck and Filatotchev.

Perceived or actual contributions that fall short of other members' expectations can seriously undermine team cohesion. Before this leads to irretrievable breakdowns, open discussion of the problems may help resolve problems. It may be that unexpected and unavoidable demands have meant that a team member is unable to deliver what was initially promised at the expected time. Where there is a continuing research program, it may be feasible to delineate a subset of areas where particular team members may contribute rather than having an expectation that all members will contribute equally to all outputs. In this way, the composition of teams may be quite fluid.

Some teams may be maintained over long periods while others may be just one-off or short-lived. The longevity of a team's collaborative efforts may not be evident at the outset. An initial team collaboration may be viewed as taking out an option for future collaborations, which may or may not be exercised. What the subsequent opportunities are may not be known at the outset and may only emerge as a result of the collaboration.

Over time, of course, team members may want or need to pursue other interests and projects but may still be able to continue to work together. Some members may need to carve out their own trajectory to provide a clear signal of their contribution to a field to Tenure and Promotions committees. Pursuing other opportunities can be beneficial too in bringing new insights that can reinvigorate an initial research collaboration.

Professional Development

How a sustained publishing record can be delivered involves the professional development of scholars. Much of the focus of training has typically been on doctoral students and junior faculty through colloquia at conferences such as the Academy of Management Conference. However, mid-career academics also need continuing support. The bar to get into top journals rises significantly over time. Meeting increases in the "industry standard" quantitative and qualitative research methods expected of papers aimed at top journals may be particularly critical. But the need for professional development goes further as editorial and reviewer demands regarding the framing and contribution of papers also change over time.

Research Grants

Obtaining research grants can result in additional resource in terms of time, as they may allow for buyouts from teaching and administration, as well as providing for the recruitment of researchers. Research grants from governmental funding bodies increasingly require evidence that the work will have impact besides academic journal output. Research grants from governmental funding bodies are typically highly competitive and therefore quite lumpy as rejection rates are high. Research funding from industry and commerce is also increasingly difficult to come by and may rely very much on the researcher having established a reputation in a particular area. The objectives of research funders in industry and commerce may be quite specific, focused on issues of immediate concern and involve confidentiality issues. However, the trick is to design studies that allow access to novel data that, while meeting the needs of commercial funders, can also allow novel research questions to be addressed that will be publishable in top journals. In an environment where there is a need to demonstrate research impact, this kind of research funding can be a useful source.

For example, building on the reputation we had developed on private equity and management buyouts, the European Private Equity and Venture Capital Association commissioned CMBOR in 2008 to conduct a survey of employee relations in private equity backed companies. This was driven by concerns being raised by trade unions and the European Parliament about the supposed adverse impact on union recognition and consultation following a private equity backed buyout. Our study, which involved putting together a team including myself and others with expertise in private equity and those with expertise in industrial relations and HRM, provided rigorous evidence to counter the critics but also enabled us to publish several papers in academic journals (notably *Human Relations*, *Industrial Relations* and *Academy of Management Perspectives*), as well as being able to construct an impact case study for the U.K. Research Excellence Framework exercise in 2013.

CONCLUSIONS

In this chapter I have attempted to analyze how the challenges in sustaining a publications career can be addressed. Sustaining a publications career involves taking a wider view of what publication means that goes beyond traditional academic articles in the field that one began with to include other complementary forms of publication and diversification into related domains. Sustaining a publications career also requires scholars to engage in strategic entrepreneurship that involves both the continual creation and recognition of publishing opportunities and the development of the resources to realize such opportunities. This strategic entrepreneurship is facilitated by the development of both adaptable human capital and a broadly based social capital.

Undoubtedly, there are different routes to sustaining a publications career. The analysis presented here provides some insights into how scholars at different stages in their careers can map out a route that fits their interests and circumstances.

NOTE

* A shorter, family firm research-oriented version of this chapter was published as Wright and Sharma (2013).

REFERENCES

Aguinis, H., I. Suarez-González, G. Lannelongue and H. Joo (2012). 'Scholarly impact revisited', *Academy of Management Perspectives*, **26** (2), 105–132.

Alvarez, S.A. and J.B. Barney (2007). 'Discovery and creation: Alternative theories of entrepreneurial action', *Strategic Entrepreneurship Journal*, **1** (1–2), 11–26.

Barney, J., M. Wright and D. Ketchen (2001). 'The resource-based view of the firm: Ten Years after 1991', *Journal of Management*, **27** (6), 625–642.

Bartunek, J., S. Rynes and R. Daft (2001). 'Across the great divide: Knowledge creation and transfer between practitioners and academics', *Academy of Management Journal*, **44**, 340–355.

Boice, R. (1992). *The New Faculty Member*. San Francisco: Jossey-Bass.

Clark, T., S.W. Floyd and M. Wright (2006). 'On the review process and journal development', *Journal of Management Studies*, **43** (5), 655–664.

Clark, T., S.W. Floyd and M. Wright (2013). 'In search of the impactful and the interesting: Swings of the pendulum?', *Journal of Management Studies*, **50** (8), 1358–1373.

Clark, T. and M. Wright (2009). 'So farewell, then … Reflections on editing the *Journal of Management Studies*', *Journal of Management Studies*, **46** (1), 1–9.

Clark, T., M. Wright, Z. Iskoujina and P. Garnett (2014). 'JMS at 50: Trends over time', *Journal of Management Studies*, **51** (1), 19–37.

Coase, R. (1992). 'The institutional structure of production', *American Economic Review*, **82** (4), 713–719.

Estes, B. and B. Polnick (2012). 'Examining motivation theory in higher education: An expectancy theory analysis of tenured faculty productivity', *International Journal of Management, Business and Administration*, **15** (1), 1–7.

Filatotchev, I. and M. Wright (2011). 'Agency perspectives on corporate governance of multinational enterprises', *Journal of Management Studies*, **48** (2), 471–486.

Gedajlovic, E. and M. Carney (2010). 'Markets, hierarchies and families: Toward a transaction costs theory of the family firm', *Entrepreneurship Theory and Practice*, **34** (6), 1145–1172.

Gedajlovic, E., B. Honig, C. Moore, T. Payne and M. Wright (2013). 'Social capital and entrepreneurship: A schema and research agenda', *Entrepreneurship Theory and Practice*, **37** (3), 455–478.

Harrison, J. (2006). 'Post-tenure scholarship and its implications', *University of Florida Journal of Law and Public Policy*, **17**, 139–164.

Hollenbeck, J. and M. Mannor (2007). 'Career success and weak paradigms: The role of activity, resiliency, and true scores', *Journal of Organizational Behavior*, **28**, 933–942.

Hoskisson, R., L. Eden, C.M. Lau and M. Wright (2000). 'Strategies in emerging markets', *Academy of Management Journal*, **43** (3), 249–267.

Ireland, R.D., M.A. Hitt and D.G. Sirmon (2003). 'A model of strategic entrepreneurship: The construct and its dimensions', *Journal of Management*, **29** (6), 963–989.

Link, A.N., D.S. Siegel and M. Wright (2015). *The Chicago Handbook of University Technology Transfer and Academic Entrepreneurship*. Chicago, IL: University of Chicago Press.

Meuleman, M., A. Lockett, M. Manigart and M. Wright (2010). 'Partner selection decisions in interfirm collaborations: The paradox of relational embeddedness', *Journal of Management Studies*, **47**, 995–1019.

Park, S. and M. Gordon (1996). 'Publication records and tenure decisions in the field of strategic management', *Strategic Management Journal*, **17**, 109–128.

Podsakoff, P.M., S.B. MacKenzie, N.P. Podsakoff and D.G. Bachrach (2008). 'Scholarly influence in the field of management: A bibliometric analysis of the determinants of university and author impact in the management literature in the past quarter century', *Journal of Management*, **34**, 641–720.

Siegel, D.S. and M. Wright (2015). 'University technology transfer offices, licensing, and start-ups', in A.N. Link, D.S. Siegel and M. Wright (eds), *The Chicago Handbook of University Technology Transfer and Academic Entrepreneurship*. Chicago, IL: University of Chicago Press.

Starbuck, W. (2005). 'How much better are the most prestigious journals? The statistics of academic publication', *Organization Science*, **16**, 180–200.

Steier, L.P., J.H. Chua and J.J. Chrisman (2009). 'Embeddedness perspectives of economic action within family firms', *Entrepreneurship Theory and Practice*, **33** (6), 1157–1167.

Ucbasaran, D., P. Westhead and M. Wright (2008). 'Opportunity identification and pursuit: Does an entrepreneur's human capital matter?', *Small Business Economics*, **30** (2), 153–173.

Ucbasaran, D., P. Westhead, M. Wright and M. Flores (2009). 'The nature of entrepreneurial experience, business failure and comparative optimism', *Journal of Business Venturing*, **25** (6), 541–555.

Uzzi, B. (1997). 'Social structure and competition in interfirm networks: The paradox of embeddedness', *Administrative Science Quarterly*, **42** (1), 35–67.

Wilson, N., M. Wright and L. Scholes (2013). 'Family business survival and the role of boards', *Entrepreneurship Theory and Practice*, **37** (6), 1369–1389.

Wright, M., B. Clarysse, P. Mustar and A. Lockett (2007). *Academic Entrepreneurship in Europe*. Cheltenham, U.K. and Northampton, MA: Edward Elgar.

Wright, M. and J. Coyne (1985). *Management Buyouts*. Beckenham, U.K.: Croom Helm.

Wright, M., I. Filatotchev, R. Hoskisson and M. Peng (2005). 'Strategies in emerging markets: Challenging the conventional wisdom', *Journal of Management Studies*, **42** (1), 1–34.

Wright, M. and P. Sharma (2013). 'Sustaining a publications career', *Family Business Review*, **26**, 323–332.

6. Why publish in Asia management journals?

Daphne W. Yiu

INTRODUCTION

Traditionally, region-focused journals are viewed as a secondary or second-tiered outlet for publications for "marginalized" research that carries a theme of a regional phenomenon and/or use regional data. Nonetheless, with the fast growth and increasing significance of Asian countries in the global economy, Asia management journals have recorded skyrocketing numbers of manuscript submissions and increasing impact factors in recent years. For example, the *Asia Pacific Journal of Management* (APJM) has a five-year citation impact factor of 3.00 as stated in the ISI Journal Citation Reports for 2013. The 2013 impact factor places APJM as the 24th most influential management journal among all the 172 tracked. APJM receives over 800 manuscripts per annum and publishes 35–40 articles.

This chapter aims to provide a general discussion of the similarities and differences in publishing Asian research in Asia management journals as compared to those in North America with regard to publication-related issues viewed and experienced by myself as author, reviewer, and editor at Asia management journals in the past decade. I will particularly use APJM as the focal Asia management journal in my illustrations. In addition, to echo the recent advocacy on the future direction of Asia management journals, I will discuss if and how these journals publish more indigenous research.

ASIA MANAGEMENT JOURNALS VS. WESTERN MANAGEMENT JOURNALS

The Rules of the Game

When tracing the development of APJM, it is interesting to find the resemblance of an indigenous local firm undergoing a gradual internationalization path. Founded in 1983, APJM was a journal established by the dean of the business school at the National University of Singapore as an in-house publication for MBA and graduate students (Lee, 2007). Subject to tremendous barriers and pains during its childhood and adolescence, APJM started to catch international attention and, in 1998, was formally affiliated with the Asia Academy of Management, the official affiliate of the Academy of Management, with the mission to "encourage contextualized management research with Asian relevance towards contribution to global scholarship" (Lau, 2007: 401). Since then, APJM has grown to be a highly reputable and the most prestigious journal in Asian management research (see Peng, 2007 for the achievements of APJM).

With such a historical development, together with the development of Asian business schools towards the American system, recruitment of faculty members from North America, a reward system striving for publishing in higher ranked journals that are often U.S.-based, affiliation with American academic associations, and collaboration with U.S. publishers, Asia management journals like APJM highly resemble many of the top-tiered U.S. management journals. As commented by Leung (2007: 512), "the downside of the adaptive response to the pressure to publish in highly cited journals is that virtually all Asia management research falls within the confines of well-known Western theories." The adaptation and institutionalization process has resulted in conformity towards how editors and reviewers evaluate publishable research, as well as enabled academic stakeholders to make sense of what a top-tiered Asia management journal should look like. Particularly, Pfeffer (2007) highlighted that what seems to signal the quality of a research or journal rank is the attraction to theory and methodological sophistication. To gain legitimacy, many Asia management journals are run just like the American and other global ones, and the expectations of "quality" are very similar, such as novelty and importance of research questions, theoretical contributions, logical adequacy and consistency, empirical rigor and coherence between theory and empirics, relevance and implications to academic and practitioner communities, and so on.

Regional relevance, global impact

Does Asia management matter? How distinct is Asia management from management elsewhere? This question has been pondered by many Asia management scholars, editors, and reviewers in the publication process of Asia management journals. In his reflection on Asia management in the 21st century, Hofstede (2007: 412) commented, "management problems basically have remained and will remain the same over time, and that their solutions differ less from period to period than from part of the world to part of the world, and even from country to country." Given that management problems themselves do not change over time but management thinking differs from one country to another as a function of the local culture, universal solutions to management problems do not exist. So, the key for Asian-based management research to contribute to global management is to study the contextual boundaries of management knowledge, and researchers need to trade ideas across borders and the cultural limits of their own thinking (Hofstede, 2007; Meyer, 2006).

As stated in the objectives of APJM, two out of the three key features of the journal are about regional relevance: focusing on key management and organizational trends in the region, and being the first and most prominent management journal published in and about the fastest growing region in the world. Given the trajectory of the fast growing economies with substantial economic turbulence and institutional upheavals in Asia, timely research on emerging business phenomena and management issues that can provide explanations, predictions, and insights are important in their own right. To facilitate regionally relevant research, an effective and efficient way is to organize "Special Issues" on timely local phenomena that may contribute to global understanding of the Asian context. For example, after the Global Economic Crisis in 2008, a Special Issue "Varieties of Asian Capitalism: Toward an Institutional Theory of Asian Enterprise" was published in 2009, which challenged the often presumed superiority of the liberal market model of capitalism and reinstated how alternative models of capitalism may be preferable for developing economies in Asia (Carney, Gedajlovic, and Yang, 2009). The concept and view of "varieties of capitalism" (VoC) has also addressed the limitations of institutional theory that has yet to explain the immense variations within and between national economies and provides a third leg to examine institution–firm relationships. The VoC perspective can be fruitfully applied in the Asian context by delineating the complex institutional dynamics existing in Asian capitalism, thus realizing the full potential of regional relevance; at the same time, through the theory-building process, by contextualizing the institution–firm phenomenon from a co-evolutionary and actor-centered view, the VoC model presents a challenge to mainstream scholars investigating traditional capitalism in a Western context, thus exerting global impact on the rethink of the Western model of market capitalism.

Recently, a Special Issue "Entrepreneurship, poverty, and Asia: Moving beyond subsistence entrepreneurship through Entrepreneurship and Innovation" (Bruton, Ahlstrom, and Si, 2015) has been launched to address the poverty problem in Asia, a topic that has been largely unexplored by business scholars in spite of the close linkage between business and poverty and over half of Asia's total population living on approximately $2 a day. As entrepreneurship is a fundamental engine of economic growth (Baumol, Litan, and Schramm, 2009), Bruton and his colleagues (2015: 5) advocated that entrepreneurs should move beyond subsistence entrepreneurship, which is referred to as "ventures in settings of poverty in which a new venture offers little in terms of the potential to significantly improve the entrepreneur's life or that of the entrepreneur's family," and create new entrepreneurial ventures and initiatives, such as micro-lending, social entrepreneurship, base of the pyramid (BoP) initiatives, and so on, to empower the poor to break out of poverty. This Special Issue is pioneering. Not only has it laid the foundation for the future pursuit of entrepreneurship as a solution to poverty, but it has also undoubtedly provided new approaches and insights to policy makers and entrepreneurs regarding the formation of entrepreneurial growth policies in different countries. This indicates a strong dedication of APJM to be the first to publish underexplored yet important business issues that are of critical relevance to the business community and region.

Puffer, McCarthy, and Peng (2013) demonstrated how to bridge local relevance and global impact in their Special Issue on "Favors in the Global Economy," exploring and demonstrating how a seemingly regionally salient, culturally specific construct plays an important role in the global business transactions. This sounds like an old topic, but it has never systematically been examined in the management discipline. The construct of favors is found to be multidimensional and complex, conveying different meanings and expectations across different cultures. The Special Issue focuses attention on a timely topic that fits with concurrent Special Issue and conference themes in the broader management academy, including the Special Research Forum "West Meets East: New Concepts and Theories" at the *Academy of Management Journal* and the theme "The Informal Economy" of the Academy of Management annual meeting in 2012.

In conclusion, as compared with top-tiered international business and management journals in the West, Asia management journals seem to put more weight on publishing context-relevant research with topics that are timely and of growing importance in the region, which at the same time also spur global awareness and hence tighten connection with practice.

Contributions: the rigor/relevance tradeoff?

Asia management research has been treated more as an area study that relies heavily on applying Western management theories but rarely on the development of new theories (Lau, 2002; Tsui, 2004; White, 2002). The lack of theoretical contribution and questioning about the generalizability of research findings are often the main reasons for reviewers to suggest a rejection in Asia management journals. This raises a fundamental question that has been asked by many Asia management researchers: Is the notion of "making theoretical contributions" a hindrance to publishing "interesting" and "novel" research that is of high local or regional relevance? Obviously, "theoretical contribution" often refers to the addition of knowledge to mainstream theories that are developed using Western logic, measurements developed and validated in the West, as well as data and sample collected in the West (Leung, 2007, 2012; Lau, 2006).

One could have expected that the role of theory did not carry a significant weight at the early stage of Asia management publications. Nonetheless, in the past decade or so, there have been numerous reflections on and suggestions for the "levels of the theoretical contributions" of publications in Asia management journals, such as the classifications into "theory application, theory extension, and development of a new theory" by Lau (2006); contextualizing theory (theories *in* context) and theorizing about context (theories *of* context) by Whetten (2009); and context-insensitive (contextualization in *what*), context-sensitive (contextualization in *how*), and context-specific (contextualization in *why*) by Jia, You, and Du (2012). To produce more high-impact articles to be published in Asian management journals, learned societies including the Asia Academy of Management (AAOM) and the International Association of Chinese Management Research (IACMR) have sought to blend Asian management research with that of the West and thereby enhance the research skills of Asian management scholars, especially the younger generations. Asian scholars' skills have been elevated substantially and quickly in the past decade (Leung, 2007). There are signs that more Asian contributions are appearing in mainstream management research, both in terms of extending management theories with contextualized constructs and variables and developing contextualized theories to examine context-specific phenomenon, although the latter has accounted for a much smaller proportion so far (Jia et al., 2012; Lau, 2006; Whetten, 2009). In general, the tradeoff between rigor and relevance is getting smaller.

TOWARDS THE NEXT ERA OF ASIAN MANAGEMENT RESEARCH

More than ten years ago, Leong and Leung (2004) predicted that the "adopted Western approach," due to the institutional pressure to publish in high-impact journals in the West in many Asian business schools, will prevail in Asia eventually, while the "Asian approach," focusing on indigenous research, will be marginalized and the "integration approach" will be difficult to implement. Such a claim has been realized over the past decade with the pendulum swinging towards adopting Western theories in the Asian context. A significant drawback of such an "internationalization or Westernization" approach is that the value-added of Asia management research is diminishing. Leung (2009) criticized the fact that such an adaptive approach has shaped Asian researchers to imitate publications in the top-tier management journals in the West, with expectations such as favoring deductive rather than inductive research, deriving research ideas from well-known mainstream theories in the West instead of nascent regional theories, and demonstrating as much methodological rigor as possible. As a consequence, "Asian researchers tend to publish on research topics that are well known in the West" (Leung, 2007: 512). It is also my observation in the past few years that the style and findings of Asia management research cannot be distinguished from mainstream international business research published in the West. Or to put it another way, do we need to continue to claim that "Now the Chinese can produce a Xiaomi that looks very much like an iPhone?" The "homogenizing tendencies of organizational studies" (March, 2005: 5) may adversely affect the development of global management knowledge and even hamper scientific progress (Tsui, 2007).

Recently, there has been an increasing call for making Asia management research more regionally relevant by conducting more indigenous, context-specific research (Jia et al., 2012; Leung, 2012; Meyer, 2006; Tsui, 2013; Whetten, 2009). So, it sounds like that the swing is shifting back to the emphasis on regional and local relevance. In Tsui's editorial introduction (2009: 1), she advocated that "Based on the principle of autonomy of inquiry and heeding the warning of the constraint of normal science, the Chinese management research community can shape its own future by engaging in research that may contribute to global management knowledge and address meaningful local management problems." I share her view that we definitely need high-impact research, but what we need more is the researcher's pure pursuit of scientific discovery and theoretical innovations that can develop more new and global knowledge.

Many editorial teams of Asia management journals are discussing how to make Asia management journals stand out more and how they can be distinguished more from Western journals. A defensive reason for doing this is the huge competition for quality manuscripts and the challenge of how to create differentiation from both mainstream international business and regional-focused journals; while a more proactive reason is that journals like APJM have "grown up" and are well-recognized in the international arena; therefore, it is ripe for them to take more ambitious moves. Editors and established scholars are increasingly calling for the development of truly universal theories by conducting indigenous management research in the region. In conclusion, I will provide three suggestions about how we can approach such an ambitious move.

Understand the Context Deeply

Undoubtedly, the "soul" of Asia management research is its "context." However, Asia management researchers have not treated the unique context of Asia seriously and rigorously so far. Why should we treat the context seriously? In the opening of this chapter, I restated Hofstede's (2007) comment on the importance of Asia management research in that research and theories coming out of one cultural context may not be applied to other cultural contexts. Because of the context-dependent assumptions of theories (Whetten, 2009), there is a "need" to conduct indigenous research in order to develop theories that can best explain regional or locally relevant phenomena (Leung, 2012). How can the context be treated rigorously? The Asian economic ascendance provides ample opportunities for exploratory research in Asia. If we can understand emerging and newly developed business phenomenon deeply and examine them rigorously, it is possible that an exploratory, indigenous theory can contribute to the development of truly universal theories. According to Leung (2009, 2012) and Whetten (2009), there are several ways that Chinese or Asian researchers can develop original and trailblazing universal theories: demonstrating the boundary conditions of a Western theory when applying it in the Asian cultural context; showing the superiority of an indigenous theory developed in Asia over a Western theory in the Asian context; and identifying when and where the indigenous theory developed in Asia can be applied to another cultural context. By synthesizing indigenous research from diverse cultural contexts, we may ultimately arrive at truly universalistic theories (Yang, 2000).

Ambicultural Approach

To instill new ideas and perspectives into global management, Chen and Miller (2011) proposed an ambicultural approach to bridge the global divide between the East and the West by integrating the best practices of the East and the West, or the so-called "self-other integration," identifying commonalities and applying universalities in both the Eastern and Western settings, and transcending paradigmatic differences and integrating extremes. By so doing, Asian researchers can be enlightened by expansive new paths of scholarly, managerial, and human pursuits. The ambicultural approach echoes Mao Zedong's (1967) key message in *On Contradictions*, in which he highlighted that the fundamental cause of the development of a thing lies in the contradictoriness with it. Instead of choosing one of the two contradictory paths, it is critical to take both simultaneously because it is in the tension between the two that new insight is most often generated. Barney and Zhang (2009) suggested that this may also be the case with the evolution of Chinese and Asian management research. To facilitate the process of integrating Eastern and Western management research, Asian researchers should not criticize those who are focusing on extending Western management theories to the Asian context or those who are seeking to derive logics and formulate theories from the local context. Instead, it is through the continuous efforts of studying contextual differences that one may develop new and universal theories.

Uphold the Spirit of Scholarship

Finally, Asian researchers are strongly encouraged to undertake the purest pursuit of scientific discovery. As Tsui (2009: 3) suggested, "it is time for the Chinese management research community to chart its own course in developing valid knowledge and contributing to scientific progress, thus achieving both rigour and relevance, the dual criteria of good applied science." The same is true for Asia management scholars who should leave the ivory tower and be critical of the relevance and usefulness of the research questions, theories, and methods in addressing phenomena in their own contexts (Pfeffer, 2007; Tsui, 2009). It is interesting to learn from the former editor of APJM that many of the few exploratory research papers were not published because the research did not provide an answer to the research question (Ahlstrom, 2011). So, despite standing strong against the current, the Asian management communities should be more courageous in striving for scientific discoveries and the development of Asian-based universal theories (Leung, 2009; Tsang, 2009).

To end the chapter, I would like to provide some more concrete guidance to authors who are dedicated to making meaningful contributions to Asia management research.

- Discoveries of context-specific phenomenon. Explore and discover substantively important yet under-studied phenomena in the context that can bring new insights to the field of organization and management in general. What makes Asia research stand out from context-free studies is always its context-specific nature, which will inform the academic community about timely management and organizational issues in the Asian context. It is not surprising to see manuscripts submitted to Asia management journals in which the authors did not make any reference to the Asian context in explaining the motivation for the study nor provide implications of their findings for the Asia management context.
- Theorizing vs. theoretical contributions. A majority of the typical manuscripts received by Asia management journals are about theorizing a phenomenon in a context, with solid literature review, employing mainstream management theories on which to develop a set of concrete hypotheses. Nonetheless, theoretical contributions are lacking. Authors are often reminded to test whether their hypotheses still hold if the country context is omitted in their hypothesis statements. As mentioned above, authors are strongly recommended to make use of the context to challenge and/or modify existing theories, or even to build an original and universal theory from the context.
- Crafting and writing. Many Asia management journals are developmental and have a mission to train Asian scholars towards a universal standard of publication. This, to a large extent, is due to the lack of crafting and writing skill development in the educational background of universities in Asia. As such, authors are strongly recommended to devote efforts in strengthening and fine-tuning skills in crafting their manuscripts. A lot of times editors and reviewers have to guess what the true motivations and contributions of the study are. Effective communication from the authors would certainly keep readers' attention and interest in reading the manuscript.

REFERENCES

Ahlstrom, D. (2011), 'On the aims and scope of the *Asia Pacific Journal of Management*: What does APJM really seek to publish?', *Asia Pacific Journal of Management*, **28** (2), 215–219.

Barney, J.B., and S. Zhang (2009), 'The future of Chinese management research: A theory of Chinese management versus a Chinese theory of management', *Management and Organization Review*, **5** (1), 15–28.

Baumol, W.J., R.E. Litan, and C.J. Schramm (2009), *Good Capitalism, Bad Capitalism, and the Economics of Growth and Prosperity*. New Haven, CT: Yale University Press.

Bruton, G.B., D. Ahlstrom, and S. Si (2015), 'Entrepreneurship, poverty, and Asia: Moving beyond subsistence entrepreneurship', *Asia Pacific Journal of Management*, **32** (1), 1–22.

Carney, M., E. Gedajlovic, and X. Yang (2009), 'Varieties of Asian capitalism: Toward an institutional theory of Asian enterprise', *Asia Pacific Journal of Management*, **26** (3), 361–380.

Chen, M.J., and D. Miller (2011), 'The relational perspective as a business mindset: Managerial implications for East and West', *Academy of Management Perspectives*, **25** (3), 6–18.

Hofstede, G. (2007), 'Asian management in the 21st century', *Asia Pacific Journal of Management*, **24** (4), 411–420.

Jia, L., S. You, and Y. Du (2012), 'Chinese context and theoretical contributions to management and organization research: A three-decade review', *Management and Organization Review*, **8** (1), 173–209.

Lau, C.M. (2002), 'Asian management research: Frontiers and challenges', *Asia Pacific Journal of Management*, **19** (2–3), 171–178.

Lau, C.M. (2006), 'Achievements, challenges and research agendas for Asian management research studies', *Asian Business and Management*, **5** (1), 53–66.

Lau, C.M. (2007), 'The first decade of the Asia Academy of Management', *Asia Pacific Journal of Management*, **24** (4), 401–410.

Lee, S.A. (2007), 'APJM and NUS, 1980–90', *Asia Pacific Journal of Management*, **24** (4), 395–396.

Leong, F.T.L., and K. Leung (2004), 'Academic careers in Asia: A cross-cultural analysis', *Journal of Vocational Behavior*, **64** (2), 346–357.

Leung, K. (2007), 'The glory and tyranny of citation impact: An East Asian perspective', *Academy of Management Journal*, **50** (3), 510–513.

Leung, K. (2009), 'Never the twain shall meet? Integrating Chinese and Western management research', *Management and Organization Review*, **5** (1), 121–129.

Leung, K. (2012), 'Indigenous Chinese management research: Like it or not, we need it', *Management and Organization Review*, **8** (1), 1–5.

March, J.G. (2005), 'Parochialism in the evolution of a research community: The case of organization studies', *Management and Organization Review*, **1** (1), 5–22.

Meyer, K.E. (2006), 'Asian management research needs more self-confidence', *Asia Pacific Journal of Management*, **23** (2), 119–137.

Peng, M.W. (2007), 'Celebrating 25 years of Asia Pacific management research', *Asia Pacific Journal of Management*, **24** (4), 385–393.

Pfeffer, J. (2007), 'A modest proposal: How we might change the process and product of managerial research', *Academy of Management Journal*, **50** (6), 1334–1345.

Puffer, S.M., D.J. McCarthy, and M.W. Peng (2013), 'Managing favors in a global economy', *Asia Pacific Journal of Management*, **30** (2), 321–326.

Tsang, E.W.K. (2009), 'Chinese management research at a crossroads: Some philosophical considerations', *Management and Organization Review*, **5** (1), 131–143.

Tsui, A.S. (2004), 'Contributing to global management knowledge: A case for high quality indigenous research', *Asia Pacific Journal of Management*, **21** (4), 491–513.

Tsui, A.S. (2007), 'From homogenization to pluralism: International management research in the academy and beyond', *Academy of Management Journal*, **50** (6), 1353–1364.

Tsui, A.S. (2009), 'Editor's introduction – autonomy of inquiry: Shaping the future of emerging scientific communities', *Management and Organization Review*, **5** (1), 1–14.

Tsui, A.S. (2013), 'The spirit of science and socially responsible scholarship', *Management and Organization Review*, **9** (3), 375–394.

Whetten, D.A. (2009), 'An examination of the interface between context and theory applied to the study of Chinese organizations', Management and Organization Review, **5** (1), 29–55.

White, S. (2002), 'Rigor and relevance in Asian management research: Where are we and where can we go?', *Asia Pacific Journal of Management*, **19** (2), 287–352.

Yang, K.-S. (2000), 'Monocultural and cross-cultural indigenous approaches: The royal road to the development of a balanced global psychology', *Asian Journal of Social Psychology*, **3**, 241–263.

Zedong, M. (1967), *Selected Works of Mao Zedong*. Beijing: Foreign Languages Press.

7. Squeezing lemons to make fresh lemonade: how to extract useful value from peer reviews[*]

William H. Starbuck

A GOLDEN RULE

Many years ago, feedback from an editor induced me to formulate a rule that proved very valuable, so valuable that, after some years, I began to call it my Golden Rule. Other authors will find this rule useful. It states:

No reviewer is ever wrong!

This rule is valuable partly because it makes an assertion that seems patently ludicrous and bizarre. Obviously, any human being, even an editor or reviewer, may err. Sometimes editors or reviewers make comments that appear stupid or they recommend changes that are unethical or methodologically incorrect. Occasionally reviewers seem arrogant, disrespectful and even nasty. Therefore, to declare that reviewers' comments are never wrong might appear irrational, but this apparent irrationality draws attention to a more fundamental truth: Editors and reviewers are only reporting what they thought when they read your paper and every editor and every reviewer is a potentially useful example from the population of potential readers. Indeed, a reviewer is likely to be a better source of information than a typical reader is in that a reviewer probably reads more carefully than a typical reader does and nearly every reviewer plows through an entire paper instead of giving up in disgust after a few pages.

The central purpose of my Golden Rule is to remind me to regard reviewers' comments not as judgments about the value of my research or the quality of my writing, but as data about potential readers of my paper. If a reviewer interprets a statement differently than I intended, other readers, possibly many other readers, are likely to interpret this statement differently than I intended, so I should revise the statement to make similar misinterpretations less likely. If a reviewer thinks I made a methodological error, other readers, possibly many of them, are also likely to think that I made this error, so I should revise my paper to explain why my methodology is appropriate. If a reviewer advises me to cite literature that I see as irrelevant, some other readers are also likely to think this literature is relevant, so I should explain why it is not relevant. In general, I should attend very conscientiously to the honest reactions of anyone who has read my words rather carefully. These are much more realistic data than the polite but superficial comments of close colleagues, who may have read hastily and who do not want to hurt my feelings. Valid data about readers' reactions are hard to obtain and good data can never be "wrong."

My Golden Rule does not ask me to follow reviewers' advice blindly. Absolutely not! Editors and reviewers often give bad advice. Their advice derives from their interpretations of what they thought I was trying to say, which may not be what I actually intended to say. Often, reviewers conflict with each other, or what reviewers advise conflicts with advice from my colleagues, so I have to decide what advice is more useful. Most of the time, reviewers' advice also conforms to widely accepted but incorrect beliefs about proper methodology. Reviewers and especially editors often see radically deviant ideas as incorrect or implausible. Indeed, there would be no point in doing research if all widespread beliefs were reliably correct.

Editorial practices have serious deficiencies, the main deficiency being the assumption that reviewers should select papers for publication. The act of rendering judgment creates a hierarchical relationship between a reviewer and an author that benefits neither of them and that often keeps innovative research from appearing in prestigious journals.

"Peer review" should mean that reviewers and authors are equals. However, most editors – and most reviewers – act as if reviewers have more competence than authors do and as if reviewers' evaluations have more validity than authors' evaluations do. Editors also typically act as if they themselves have the wisdom and knowledge to impose constraints on papers. Such behaviors create power differences that not only contradict the concept of peer review but also invite reviewers and editors to indulge their idiosyncrasies. As Lord Acton's hoary dictum implies, editorial power tends to corrupt and absolute editorial power ... . Very few editors or reviewers can refrain from thinking: "I could say this better," "I see a more interesting problem," or "I could design a better study."

Authors also find it extremely difficult to look upon editors or reviewers as peers. For authors, feedback from journals has implications for social status, job security and self-image. Thus, authors defensively tend to interpret all editorial comments as critical judgments. Even when a reviewer intends to say "perhaps this might be a useful suggestion," the author is likely to hear "do this or I will recommend that the journal reject your paper" (see also Chapters 16 and 17 in this volume).

Before, during and after my period as the editor of *Administrative Science Quarterly* (*ASQ*), a botanist copyedited the accepted papers. *ASQ* employed this botanist as a way to foster effective communication to an interdisciplinary audience, the premise being that a management paper that a botanist could understand would also be understandable to a wide variety of readers. Over time, however, the botanist made ever more detailed demands of authors and grew increasingly disdainful of authors' own writing. Authors sometimes protested the botanist's style preferences or the tone of the botanist's remarks. A crisis arose when the botanist wrote on the paper of a very famous and distinguished author, "This looks like the ramblings of a senile old man speaking before a Rotary Club!" Thereafter, with every copyedited paper sent back to an author, I sent a letter explaining (a) that the copyeditor was a botanist, (b) that *ASQ* used a botanist to copyedit precisely because the botanist might not understand nuances and jargon and (c) that the author was free to ignore the botanist's suggestions and comments because they were merely suggestions. Of course, I also told the botanist what I was telling authors. The botanist's comments developed a different tone and authors never again complained about the botanist's suggestions, yet it appeared that authors were following those suggestions more thoroughly than before. More tactful and explanatory editorial suggestions were persuading authors who had the right to ignore the suggestions unless they improved the papers.

Editorial processes might be more effective if editors would frequently tell authors to regard the ideas of reviewers – and of the editors themselves – as mere suggestions for possible improvement rather than as commands.

The next section of this chapter summarizes studies of editors and reviewers. These studies indicate that reviewers usually disagree with each other and give mutually inconsistent advice to authors, and reviewers make inaccurate predictions about the impacts that papers will have on their fields. Reviewers' biases imply that they go beyond the actual texts of papers and take account of data that may signal authors' levels of competence. Two ensuing sections propose how authors should think about and react to feedback from journals. A final section suggests the possibility of a better future for peer review.

EVALUATIONS BY EDITORS AND REVIEWERS HAVE EARNED SKEPTICAL READING

Editing *ASQ* also exposed me to statistical evidence about the unreliability of reviewers' judgments. As an author, I had received several pairs of reviews that contradicted each other, but I had interpreted these contradictions as mere variations in personal experience. As an editor, however, I took note of the very high frequency with which pairs of reviewers gave me inconsistent advice about publication and desirable changes. After I had accumulated reviews of several hundred papers, I observed that about 25 percent of the reviewers recommended acceptance, 25 percent recommended revisions and 50 percent recommended rejection. I also calculated the correlation between reviewers' recommendations to accept, revise or reject. The correlation between reviewers was only 0.12. Thus, knowing the recommendations of one reviewer gave no basis for predicting the recommendations of a second reviewer.

I have found six instances in which editors published the frequencies of reviewers' recommendations (Starbuck, 2005). Acceptance recommendations ranged from 9 percent to 14 percent, revision recommendations from 25 percent to 44 percent and rejection recommendations from 46 percent to 66 percent.

I have also found 15 instances in which editors published statistics about the agreement between reviewers (Starbuck, 2003, 2005). These correlations ranged from 0.05 to 0.37, with an average of 0.18. Further, Gottfredson (1977, 1978) found that psychologist reviewers distinguish between the quality of a paper and its probable impact on its field, but reviewers' ratings of impact correlate only 0.14 with later citations. In fact, the practical correlation is nil because reviewers' ratings of impact correlate only 0.03 with later citations for papers that receive few citations, implying that positive correlations between reviewers arise entirely from above-average papers. Because citations and ratings of papers have lognormal distributions, positive correlations between reviewers are attributable to only about 20 percent of the papers (Starbuck, Aguinis, Konrad and Baruch, 2008).

A graph may clarify the practical implications of these statistics. Figure 7.1 graphs the agreement–disagreement for 1000 pairs of simulated reviewers whose evaluations resemble the published data about actual reviewers. The figure shows finely measured evaluations by these imaginary reviewers just before they convert their evaluations into discrete recommendations about readiness for publication. The circular area formed by most of the dots indicates that the correlation between

Figure 7.1   Simulated evaluations of 1000 papers by pairs of reviewers

reviewers is near zero for papers that reviewers evaluate as near or below average. However, there is an overall positive correlation between reviewers because agreement about the good and excellent papers produces the conical projection to the upper right.

Table 7.1 shows the data from Figure 7.1 in a different way – with the reviewers' evaluations converted into recommendations to accept, revise or reject. The frequencies of these recommendations approximate the frequencies published by journals.

The published statistics imply that, on average, journals reject over half of the best papers that they receive. Journals having more prestige receive more submissions, which give them more opportunities to publish the best papers, so they publish more of the best papers. However, erratic publication decisions mean that all journals, including the most prestigious ones, often reject superior papers while choosing to publish inferior ones. The most prestigious 20 percent of journals publish almost half of the best papers they review and they publish less than one-seventh of the worst papers they review (Starbuck, 2005). At the same time, erratic publication decisions cause about half of the best articles to appear in second-tier or third-tier journals.[1]

Undoubtedly, some editors and reviewers make erratic evaluations and provide incorrect feedback because they devote insufficient time to reading papers and writing clear comments about them. However, the main reason editors and reviewers make disparate evaluations is that the reviewing tasks are too difficult. Although most reviewers and editors are trying, their evaluation tasks exceed their cognitive and communication abilities. Calculations indicate that reviewers' advice to editors is so unreliable that having evaluations from five reviewers would yield no better editorial decisions than evaluations by two reviewers do.

Table 7.1   Reviewers' recommendations to editors

Recommendations by two reviewers	Percentage of manuscripts
Accept–Accept	6%
Accept–Revise	6%
Accept–Reject	13%
Revise–Revise	8%
Revise–Reject	37%
Reject–Reject	30%

Two factors make highly unreliable evaluations both desirable and necessary. Firstly, social scientists disagree about the nature of knowledge, the purposes of scholarly publication, the character of good research methodology, the social functions of scholarly journals and the proper roles of editors and reviewers (Starbuck, 2014). Many behavioral scientists concede that human knowledge is socially constructed, but some believe they are creating knowledge that will have very stable value and relevance for decades or centuries whereas others see their research as updating reports about current events or as translations of ancient generalizations into contemporary language. In addition to publishing excellent papers, journal editors seek to gain circulation, to earn readers' respect, to nurture inexperienced authors and to bring about changes in scholars' beliefs and methods (Starbuck et al., 2008). Very often authors misrepresent how they conducted research by saying they derived hypotheses by reading previous studies before they gathered data, whereas they actually analysed their data before they proposed hypotheses, then they searched for previous studies to support these ex post hypotheses (Bedeian, Taylor and Miller, 2010; Bones, 2012; Kepes and McDaniel, 2013). Authors also overstate the validity of their inferences by making numerous calculations under differing assumptions, but then they disregard the implications of this data mining when they calculate statistical significance (Simmons, Nelson and Simonsohn, 2011). One result is that researchers claim to have found convincing support for 75–90 percent of their hypotheses (Mazzola and Deuling, 2013).

Because so many researchers violate the assumptions underlying their published statistical tests, high percentages of their claimed "findings" are incorrect and unreproducible (Ioannidis, 2005a). These deceptions turn claims about the significance or meaningfulness of "findings" into hollow charades, yet scholars defend the charades by saying something like, "this is standard practice in our literature" (Starbuck, 2014). Open use of such justifications suggests that many scholars may see research as a way to demonstrate membership in a social group rather than as a way to generate useful knowledge. Certainly, if people cannot agree about what they should be trying to accomplish, it is better for them to disagree with each other and thereby to portray the diversity of values they hold and the goals they pursue.

Secondly, scholarly papers have many and diverse properties: authors' writing skill, authors' prestige, the prestige of authors' employers, the structures of logical arguments, the amounts and relevance of reviewed literature, the currency of topics, researchers' access to relevant data, various properties of data, implications for practices, implications for past or future research. Gottfredson (1978) identified 83 distinct properties that 299 reviewers mentioned in their comments. Although some of them correlate with each other, these properties do not fall into a logical hierarchy. Every paper has some properties that can elicit reviewers' dissatisfaction. Every paper contains some poorly phrased statements. Every paper fails to mention some relevant literature. Every paper makes some arguments that have unclear reasoning. Every theory overlooks some potentially important contingencies. Every design for a study has some defects. All data have some limitations and defects. Every analytic technique makes some unrealistic assumptions. Every useful study demonstrates its own inadequacy by revealing some aspects of the studied situation(s) that the researchers did not anticipate. One finding of every empirical study is that the study had some limitations and authors point these out. As a result, for a large majority of papers, reviewers find it much easier to complain about liabilities than to praise assets. However, reviewers do not agree with each other about which liabilities warrant complaints.

Gottfredson (1978), Gottfredson and Gottfredson (1982) and Wolff (1970) found that reviewers for psychological journals agree strongly that papers ought to exhibit some general, qualitative properties: Mainly, the research should address an important and interesting problem, not a trivial, ho-hum problem. Research should not have glaring errors. As well, the paper should exhibit good writing style and should discuss findings, not merely report them. However, when reviewers react to specific papers, their agreement plummets, as they focus on different properties of the paper and they assign different priorities to these properties. Indeed, the properties that draw the strongest agreement from reviewers when stated as generalities are also the properties that draw the weakest agreement from reviewers when they characterize specific papers (Gottfredson, 1978). Reviewers are especially prone to disagree about whether research is interesting or important and about what researchers have done wrong. The result is erratic quality for the range of published papers: Mazzola and Deuling (2013) found that many published papers had tested unstated hypotheses, had failed to test stated hypotheses or had drawn inferences about hypotheses that they neither stated nor tested. If people cannot agree about the relative importance and qualities of stimuli, it is better for them to make mutually inconsistent judgments that reveal the uncertainty surrounding their evaluations.

Studies of evaluations by editors and reviewers have disclosed biases that suggest they supplement the information they gain from merely reading papers. These studies imply that authors receive feedback that is more favorable if they say they have had other papers accepted for publication, write in idiomatic English, use mathematical formulas even if nonsensically, report findings that support widely held beliefs and have return addresses at highly prestigious schools.

Reviewers seem to be groping for clues about authors' excellence or mediocrity. Nylenna, Riis and Karlsson (1994) found that reviewers gave higher ratings to a paper in English than to the same paper in the native language shared by the author and reviewers. Mahoney, Kazdin and Kenigsberg (1978) inferred that reviewers were more likely to render favorable evaluations about papers that cited in-press studies by the papers' authors. Eriksson (2012) reported that readers with backgrounds in the humanities or social sciences gave higher evaluations to abstracts that included a sentence about a mathematical model that actually had no relevance to the research; readers with backgrounds in the physical sciences did not show such a bias.

Perhaps the most discussed and controversial study of peer review was one by Peters and Ceci (1982), who resubmitted 12 papers to the journals that published them just 18 to 32 months earlier. All 12 journals were highly regarded and all of the papers had authors who worked in prestigious psychology departments. However, the resubmitted papers had fictitious authors with return addresses at obscure schools. The resubmissions went to 38 editors and reviewers. Three of these 38 people recognized that the papers had already been published, which cut the sample to nine papers and 18 reviewers. Sixteen of the 18 reviewers recommended rejection and the editors rejected eight of the nine papers.

The most prevalent reasons for rejection were "serious methodological flaws," including inappropriate statistical analyses and faulty study design.

Reviewers' comments about research methodology may cloak other biases. Mahoney (1977, 1979) submitted five papers to 75 people who had recently reviewed for the *Journal of Applied Behavior Analysis*. The papers were nearly identical except that some of them reported negative results, some reported positive results and some reported mixed results. Mahoney chose reviewers whose own publications suggested they would prefer positive results, and indeed these reviewers did generally give higher ratings of scientific contribution to papers that reported positive results and they were much more likely to recommend acceptance or minor revision of papers that reported positive results. The inter-rater correlations were 0.30 for recommendations about publication and ratings of scientific contribution, but close to zero for ratings of methodology, relevance and the quality of discussion. The evaluated papers all had identical methodology, yet the ratings of methodology correlated 0.94 with recommendations about publication. That is, reviewers found methodological faults in studies presenting evidence that contradicted the reviewers' own published work and they applauded the methodology of studies offering evidence to support the reviewers' own published work.

Junior scholars and senior ones may have different biases when they act as reviewers. One junior scholar told me in private: "When I first started reviewing, I was terrified of two kinds of errors: giving a negative evaluation to a 'good' paper, and giving a good evaluation to a 'bad' paper; either result, I feared, would lead me to look incompetent in the eyes of the editor. My fellow junior scholars privately expressed the same fears." Senior scholars may think of themselves as experts, and experts often make less accurate predictions than nonexperts do. Various studies have documented this pattern for predictions about conflict resolution, economic trends, ecological changes, political trends, tennis victories and stock investments. One factor is that experts' predictions often over-emphasize a few specific details while underemphasizing general patterns. Thus, reviewers and editors who regard themselves as experts may make inaccurate predictions about papers' impact and importance. McBride, Fidler and Burgman (2012) provide a long bibliography.

Editors may be more likely to make significant evaluation errors than reviewers are. Whereas reviewers can focus solely on the properties of the manuscript before them, editors have to attend to the social status and financial viability of their journals, which implies that editors must demonstrate conformity to widespread social norms. For example, a reviewer can advise an author to use an unconventional statistical analysis whereas an editor – aware that methodology is a formal ritual that persuades readers to have respect for researchers' work – may recommend using a statistical analysis that matches readers' expectations (Starbuck, 2014). Editors generally know authors' names and institutions, and authors and everyone else know the editors' names and institutions. Thus, editors have reasons to protect their personal reputations and social relationships. As established scholars, editors are more likely than are many reviewers to encounter papers that relate to their own prior research. Bedeian (2008) has reported that many editors force authors to include statements in their papers with which the authors disagree.

Laband (1990) studied comments by editors and reviewers and authors' reactions to these comments for 89 papers that had appeared in top journals. He inferred that reviewers' comments had significantly increased the numbers of citations to the published papers, but editors' comments had not affected citations. He concluded that editors add little value to manuscripts except by choosing reviewers well.

Silera, Leeb and Beroc (2015) studied 1008 papers that authors had once submitted to three prestigious medical journals; 808 of these papers eventually appeared in various journals. The editors of the prestigious journals had desk-rejected 772 papers and had not sent them to reviewers; after 571 of these desk-rejected papers appeared in other journals, they averaged 70 citations. Of the papers sent to reviewers for the prestigious journals, the editors rejected 187; these rejected papers averaged 95 citations after publication in other journals. Thus, Silera et al. inferred that the papers chosen for review were better, on average, than those that editors had desk-rejected. However, the editors performed very poorly as evaluators of the most outstanding papers. Nearly all of the published papers attracted comparatively few citations, but 14 papers had drawn many more citations than the others had. Of these 14 papers that drew many citations, editors for the most prestigious journals had desk-rejected 12, and one of these heavily cited papers was desk-rejected by the editors for two of the most prestigious journals. Silera et al. (2015: 365) opined,

> ... it seems that distinguishing poor scientific work is easier than distinguishing excellent contributions. However, the high rate of desk-rejections among extremely highly cited articles in our case studies suggests that although peer review was effective at predicting "good" articles, it simultaneously had difficulties in identifying outstanding or breakthrough work. In turn, the complexity of science appears to limit the predictive abilities of even the best peer reviewers and editors.

Although the inferences by Silera et al. seem plausible, they may overstate editors' aversion to research that attracts many citations. At least, Silera et al. did not investigate whether later studies had confirmed the findings reported in the highly cited papers. Ioannidis (2005b) found that subsequent research had failed to confirm the findings of 36.8 percent of highly cited papers, as compared with 24.4 percent of a random sample that had not been highly cited. Thus, highly cited papers were about 50 percent more likely to have reported findings that were overstated or wrong.

Laband and Piette (1994) investigated the effects of favoritism by editors. Papers by authors having personal connections with editors were more likely to become lead papers, and these papers attracted significantly more citations after publication. Laband and Piette (1994: 194) inferred that "although journal editors occasionally publish subpar papers authored by colleagues and former graduate students, on balance their use of professional connections enables them to identify and 'capture' high-impact papers for publication." Medoff (2003: 434) drew a similar conclusion:

> articles authored by those with editorial connections, particularly serving on the publishing journal's editorial board, are both statistically and numerically of higher quality ... The empirical results support the proposition that journal editors, in order to reduce the search costs involved in identifying high-quality manuscripts, use personal ties and institutional connections to persuade high-quality authors to submit their papers to them. Journal editors/coeditors attract these submissions by inducing high-quality authors to serve on their editorial boards as well as by offering constructive comments and suggestions on a high-quality author's paper, reducing the author's transaction cost of publishing.

The next two sections of this chapter offer some thoughts about the implications of the foregoing studies and propose how authors might deal with reviewers' comments.

WHY SUCH STATISTICS MATTER

Of course, everyone who has submitted several papers to journals has experienced inconsistent reviews, and every academic has heard many stories about the inconsistent reviews received by colleagues. Nevertheless, such experiences inevitably leave authors wondering if they are especially unfortunate, if other authors of more talent and greater skill receive helpful, positive reviews. The overall negative tone of editorial feedback induces some scholars to withdraw from publishing altogether, and the difficulty of satisfying editors and reviewers persuades scholars to eschew publication in prestigious journals. After Gans and Shepherd (1994) asked 140 leading economists what they thought about review processes, many respondents told stories about very influential papers that journals had rejected, and some wrote "several blistering pages."

Statistical studies put individual experiences in perspective and provide evidence that almost all authors must deal with conflicting demands, some of which seem to be unwise. Reviewers rarely agree about what researchers did wrong or the importance of research topics; they agree weakly about papers' scientific contributions and worthiness for publication; and their ratings of scientific contribution correlate very weakly with later citations of published papers.

The reactions to this situation have been remarkably diverse, as demonstrated by the numerous commentaries accompanying the papers by Cicchetti (1991) and by Peters and Ceci (1982). Peer review arouses strong emotions, beliefs and ambitions. It angers, it reassures, it intimidates, it tramples egos and it puffs them up. For some people, peer review demonstrates the vacuousness and unreliability of social science, whereas other people see peer review as evidencing the substance and reliability of social science. Responses range from abstract to quibbling, from idealistic to pragmatic, from outraged to philosophical (Baumeister, 1990; Bedeian, 1996a, 1996b; Holbrook, 1986). There has also been much writing, research and discussion about the advantages and disadvantages of using citation counts as evidence about peer review, paper visibility, paper quality, journal prestige and journal quality; Osterloh and Frey (2015) provide a long bibliography.

Harnad (1986) opined that attitudes about peer review depend on whether people believe that most published research is "significant and essential" or "neither significant nor essential." However, this phrasing understates the role of social construction. It is people, acting collectively, that define "significant and essential." Processes of communication, social influence and consensus building transform the insignificant into the significant, the inessential into the essential, the irrelevant into the interesting, perceptions into facts, conjectures into theories and beliefs into truths. Davis (1971) inferred that influential contributions to sociology have presentational ingredients that create tension in readers and make the topics seem "interesting."

Debates about what is "significant and essential" have strong effects on the development of widely shared perceptions and beliefs. Kuhn (1970) argued that some scientific fields develop around stable paradigms that state criteria for choosing problems and methods of research; a new paradigm emerges only when doubt about an existing paradigm grows strong and spreads widely. Such is not the world of management thought, however, where paradigms are multitude, vague and ever changing. Researchers do not behave as if consensus declares certain beliefs and perceptions to be correct. Editors insist that studies must make "theoretical contributions" rather than demonstrate the effectiveness of existing theories. Therefore, almost every author dismisses prior findings and claims to have discovered support for new hypotheses. Minor revisions of existing theories get distinctive names and attract enthusiastic adherents (Starbuck, 2009).

One consequence is that research ideas tend to follow dialectic trajectories: A new assertion elicits a contrary assertion; indeed, merely stating a hypothesis may be sufficient stimulus to elicit a contrary hypothesis. The ensuing debates often yield syntheses that combine the opposing hypotheses in more complex frameworks; such integration expands perceptions. Nevertheless, until such syntheses occur, the proponents of alternative viewpoints continue to quarrel about terminology and methodology. Partly because researchers have not agreed about what they know, knowledge has not accumulated and today's theories have no more explanatory power than do those in use fifty years ago (Webster and Starbuck, 1988).

HOW AUTHORS CAN DEAL WITH THIS ENVIRONMENT

The statistical evidence about editors and reviewers can be liberating because it shows that ultimate decisions about what is right must come from inside authors, expressing their own expertise, ways of thinking and ethics. Editors and reviewers are unreliable judges of the value of scholarly papers; journals that are more prestigious publish better papers mainly because authors submit better papers to them. Although authors should pay careful attention to the comments of editors and reviewers, authors dare not depend on editors and reviewers to tell them what to do. We are indeed peers even though social roles induce some of us to behave as if they are superiors.

Because comments from editors and reviewers rouse strong emotions, authors may find it useful to follow a step-by-step procedure that distributes the issues over time.

Issue 1

Did the editor desk-reject the paper? And, did the editor state a reason for this action? A desk-reject may mean little except that an over-loaded editor made a mistake. Even so, you should reduce the probability of another mistake of the same sort. You might have sent the paper to the wrong journal. Does the paper cite several recent studies in that journal? Does the paper make a meaningful contribution to an ongoing conversation in that journal? If the answers are "yes," the current version of the paper does not present itself effectively. You ought to rewrite the paper's title, abstract and introduction to clarify the paper's importance and contribution.

Issue 2

Are you ready to act calmly and analytically? Coping with editorial feedback requires managing yourself – your ego and your emotions. You are disappointed and possibly offended; you want to protest or correct misunderstandings. However, it is a mistake to undertake revisions while you are feeling this way. Wait several weeks and reread the reviewers' comments about once a week. Eventually, you will become able to regard the reviewers' comments as data about your potential audience. Eventually, you will see why the reviewers are not wrong. They are just fallible humans struggling with difficult tasks.

Issue 3

You should analyse reviewers' comments carefully and make corresponding changes in your paper no matter what the editor said about publishing the paper – accept, revise or reject. Those comments reveal how readers reacted to the paper; if you do not like those reactions, you have to change the stimuli that evoked them.

How should you react to the reviewers' comments? Examine each sentence, asking why the reviewer made that statement, and then make a corresponding change in the paper. Every comment by a reviewer warrants changes. Make notes about every change you make and why you made it. What is the reviewer's interpretation? An alternative phrasing might help. You might need to add detail or to explain an assumption. If a reviewer suggests there is something you do not know, show your knowledge, but first consider the possibility that you ought to read some additional literature. If a reviewer says you used the wrong methods, explain why you used those methods, but first consider the possibility that the reviewer might know better methods!

Beware, however, of a lurking trap. Reviewers' comments generally encourage authors to add to their papers. These additions can make the paper too complex and too difficult to read, and can result in it lacking a main theme. Ultimately, your paper must have a clear topic and clear findings.

As an editor, I observed that only about half of the authors who received invitations to revise actually submitted revised manuscripts that differed noticeably from their earlier manuscripts. The other half of these authors either submitted very superficial revisions or never resubmitted. Thus, authors' motivation and belief in their work play large parts in determining whether their papers make it into print. Some authors respond to feedback by withdrawing or refusing to comply, whereas other authors respond by demonstrating persistence and a degree of compliance.

Issue 4

Should you send the revised paper back to the journal that rejected it? An editor's decision to reject a paper may be worthy of appeal (see Chapter 18 in this volume). A central question is whether you had submitted the paper to the best possible journal. If you did, then you should resubmit it to the same journal. Before doing so, however, you should make very conscientious efforts to satisfy the reviewers, either by correcting problems or by explaining better why these are not actually problems. Many editors are willing to listen to tactful and rational appeals of their decisions. Of my four most-cited papers, two were rejected by the journals that later published them.

Issue 5

If you are sending the revised paper back to the original journal, have you explained your revisions well? Editors and reviewers expect to receive detailed explanations of the revisions authors made in response to their comments (Liu, 2014). These explanations are partly symbols of deference, of course, but they also serve to focus reviewers' attention on elements that they actually challenged earlier, which makes it less likely that the reviewers will raise entirely new issues on the next iteration.

Issue 6

If you are not sending the revised paper back to the original journal, where should you submit it? What is the most appropriate journal? Match the properties of your paper against the properties of typical papers in each candidate journal. Has this journal recently published papers on related topics? Do papers in this journal use statistical methods or qualitative ones?

The foregoing procedures are useful in today's publication environment, but the environment has been changing and appears likely to change even more over the coming years. The final section of this chapter points to the possibility of more useful peer review.

PEER REVIEW COULD HAVE A BETTER FUTURE

Academic publication has been changing, and it seems certain to change much more. Technology is challenging journals to show that they can be useful. However, unreliable peer review is an Achilles heel that could, perhaps should, put journals out of business.

Peer review originated because publishing was expensive. Each published page had a significant cost, so editorial budgets limited the numbers of pages. Libraries had to choose which journals to purchase. Journal publishers held editors to annual page limits. University administrators and scholars generally interpreted peer review as a mild validation of the quality of scholarly publications.

Then, peer review gained financial leverage. In the late 1980s, popular magazines began to publish ratings of schools and colleges and some of these ratings took account of the journals in which professors published. Publication in prestigious journals had some influence on students' applications and donors' willingness to give. Around 2000, word spread that the wealthiest and most prestigious departments and schools were placing great emphasis on publishing in the most prestigious journals – so-called "A journals" (Starbuck, 2005).

Publishing no longer has to be expensive. Scholars read journals online and libraries provide computer terminals instead of printed books and journals. Additional pages online cost almost nothing. Many scholars are making their papers available through online databases (e.g., SSRN, ResearchGate) and their universities' websites. New journals are appearing daily and the total number of journals is exploding. In early 2014,

Forgues and Liarte (2014) reported that open-access journals numbered around 10 000 and that 68 percent of these charge nothing for their services.

So, what value can editors and editorial boards offer? As long as university administrators see journal prestige as a very important factor in attracting donations and students, scholars will seek to win endorsements by editorial boards composed of prestigious editors and reviewers (Davis, 2014). However, that seems to be an embarrassingly poor rationale in the face of evidence about the ineffectiveness of editors and reviewers.

A more promising rationale for the existence of editors and reviewers would be improved communication. Instead of focusing on whether to publish, editors could focus on how to make papers clearer, more persuasive and more interesting. Although editors and reviewers sometimes use criteria that are not legitimate and they may have concealed motives, improved editorial practices could moderate both tendencies. For example, editors could make doubly sure that nothing in a paper hints at the author's identity, place of employment or previous publication history. Editors could tell reviewers that they should phrase their comments to authors as suggestions for improvement, not as necessary changes. Editors could tell authors that they should only follow reviewers' advice if they believe changes will improve their papers. Editors could act less as authorities or judges and more as coaches and peers. Indeed, peer review could become what it claims to be.

NOTES

* This chapter is an updated revision of a paper that appeared in the *Journal of Management Inquiry*, 2003, **12**, 344–351. However, this chapter differs rather substantially from the earlier paper. Thanks to Jeffrey Gish, Andrew Nelson, Andreas Schwab, and the editors of this book.
1. Search engines have been making less prestigious journals more visible. Acharya et al. (2014) reported that whereas the non-elite journals published only 27 percent of the most-cited papers in 1995, the non-elite journals published 47 percent of the most-cited papers in 2013. In addition, authors have been using online media to attract readers to their papers.

REFERENCES

Acharya A., A. Verstak, H. Suzuki, S. Henderson, M. Iakhiaev, C. Chiung, Y. Lin and N. Shetty (2014). *Rise of the Rest: The Growing Impact of Non-elite Journals*, Google Inc., 9 October 2014.
Baumeister R.E. (1990). 'Dear journal editor, it's me again: Sample cover letter for journal manuscript resubmissions,' *Dialogue*, **5** (Fall), 16.

Bedeian A.G. (1996a). 'Thoughts on the making and remaking of the management discipline,' *Journal of Management Inquiry*, **5**, 311–318.

Bedeian A.G. (1996b). 'Improving the journal review process: The question of ghostwriting,' *American Psychologist*, **51**, 1189.

Bedeian A.G. (2008). 'Balancing authorial voice and editorial omniscience: The "It's my paper and I'll say what I want to"/"Ghostwriters in the sky" minuet,' in Y. Baruch, A. Konrad, H. Aguinis and W.H. Starbuck (eds.), *Opening the Black Box of Editorship*, Basingstoke: Palgrave Macmillan, pp. 134–142.

Bedeian A.G., S.G. Taylor and A.N. Miller (2010). 'Management science on the credibility bubble: Cardinal sins and various misdemeanors,' *Academy of Management Learning and Education*, **9**, 715–725.

Bones A.K. (2012). 'We knew the future all along: Scientific hypothesizing is much more accurate than other forms of precognition – a satire in one part,' *Perspectives on Psychological Science*, **7** (3), 307–309.

Cicchetti D.V. (1991). 'The reliability of peer review for manuscript and grant submissions: A cross-disciplinary investigation,' *Behavioral and Brain Sciences*, **14**, 119–186 (includes 33 pages of comments by others and a response by Cicchetti).

Davis G.F. (2014). 'Editorial essay: Why do we still have journals?' *Administrative Science Quarterly*, **59** (2), 193–201.

Davis M.S. (1971). 'That's interesting! Towards a phenomenology of sociology and a sociology of phenomenology,' *Philosophy of Social Science*, **1**, 309–344.

Eriksson K. (2012). 'The nonsense math effect,' *Judgment and Decision Making*, **7** (6), 746–749.

Forgues B. and S. Liarte (2014). 'Academic publishing: Past and future,' *M@n@gement*, **16** (5), 739–756.

Gans J.S. and G.B. Shepherd (1994). 'How are the mighty fallen: Rejected classic articles by leading economists,' *Journal of Economic Perspectives*, **8**, 165–179.

Gottfredson D.M. and S.D. Gottfredson (1982). 'Criminal justice and (reviewer) behavior: How to get papers published,' *Criminal Justice and Behavior*, **9** (3), 259–272.

Gottfredson S.D. (1977). 'Scientific quality and peer-group consensus' (Doctoral dissertation, Johns Hopkins University), *Dissertation Abstracts International*, **38**, 1950B (University Microfilms No. 77-19).

Gottfredson S.D. (1978). 'Evaluating psychological research reports: Dimensions, reliability, and correlates of quality judgments,' *American Psychologist*, **33** (10), 920–934.

Harnad S. (1986). 'Policing the paper chase,' *Nature*, **322**, 24–25.

Holbrook M.B. (1986). 'A note on sadomasochism in the review process: I hate when that happens,' *Journal of Marketing*, **50** (July), 104–106.

Ioannidis J.P.A. (2005a). 'Contradicted and initially stronger effects in highly cited clinical research,' *JAMA: The Journal of the American Medical Association*, **294** (2), 218–228.

Ioannidis J.P.A. (2005b). 'Why most published research findings are false,' *PLoS Medicine*, **2** (8), e124.

Kepes S. and M.A. McDaniel (2013). 'How trustworthy is the scientific literature in industrial and organizational psychology?' *Industrial and Organizational Psychology*, **6** (3), 252–268.

Kuhn T.S. (1970). *The Structure of Scientific Revolutions* (2nd edn.), Chicago: University of Chicago Press.

Laband D.N. (1990). 'Is there value-added from the review process in Economics? Preliminary evidence from authors,' *Quarterly Journal of Economics*, **105**, 341–352.

Laband D.N. and M.J. Piette (1994). 'Favoritism versus search for good papers: Empirical evidence regarding the behavior of journal editors,' *Journal of Political Economy*, **102**, 194–203.

Liu L.A. (2014). 'Addressing reviewer comments as an integrative negotiation,' *Management and Organization Review*, **10** (2), 183–190.

Mahoney M.J. (1977). 'Publication prejudices: An experimental study of confirmatory bias in the peer review system,' *Cognitive Therapy and Research*, **1**, 161–175.

Mahoney M.J. (1979). 'Psychology of the scientist: An evaluative review,' *Social Studies of Science*, **9** (3), 349–375.

Mahoney M.J., A.E. Kazdin and M. Kenigsberg (1978). 'Getting published,' *Cognitive Therapy and Research*, **2**, 69–70.

Mazzola J.J. and J.K. Deuling (2013). 'Forgetting what we learned as graduate students: HARKing and selective outcome reporting in I–O journal articles,' *Industrial and Organizational Psychology*, **6** (3), 279–284.

McBride M.F., F. Fidler and M.A. Burgman (2012). 'Evaluating the accuracy and calibration of expert predictions under uncertainty: Predicting the outcomes of ecological research,' *Diversity and Distributions*, **18**, 782–794.

Medoff M.H. (2003). 'Editorial favoritism in economics?' *Southern Economic Journal*, **70**, 425–434.

Nylenna M., P. Riis and Y. Karlsson (1994). 'Multiple blinded reviews of the same two manuscripts: Effects of referee characteristics and publication language,' *JAMA: The Journal of the American Medical Association*, **272**, 149–151.

Osterloh M. and B.S. Frey (2015). 'Ranking games,' *Evaluation Review*, **39** (1), 102–129.

Peters D.P. and S.J. Ceci (1982). 'Peer-review practices of psychological journals: The fate of published articles, submitted again,' *Behavioral and Brain Sciences*, **5**, 187–255 (includes 50 pages of comments by others and a response by Peters and Ceci).

Silera K., K. Leeb and L. Beroc (2015). 'Measuring the effectiveness of scientific gatekeeping,' *PNAS (Proceedings of the National Academy of Sciences)*, **112** (2), 360–365.

Simmons J.P., L.D. Nelson and U. Simonsohn (2011). 'False-positive psychology: Undisclosed flexibility in data collection and analysis allows presenting anything as significant,' *Psychological Science*, **22** (11), 1359–1366.

Starbuck W.H. (2003). 'Turning lemons into lemonade: Where is the value in peer reviews?' *Journal of Management Inquiry*, **12**, 344–351.

Starbuck W.H. (2005). 'How much better are the most prestigious journals? The statistics of academic publication,' *Organization Science*, **16**, 180–200.

Starbuck W.H. (2009). 'The constant causes of never-ending faddishness in the behavioral and social sciences,' *Scandinavian Journal of Management*, **25** (1), 108–116.

Starbuck W.H. (2014). 'Why and where do academics publish?' *M@n@gement*, **16** (5), 707–718.

Starbuck W.H., H. Aguinis, A.M. Konrad and Y. Baruch (2008). 'Tradeoffs among editorial goals in complex publishing environments,' in Y. Baruch, A. Konrad, H. Aguinis and W.H. Starbuck (eds.), *Opening the Black Box of Editorship*, Basingstoke: Palgrave Macmillan pp. 250–270.

Webster J. and W.H. Starbuck (1988). 'Theory building in industrial and organizational psychology,' in C.L. Cooper and I. Robertson (eds.), *International Review of Industrial and Organizational Psychology 1988*, Chichester: Wiley, pp. 93–138.

Wolff W.M. (1970). 'A study of criteria for journal manuscripts,' *American Psychologist*, **25**, 636–639.

PART II

Resolving practical key issues

Section II.I

Becoming a scholar

8. Rules of the game

Denny Gioia

Isaac Newton – a semi-modest man despite his genius – once said that, "If I have seen far, it is because I have stood on the shoulders of giants." Pablo Picasso – not quite so modest, but just as insightfully clever – said that, "Good artists copy; great artists steal," by which he meant that great artist's take the essence of a good idea and transform it in their own image. I have an undeserved foot in both these august camps. I stand tippy-toed on a lot of broad shoulders to survey the mindscape of our field, but I also consider myself an equal-opportunity kleptomaniac. I will steal from anybody. Well, not exactly steal, but I am prone to borrowing the spirit of others' wisdom and transmogrifying it for my own purposes.

When I started out in the field, the whole business of publishing in the organization sciences was an intimidating if intriguing mystery. Having come from a doctoral program that did not emphasize publishing only made uncovering the arcane secrets of the process even more mysterious. Hmmm. How to begin to decipher a figurative Rosetta Stone? As a faux ethnographer, I began to ask various published scholars for their insights, their heuristics, their received wisdom, their "rules of the game" of publishing. In addition to my own colleagues, anytime a visiting scholar showed up at Penn State I'd make it my business to pick their brains (which is what I do for a living anyway – see Gioia, 2004). Over the years, I have assembled quite a lot of informal rules. I at least had the good sense to steal with a tip-of-the-hat attribution to the person from whom I stole the spirit of a rule worth internalizing.

Herewith, then, is a selection from my assemblage of rules, named in honor of the person from whom I purloined it – even if these rules are my (probably bastardized) interpretations of what they actually said. All have a specific theft victim's name, except in the first and last instance, because the first, "Somebody's Statement," has achieved the status of received folk wisdom that is woven into the fabric of our field, and the last, "Nike's Rule," is named for a mythological figure whose name was swiped by a corporate entity (thus demonstrating that I am not the only thief in the realm). A small bit of probably unnecessary commentary accompanies each entry. You should forgive the forced alliteration in the names of the rules. Sometimes I just can't help myself.

Somebody's Statement*: Publish or perish!* It is worth beginning with this old cliché, because publishing is the currency of the realm and you ignore this hackneyed (if nonetheless wise) counsel at your peril. My old prof, Bill Hodge's, perennial advice was "always have options." Publishing is the best way to keep your options open in this field.

Susman's Standard (named for Gerry Susman): *Two good publications per year keep the wolf away from the door.* Earlier in his career Gerry would close up his writing shop for the year as soon as he had two good hits (an "A" and a something else reputable). Wish I didn't have the publishing disease and could bring myself to live by this wisdom. Might make for a more balanced life.

Manz's Method (Chuck Manz): *More shots on goal means more goals.* No, it's not cynical. It's actually insightful. The metamessage here is to be prolific. But, remember, the product has your name on it, so you can't try to foist off garbage.

Mejia's Model (Luis Gómez-Mejía): *Target every manuscript to a specific journal.* Pay attention! Don't be oblivious! Journals have hallmarks. Look for what they're looking for.

Sim's Statute (Hank Sims): *Work on the things that are closest to publication.* A dose of pragmatic wisdom. Most of us are easily distractible. Too many balls in the air. Which one to snare, chew on, and polish? [Somebody call the mixed metaphor abuse hotline, quick!] Sims statute solves this problem with a simple heuristic.

Locke's Law (Ed Locke): *Don't take no for an answer.* Never give up on a paper. Never, never, never give up as some famous Englishman so famously said.

Meyer's Maxim (Alan Meyer): *You want to be read, not just published.* A really good observation. Do it like you mean it. Intend not just to get it published; intend for people to read it. I'll even add a corollary: Do it so people will cite it. Yes, you want to be published, you want to be read, but more importantly, you want to have other scholars use your work in their work.

Brass's Bylaw (Dan Brass): *The best predictor of future performance is past performance.* How do you know you're good at this game? You keep doing it and doing it and doing it the best you can.

Weick's Wisdom (Karl Weick): *There are few truly new ideas. Focus instead on finding a different way of seeing.* Coming up with the Grand Shazzam just isn't very likely. Instead, take an interesting idea and play with it. Look at what everyone thinks they know in a different way.

Revisit Davis's (1971) pointers for what leads people to say "That's Interesting!" and build those attributes into your projects and your papers.

Gioia's Judgments (My name is pronounced as "Joya," so you should forgive the necessary use of a homonym here, as I am not quite clever enough to come up with a term beginning with "g" that alliterates "Gioia.") Of course, when you set out on a project to swipe other peoples' wisdom, you develop a few rules of your own. Here's a selection that have served me well ...

- *The academic world can be divided into knowledge generators and knowledge disseminators. Better to be a knowledge generator.* You probably wouldn't be reading this little chapter if you saw yourself primarily as a disseminator of other people's ideas (a teacher), rather than a generator of ideas (a theorist/researcher).
- *The academic world can be divided into readers and writers. Better to be a writer.* Quiz #1: Do you (a) think to write or (b) write to think? The effective people who publish answer with (b). Quiz #2: Do you (c) read to write or (d) write to read? Guess which tactic the effective publishers use? (If you think it's (c), rethink it.)
- *Rhetoric matters.* In our field argumentation matters most. Data/results/findings can mean lots of different things to lots of different people. In the face of the kind of ambiguity associated with our field, you need to learn to structure ambiguity for others (I call that *sensegiving*). You do that in a manuscript by arguing well. And you do *that* by becoming a rhetorician.
- *Write something every day. Writing is rewriting. Revise, Revise, Revise.* Writing for publication is a craft honed by deliberate practice (Colvin, 2008). The key to my professional identity is my sense that, among my many identities, above all *I am a writer*. So I write something every day (even if some days it's just a well-crafted email).
- *It's all personal but you can't take it personally.* If you take yourself seriously as a writer, you are putting yourself out there whenever you submit a paper for publication. Your work is who you are. Odds are, however, that you're going to be rejected, sometimes even with a dreaded RWS (Rejection With Scorn). *Illegitimi non carborundum!* (loosely translated as "Don't let the bastards get you down!").

I conclude with two pearls that have served as my metaguides:

Castaneda's Counsel (Carlos Castenada): *Find a path with a heart.*
This was the core message from Castenada's *The Teachings of Don Juan.*
It sounds like a new-age idealistic platitude, but it is nonetheless good
counsel. It's also not that easy to do. Successful publishing too often
seems like opportunistic publishing – joining in on any project that might
look like it has publication potential. Don't do that. A small witticism
around my shop is that we counsel junior faculty that having three
streams of research is too many and having one stream is too few, so ...
do the math. In the end, you want to be known for something. You can't
be known for something if you're acting like you want to be known for
everything. Find a path with a heart. Be known for that.

Nike's Rule (Corporate America): *Just do it!* (Yes, I will even steal
from disembodied entities who are quasi-people.) Here's why I have
chosen this simplistic, pragmatic rule of the game as my parting shot: I
am often amazed at how many procrastinators and seeming perfectionists
there are in academia. Both procrastination and perfectionism are dis-
eases that are inhibitors. First, you gotta discipline the execution of your
craft by finding your own ways of working on your work without
constantly putting if off. Just do it. Second you gotta stop using the
pursuit of perfection to enable your procrastination. Get off your duff.
Just do it!

REFERENCES

Colvin, G. (2008). *Talent Is Overrated: What Really Separates World-Class
Performers from Everybody Else*, New York: Penguin.
Davis, M.S. (1971). 'That's interesting: Towards a phenomenology of sociology
and a sociology of phenomenology', *Philosophy of Social Science*, **1**, 309–
344.
Gioia, D.A. (2004). 'A Renaissance self: Prompting personal and professional
revitalization', in P.J. Frost and R.E. Stablein (eds.), *Renewing Research
Practice: Scholars' Journeys*, Stanford, CA: Stanford University Press,
pp. 97–114.

9. Learning by walking through the snow

R. Duane Ireland

For those close to my age (this means you are a part of the oldest segment of the baby boomers), you may recall that walking through the snow to attend school as a youth was thought to represent a true hardship. If lucky, a person received responses of heartfelt concern from others when telling a story about wearing boots while traipsing through snow-laden streets to arrive at school. And it is indeed true that I walked through the snow to attend elementary school in the Midwestern U.S. city in which I was born and raised.

With hindsight, I realize that walking in the snow was a positive experience in that I quickly learned the value of patience. Particularly when confronted by heavy amounts of snow, the young student is not able to reach school quickly. Additionally, snowdrifts and accumulations of snow challenge the walker to carefully plan the route to be taken. Of course, part of an effectively constructed walking route is specification of alternate paths to take when adjustments are required to deal with unexpected conditions (such as encountering ice underneath piles of snow). My experiences reveal that both developing and executing "snow walking" plans requires *patience*.

And so it is with us as scholars. In this respect, I believe that each of us must learn to be patient as we design and execute research projects. But this is difficult for us given our desire to quickly (after we complete our degrees) and continuously (throughout our careers) contribute to the literature and, potentially, to inform managerial practice in the process of doing so. This is understandable in many ways, of course, given the reality that, for most of us, research productivity is critical to our short- and long-term academic success. Patience is particularly difficult to develop for untenured faculty who have little time to publish their scholarship as the foundation for becoming "legitimate" in the eyes of their colleagues and employing institution. After all, the infamous "tenure-clock" is ticking! The reality though is that high-quality research—the kind that finds a home in top-tier outlets and that commonly is foundational to earning a promotion with tenure—is a product of carefully constructed designs and executions of them. As I explain next, there are multiple parts of the research process for which patience is critical.

As we know, specifying an interesting research question is the foundation on which impactful scholarship is built. Paraphrasing Murray Davis (1971), the first criterion people use to judge work is whether it is interesting or not. The parameters of interesting research are expansive and include organizing a study around counterintuitive arguments, using novel methods, developing an unusual dataset, and using theories to creatively examine an intriguing question of the current time. To me, the informal economy, changing corporate mechanisms, and determining the meaning of organizational size in an increasingly digitized world are examples of currently interesting phenomena. Being able to identify important questions requires one to be patient enough to take the time and energy required to integrate multiple theories and methods within the context of contemporary phenomena that are of interest to a particular audience.

The journal to which scholarly work is to be submitted is an important audience to consider. Each journal has a mission statement that describes the type of research it seeks to publish. Scholars should patiently analyse various journals' missions to find the one that is the closest match with the research project with which they are involved at a point in time. Submitting manuscripts featuring research that rests outside a journal's mission wastes precious time given that the review process is unlikely to yield the scholar's desired outcome. Similarly, scholars should carefully read articles, especially those related to their research domain, that are published in a journal to which they intend to submit their work. Journals develop different cadences with respect to how the research they publish is presented. The journal's mission, editorial review policies, and copyediting practices are examples of influences on a journal's cadence. Becoming familiar with the nature of published work in a journal increases the likelihood of preparing a manuscript that is consistent with what a given journal commonly publishes.

Assuming the role of a reviewer while designing and completing a study and when writing our manuscript is another action requiring patience. But doing this can lead to very positive outcomes. Carefully studying our own work as we anticipate a reviewer will do once s/he receives our paper from an editor increases the probability that we will proactively identify problems with our work. Once recognized of course, we can deal with those problems prior to submitting our work for review.

Aggressively challenging our work as we complete it happens only when we are able to disassociate ourselves from the fact that we ourselves are the scholar being challenged! Of course, we would much rather take the time and energy needed to identify and correct problems ourselves rather than have those problems be the source of a rejection.

There are other actions we can take to improve the chance of our work being positively received by reviewers and editors. Asking colleagues to isolate weaknesses in our arguments before we initialize work on a project, studying the latest methods to see if a recently developed one is highly appropriate for our analyses, and seeking constructive feedback from colleagues prior to submitting a manuscript are examples of actions we can take. But each of these actions too requires patience. On the other hand, exercising the patience needed to consistently take the actions proposed in this commentary has the potential to lead to publishing success. As with carefully planning the route to take to walk to school through snow-leaden territory, being patient enough to engage in patiently crafted research can result in scholarly success. To develop patience as a scholar, each of us must be confident that doing so is a path to publishing impactful research.

REFERENCES

Davis, M.S. (1971). 'That's interesting: Towards a phenomenology of sociology and a sociology of phenomenology', *Philosophy of Social Science*, **1**, 309–344.

10. Suggestions for strengthening the discussion section and increasing your odds of publication success

Donald D. Bergh

INTRODUCTION

What section of a paper do you read first? The Introduction? Did you know that many reviewers and editors read the Discussion first? Surprised? Don't be, as this section is where readers learn about how a paper's story adds uniquely to knowledge. An effective Discussion will identify the research purpose, the paper's unique insight, and then provide an elaboration of the contribution's meaning and implications. If your paper offers a new advance, the reader should find it in the Discussion. If your paper does not offer a new contribution, the reader will find that out too. In many ways, the Discussion section is where the author showcases the paper's contribution. You want it to be a big bang and not a whimper, which, I'm sorry to say, is usually what happens.

Using my experience as a long-term reviewer (20 years or so) and as an associate editor of three top journals for more than 12 years now, I want to share with you that I usually run into big problems when I read the Discussion sections of new manuscripts. These outcomes are disappointing, as authors have usually invested considerable resources in creating an impressive model and data set while reviewers discover that the authors do not leverage the uniqueness about their research to provide a new and meaningful insight.

There is good news though. Many problems with contribution can be anticipated and resolved before submission. In the following sections, I offer some suggestions on how to define and develop your paper's contributions and Discussion and align them with journals' requirements. Hopefully, these points will help you bring your paper to publication easier, faster and with more fun. And, critically, avoid the ever increasing odds of desk rejection.

SUGGESTION 1: OBJECTIVE

Consider first your motivation for writing a paper. If the purpose of writing your paper is just to publish it, then you might not invest the effort into making it interesting and novel, and your lack of enthusiasm may become apparent to reviewers and editors. If you are not interested in the work per se, then why expect the readers to become so?

When authors are passionate about their work, the motivation, argumentation and implications become exciting. Ask yourself: How can you make your paper's story poignant and compelling? If your purpose is to offer a strong, unique and confident voice to a conversation, then your story is going to be more engaging to the paper's evaluators. What is interesting about your research? Does it have broad appeal? Does it pertain to a critical social issue? Think about what makes your research interesting. Be mindful that reviewers will assess your paper's contribution in terms of the breadth and depth of the contribution and whether it is surprising and of clear importance (Rynes, 2002). You might think too about whether your paper may have a competitive advantage in the marketplace of ideas – what is rare and valuable about your paper's story (Bergh, 2003)? All of this begins with a clear definition of your work's objective and why it is important.

Imagine what Discussion sections look like when the authors are not vested in the work versus when they are. If the Discussion is boring and repetitious, focuses on empirical findings rather than on developing a story, and does not proclaim the advance and its merits, then do you really think the reviewers and editors are going to spend their time seeking out the paper's diamond in all of the rough that surrounds it?

SUGGESTION 2: MATURITY

Many papers seem to be submitted prematurely. In these papers, the conceptual stories are usually not well developed. Within the Discussion, the content tends to focus on the findings rather than linking them to supporting a story. I recommend that you prioritize your paper's story over the data and findings. Think about it like this: The evidence is used to support the contribution and is not a substitute for it. Think long and hard about what the findings and arguments really mean in terms of supporting a novel and valuable conceptual story before submitting the paper. Let your ideas ripen. Think too about what future research might sprout from your story.

Closely related to this point is the case when authors submit their papers to journals with the hope of receiving a revision outcome or to simply get feedback so as to revise the paper for submission elsewhere. Such objectives seem to ignore the major reasons why we read papers in the first place and why some succeed in the peer review process. If the contribution is not well developed, then authors will not likely receive comments on the most important aspect of their paper in the first place and will just waste the time and resources of everyone involved.

SUGGESTION 3: MOTIVATION

Contributions need to be built upon strong foundations. This matter goes for both the Introduction and Discussion. Different types of foundations exist and typically fall into one of two categories: theories or findings. Most problematic Discussion sections focus on the latter. However, if you are attempting to make a compelling case for your paper, the motivation for the contribution is generally more convincing if it is rooted in revising or expanding explanations and understandings. Can you challenge conventional wisdom?

I mentioned the problems with empirical motivations. Many submissions have a motivation of "resolving differences in reported empirical findings is the reason for my study." This approach sets off alarm bells in my mind. I remember in graduate school being told by Professor Luis Gómez-Mejía to not write papers that attempt to "add a pebble to a pile of rocks." Papers whose motivations are based on resolving differences in empirical findings can lose sight of addressing possible problems in explanations and descriptions. Frankly, if an author is really interested in addressing differences in empirical results, then adding another study to the mix is simply going to be considered as yet another pebble to support one side over the other. If the authentic objective is to resolve differences in empirical findings, then a meta-analysis that synthesizes a literature's findings and empirically assesses the strength of moderators existing across some set of studies is more appropriate than another single study. Keep in mind that reconciling different theoretical explanations for a relationship elevates the conversation to the level that becomes necessary to make a meaningful contribution. From this perspective, findings can be construed as evidence for a conceptual insight.

I see motivation as having different levels. Empirical motivations are lower and less interesting than theoretical ones, which help us explain phenomenon and behaviors. In the latter case, the data take a supporting role.

SUGGESTION 4: STRUCTURE

A strong contribution will typically have three features. First, it will be clearly articulated relative to a research question. Second, the contribution will be defined, explained and developed. Third, it will be positioned relative to existing understanding so the reader can understand how the paper's unique story extends or revises current knowledge. Organizing a discussion around these three features will help reviewers and editors clearly interpret your paper's contribution, provide them with structure for offering their reactions to it, and ensure that the value-added of your research is clear and accessible.

SUGGESTION 5: TARGETING

Finally, contribution can take different forms and types. At least three exist: (1) a new advance for theory and topic; (2) a new advance for topic, but not theory, and (3) a new advance to theory, but not to topic (Bergh, 2008). The type of contribution offered by your paper needs to align with the journal's objective. Realize that journals seek to publish specific kinds of contributions. If you are targeting a top academic journal, then your paper likely needs to offer an advance for both theory and topic (see type (1) above). If you are targeting the next level of journals, then your paper might apply extant theory in order to derive a new insight into a topic (see type (2)). Many new submissions are rejected because the type of contribution that they can offer does not align with what the journal seeks to publish. From my experience, some papers can be shifted among these types, such that a paper's publication prospects can be significantly enhanced. This development often occurs during a revision process involving highly engaged authors and reviewers working together (Bergh, 2006). Still, leave the guesswork out and be careful to choose a target journal that most closely aligns with the kind of contribution that your paper strives to offer. You will save yourself much time in the publication process.

CONCLUSION

In closing, based on my experience as a long-time reviewer and editor, most new submissions do not include several of the above points. I recommend that you carefully consider Discussion sections and what you can do to make those in your papers as strong and compelling as possible. Read them closely so you, and your readers, can better understand what any paper offers the literature.

REFERENCES

Bergh, D.D. (2008). 'The developmental editor: Assessing and directing manuscript contribution', in Y. Baruch, A.M. Konrad, H. Aguinis and W.H. Starbuck (eds), *Opening the Black Box of Editorship*. Palgrave MacMillan, pp. 114–123.
Bergh, D.D. (2006). 'Editing the 2004 Best *AMJ* Article', *Academy of Management Journal*, **49**, 197–202.
Bergh, D.D. (2003). 'Thinking strategically about contribution', *Academy of Management Journal*, **46**, 135–136.
Rynes, S. (2002). 'Some reflections on contribution', *Academy of Management Journal*, **45**, 311–313.

11. You miss 100% of the shots you don't take

Annette L. Ranft and Anne D. Smith*

You Miss 100% of the Shots You Don't Take[1]

This famous quote – you miss 100% of the shots you don't take – by ice hockey Hall of Fame player Wayne Gretzky captures what we want to address in this short chapter: the need to get your papers out and under review! Let's be clear – we are not advocating against getting friendly reviews or feedback from conferences in order to strengthen your paper. (In our roles as Associate Editors, we have certainly seen many desk rejects of papers that needed much more work before submission.) Yet, just as some may have the propensity to pull the trigger too soon when submitting to a journal, we know there are others who are slow to send their manuscripts out to a journal, if at all. These are researchers who take weeks, months, or years to tinker with a manuscript, scrapping whole sections or the entire paper, collecting more data, reading one more book or stream of research, and/or rethinking the theoretical frame. We are addressing our comments to these colleagues whom we know well – those who are tinkerers, perfectionists, slow, or simply never "take a shot" by sending a paper to a journal. We have found that this paralyzing stultification can happen at many points in a career – from a first year assistant professor who is no longer focused on deadlines imposed by a dissertation chair, to a senior researcher who has endured a spate of harsh, negative reviews about his/her stream of research or methodological approach. Our objective in this chapter is to articulate why getting a paper under review is critical. We provide suggestions to help overcome the tendency to hold onto a manuscript.

In ice hockey, if you don't take shots, you become a weak member of a team and your playing time and marketability subsequently decreases. So too in academic institutions – not getting papers out leads to lower productivity which not only hurts chances for promotion but decreases your market value if you want or need to move. As well, in many streams of research, there is a window in which papers on a topic are sought after. Further, delaying getting your manuscript under review opens the door to be "scooped" by another academic. Instead of trying to get a manuscript perfect, it would be better to get a good manuscript under review and allow reviewers to provide direction towards publication. As Golden-Biddle and Locke (2007) noted, reviewers in many cases become like co-authors, providing clear direction on the types and degree of changes needed. A "high risk" revise and resubmit can often require additional data, a new theory lens, and substantial new analyses; yet rarely does a researcher need to start over with a "white screen" for a revision. Finally, being good enough for a review should become your mantra instead of getting it perfect.

If you have a colleague or co-author who matches the above description (or see parts of yourself in this description), here are some suggestions to help you move from manuscript to submission.

- Use deadlines to force you to submit! Special issues have built-in deadlines for submission and review cycles. Use these externally derived deadlines as your own. Certainly conference deadlines provide an opportunity to complete and submit a draft. However, getting from conference paper to journal submission many times requires you to create a deadline for yourself. Committing to that deadline publically to your colleagues, co-authors, spouse, anyone who will listen and ask you about it again later, will enhance the effectiveness of your self-imposed deadlines.
- Publically stating your commitment to meet a deadline can spur you into action. While the deadline commitment can be made orally, we suggest also making a written public reminder with a white board in your office that identifies which manuscripts are targeted at which journals, with hard deadlines. Discuss the white board with colleagues (you might find some common interests). At the very least, you create personal accountability from these visible commitments. And no erasing allowed! If you must alter a deadline for submission, strike through the old deadline and put in a new deadline – again no erasing allowed!
- Identify colleagues who are productive and have a strong publication track record and learn from their habits. How do they spend their time? How do they approach readying a manuscript for submission? See if one of these colleagues would be willing to work with you. You will learn about their work habits and approach to deciding when a manuscript is ready to send out. Even if the topic areas don't naturally overlap, most academic researchers

enjoy collaborating and connecting over intriguing ideas. You bring the deep topic knowledge, and they bring the process to getting the manuscript out the door.

- Write daily and work with one or two colleagues during two or three distinct times of the week. Many graduate students we have known have used this approach – writing with another graduate student on Saturday or every other day at specified times. Consider creating a 6 a.m. to 8 a.m. writing time in the office with another early morning colleague. Share manuscripts, ask for advice, commiserate over coffee, and essentially hold one another accountable. This regular routinized approach to writing not only helps to build communities and hold you accountable, but it also makes the process of writing and revision less lonely.
- Listen to colleagues who shoot straight but not to kill. Obviously most manuscripts could benefit from another set of eyes and feedback. On manuscripts that are for initial journal submissions, give the paper to a colleague who may not know a lot about a topic to see if he or she can discern what the project is about. And, ask someone in the same domain as the manuscript to provide input, both about the manuscript and about guidance regarding where to submit the manuscript. Take the feedback as input but not unchangeable directives, and set a time limit for your revision. This becomes your submission goal date. For significant and material criticisms, it may be that the project should be narrowed, or perhaps if there is enough negative input, the project should be flushed. There is nothing worse than having a black cloud of a lingering project hanging over your head.
- Revisions are tricky, so get some advice! Once you've done so, and you've received that glorious revise and resubmit decision, a new deadline is in place for the revision. There is no time to blame the reviewers for not understanding your study or theory. No time to process emotional reactions to the lack of enthusiastic support for your obvious creativity and intellect. Often one receives advice to put the reviews aside for 24 hours. This is good advice, but also ask for a friendly read of reviewer comments during that time. This can be invaluable whether you are a new assistant professor or seasoned full professor. Some authors who are slow to send papers out for review may perceive that a large-scale revision is needed from the comments, whereas another set of eyes will identify that the editor is calling for less substantial changes. Before heading down the path of collecting more data or scrapping the methods, ask for advice and get an interpretation of the editor's comments about a

revision (and by the way, congratulate yourself for the revision from the journal, which brings us to our last point …).

- Tell the negative mouse to be quiet! Michael Lubatkin, a seriously prolific strategy scholar, described having a mouse on either shoulder – one with helpful thoughts ("That is a great insight!" "Congratulations on the revision!" "You can do this!") and another (usually with a louder voice) with negative thoughts ("You only wrote a paragraph today?" "You will never finish this manuscript"). These negative thoughts slow you down and, let's bottom line it, are just not helpful. Confidence is not built overnight, but getting manuscripts out are a visible sign that the negative mouse's arguments have been curtailed.

So, we hope that our suggestions help you to "take a shot" and submit your manuscript in a timely fashion to journals.

NOTES

*   Equal authorship.
1.   http://www.forbes.com/sites/actiontrumpseverything/2014/01/12/you-miss-100-of-the-shots-you-dont-take-so-start-shooting-at-your-goal/ (accessed January 19, 2014).

REFERENCES

Golden-Biddle, K., and K. Locke (2007). *Composing Qualitative Research*, Thousand Oaks, CA: Sage Publications.

12. Why I don't want to co-author with you and what you can do about it

David J. Ketchen, Jr.

INTRODUCTION

Time is the most precious resource that each of us manages in our professional lives. Those of us who have been fortunate enough to advance through our careers from assistant professor to associate professor to full professor and finally to chaired professor generally find that the demands on our time seem to grow as we move up the proverbial academic ladder. This forces us to make hard choices and to say "no" more than we would like. Who to embrace or reject as co-authors is one of the important choices that all academics, and especially senior faculty, must make.

My goal in this chapter is to offer some useful tips on how to be a more appealing potential co-author. In doing so, I draw inspiration from a 1985 book chapter by Dick Daft entitled "Why I recommended that your manuscript be rejected and what you can do about it" (Daft, 1985). Daft analysed his experiences as a reviewer for premier journals and distilled some guidelines for authors about how to improve their chances of having their journal submissions accepted. As a doctoral student in the early 1990s, this chapter provided me with a behind-the-scenes perspective on the review process that helped me understand what research success requires. Similarly, I hope to offer some candid advice about co-authorship based on my experiences writing 140 or so co-authored articles across the last three decades.

YOU FIND IT, YOU FIX IT

Few co-author behaviors are more frustrating than identifying a problem and then expecting others to fix it. Quite a few times I have heard from friends who were infuriated because a co-author simply pointed out a deficiency without attempting to actually solve the problem that was identified. Rather than quickly firing off an email saying "this abstract you wrote doesn't reflect our paper's contents," take the time to try rewriting the abstract instead. This sends a positive signal about your approach to collaboration and you might even come up with a great abstract. A co-authored paper is a bit like a row boat – each person with an oar in the water needs to make a good faith effort if the boat is to reach its destination with everyone still smiling. In short, don't just tell me how bad something is, make it better!

A related problem is responding to a co-author's requests for help by not being helpful. A few years ago, a friend asked a more methodologically sophisticated co-author for assistance with addressing a technical question raised by a reviewer. Rather than draft a response to the reviewer's inquiry, the co-author emailed PDFs of one or more of his/her past articles and simply stated that the answer can be found in the attached articles. You should not treat a co-author like you would a student in your class.

DON'T SANDBAG

In golf, a sandbagger is someone who cheats his or her opponents by pretending to be a worse golfer than s/he really is. This often involves, for example, inflating one's handicap so that one is put in a better position to win a tournament wherein handicaps are factored into players' scores.

Academic sandbagging occurs when someone fails to do his or her best in their role as a co-author. I was guilty of this once as a doctoral student, although naïve logic rather than ill-intent was behind it. My doctoral advisor at Penn State (Jim Thomas, who later became dean there) and I were working on a revise and resubmit for a modest journal. If accepted, this would be my first refereed article. I struggled with one of the sections that Jim had asked me to draft and I turned it over to him to fix. As an experienced writer, he could tell that it was not the best work of which I was capable. When he asked for an explanation, I noted that he could fix in a few minutes what would take me hours or even days to resolve. His face then turned an unrecognizable shade of red as he roared at me: "How do you expect to become good at this if you don't work your way through it?" I slinked out of his office, did my best on the passage in question, and never sandbagged anyone again.

I have been on the receiving side of sandbagging quite a few times. I tend to be more forgiving when a sandbagger confesses to the crime like

I confessed to Jim. But if the same person sandbags on a series of projects over time, my goal becomes to stop co-authoring with them. If a person has a reputation as a sandbagger, I avoid agreeing to co-author with them in the first place.

SAVE THE DRAMA FOR YOUR MAMA

An old saying wonders "why buy trouble when you get enough for free?" We all have drama in our lives, whether it's controversies at home, conflicts with one's supervisor, a mid-life crisis, or any number of other types of angst. Given that some drama in life is inevitable, it makes sense to avoid it in areas where it is not inevitable, such as the selection of co-authors. Indeed, one of the attractive aspects of doing academic research is that one generally gets to pick his or her co-authors as opposed to being assigned them.

A few years ago, a tenured professor sent me this email regarding a doctoral student (edited slightly to disguise the guilty): "Joe shows up at my office and says he wants to 'update me' on a research project we agreed to do together. I haven't heard anything from him in over a year. After hearing him out, I tried to gently tell him that he needs to stay in touch more, and he got all defensive. Weird!" Understandably, the professor was not excited about pursuing this project – or any other project – with the defensive doctoral student. Worse yet, the same student had shirked his work without apology on a previous project with the same professor.

In 2010, Mike Buckley and I wrote an article on "workplace divas" and how to manage them (Ketchen and Buckley, 2010). Based on our experiences with other academics and an informal survey of professionals in other fields, we suggested that workplace divas tend to have some combination of seven attributes: attention seeking, temperamental, blame avoidance, lack of perspective, overly demanding, self-importance, and self-promoting. Supervisors often try to ignore or appease such behavior; these strategies rarely work. In the research context, however, we can simply avoid divas and the associated drama by refusing to work with them. I count several of my regular co-authors among my dearest friends. I would be foolish to take time away from them and devote it to co-authoring with a workplace diva.

KEEP YOUR PROMISES

This one is pretty simple. Do what you say you are going to do. If you say you will send a co-author a draft by Tuesday, do whatever it takes to send the draft by Tuesday. Certainly unexpected glitches are inevitable and no reasonable person will be mad if a deadline is missed because a hard drive crashes or a child gets sick. But if the reason for lateness is along the lines of "I was too busy" or "I was overcommitted," then your stock as a co-author will sink. Moreover, a series of missed deadlines will undermine your attractiveness as a co-author regardless of how legitimate any individual excuse might be.

Before you break a promise, keep in mind that your co-author's work time is limited and precious. From his/her point of view, any time that s/he wastes on a bad co-author (i.e., you) could have been invested in a good co-author. A tenured scholar typically has enough quality co-authors available that there is little incentive to take a chance on "damaged goods." And because past performance is the best predictor of future performance, a scholar who becomes viewed as an undesirable co-author will have a very difficult time reversing this perception.

CONCLUSION

In sum, being an attractive co-author does not require a stellar vita or an exceptional level of brilliance. Instead, the basic recipe is pretty simple: act in good faith, always do your best, keep drama and other negative emotions out of the research process, and live up to your word. Academics that fulfill these four criteria always will have collaborators eager to work with them.

REFERENCES

Daft, R.L. (1985). 'Why I recommended that your manuscript be rejected and what you can do about it', in L.L. Cummings and P.J. Frost (eds), *Publishing in the Organizational Sciences*, Thousand Oaks, CA: Sage, pp. 193–209.
Ketchen, D.J. and M. Buckley (2010). 'Divas at work: Dealing with drama kings and queens in organizations', *Business Horizons*, **53**, 599–606.

Section II.II

Getting your methods right

13. Are your results really robust?

Bruce T. Lamont

INTRODUCTION

PhDs are trained to develop theory, collect data to test it, run analyses, write up the results, and send the paper to a journal for publication consideration. Under time pressures to get manuscripts under review, however, many scholars do not take the time to collect additional data to address potential endogeneity, alternative measures of their constructs, or other theories that may account for their anticipated findings. Nor do many scholars assess the sensitivity of their results to their sensible but possibly arbitrary methodological choices or explore why all of the results didn't turn out as expected.

Why would they? What I just outlined sounds like a lot of work and would take a lot of time. That is true. But it is also absolutely necessary if the goal is to publish in top-tier journals. By not taking these matters into consideration in the design and execution of a project, researchers are setting themselves up for failure. Without thoroughly assessing alternative explanations for one's findings, it is impossible to know if the stated interpretation is correct. And, more importantly, reviewers at our best journals are not likely to believe it. If the hurried researcher's paper makes it through the first round of review, the data and results are not likely to survive the review process without significant alterations, possibly taking the author in directions the original theory may not support, leaving him/her with a modest or uninteresting contribution and, unfortunately, an un-publishable paper ... at least in a great journal. My purpose in this brief contribution is to detail a few of things I've found useful to consider before collecting data and while analysing data for a project. The aim is to improve the odds that your data and results are robust enough to survive a rigorous review process.

BUILDING A ROBUST DATASET

Beyond the primary variables for a study, there are a few data collection issues to consider, not least of which is endogeneity. Unless you are planning a laboratory study, most management research exists in an endogenous world (Hamilton and Nickerson, 2003). It is far better to consider this while designing your study and data collection strategy than afterwards. If endogeneity is a foreign term, there are useful reference sources (e.g., Hamilton and Nickerson, 2003; Larcker and Rusticus, 2010; Semandeni, Withers, and Certo, 2014). Two of the more common forms of endogeneity are when the sample is composed of firms or people who made a choice that underlies their inclusion (self-selection bias) or when managers choose the independent variables (IVs) for specific reasons to affect the dependent variable (DV), that is, there are omitted variables correlated with the IVs and DV.

Selection and omitted variable bias may affect your results. For example, suppose you were interested in how social networks of entrepreneurs affected their firms' performance; and you plan to collect a dataset of social network factors (IVs) and firm performance (DV) for a sample of entrepreneurs in a particular industry. These data would have both types of endogeneity problems noted above. Entrepreneurs choose to be entrepreneurs and may be different from non-entrepreneurs. Their social networks may be built for a number of reasons, one of which might be to help the performance of their firm. The corrections for endogeneity all require additional data on predictors of the self-selection bias (i.e., being an entrepreneur) and/or the endogenous variables. So, this is best to address upfront when you can best get the data. When you get to creating your instrumental variables, or controls for endogeneity, but find that they aren't very good instruments despite your planning ahead, as is often the case, I have found the approach outlined in section 7 of Larcker and Rusticus (2010) to be very helpful. They show how to estimate the sensitivity/robustness of your results to "uncontrolled" endogeneity. I have usually found that when I cannot control for endogeneity, the results would not be substantively different if I were able to do so. That may not always be the case, as Shaver (1998) aptly demonstrates, but the maximum effect of endogeneity can be logically estimated using the Larcker and Rusticus procedure.

There are other data collection issues that should also be included in the design stage. For example, alternate measures you could use for your main variables should be included to assess the sensitivity of your results to alternative specifications. Authors rarely develop strong rationales for the measures they choose. Reviewers view these choices as arbitrary and frequently ask authors to consider and collect additional data for other measures. These measurement issues are most economically addressed in the design stage. And it is very helpful to push your thinking about alternative theories that might be relevant to your study. These alternate theories might suggest other predictors, potential moderators or possible mediators you might find useful to explore in a future study but would be excellent controls in this one. I have frequently found that these "indirectly" relevant data emerge as very relevant once I get to the data analysis stage. As you may be beginning to see, I don't believe you can ever have too much data; and you should rarely rely on single measures.

CONDUCTING ROBUST ANALYSES

Once you have your data, get to know it well, very well. Use the alternate measures that you collected. Examine subsamples of the dataset. Try different arbitrary choices (e.g., 5-year instead of 3-year averages or a cut-off of $500 million instead of $100 million). Use different analysis techniques. Try different endogeneity corrections. Verify their adequacy. Test your primary and alternate theories. I typically like to push the analyses in multiple ways to see which results or patterns in the results are robust and when and why any unstable results are unstable. When you find something very unexpected (e.g., significant findings in the opposite direction of previous research or insignificant results when several other studies consistently find positive results), I would strongly suggest doing post hoc analyses (and report as such), with possibly additional data, to explore logical possibilities for why you found these counterintuitive or unexpected results.

All of this data manipulation is not to be confused with data mining, or what Bettis (2012) has called "searching for asterisks." What I am advocating is a discovery process to learn why you found what you found and how stable the results may be to alternative specifications. This is useful information that will help you in the positioning of your paper and its contribution. And reporting the various approaches to analysing your data in a robustness section of your paper goes a long way to convincing the reviewer that what they are seeing is really important or at least reliable. It also means that your results are likely to remain regardless of the direction your paper may take in the review process. There will be no need to collect further data, conduct additional analyses, or use alternative measures, because you will have already done so.

CONCLUSION

Interesting data with truly robust results puts you in an excellent position to publish in our top management journals. Getting robust results can be systematic. It requires foresight in the design of a research project and diligent execution in the analyses. Always consider sources of possible endogeneity, alternate theories, and alternate measures in the design of your data collection strategy. And always push your analyses to identify the systematic, non-spurious, results in your data, those that withstand endogeneity corrections, the inclusion of various controls from other theories, and the use of alternative measures and analysis procedures. In doing so, you will be dramatically boosting your odds of publishing in our best management journals.

REFERENCES

Bettis, R. (2012). 'The search for asterisks: Compromised statistical tests and flawed theories', *Strategic Management Journal*, **33**, 108–113.
Hamilton, B. and J. Nickerson (2003). 'Correcting for endogeneity in strategic management research', *Strategic Organization*, **1**, 51–78.
Larcker, D. and T. Rusticus (2010). 'On the use of instrumental variables in accounting research', *Journal of Accounting and Economics*, **49**, 186–205.
Semadeni, M., M. Withers, and T. Certo (2014). 'The perils of endogeneity and instrumental variables in strategy research: Understanding through simulations', *Strategic Management Journal*, **35**, 1070–1079.
Shaver, J.M. (1998). 'Accounting for endogeneity when assessing strategy performance: Does entry mode choice affect FDI survival?', *Management Science*, **44**, 571–585.

14. The reviewers don't like my sample! What can I do?

Brian K. Boyd

INTRODUCTION

Let me start with the caveat that most of what I write is macro empirical research. While my examples will draw from strategy articles, the concepts are applicable to other management specialties, and other disciplines as well. I have served on a wide variety of editorial boards, including those with both a generalist (e.g., *Academy of Management Journal*, *Journal of Management*, and *Journal of Management Studies*) and a specialist (e.g, *Organizational Research Methods* and *Strategic Management Journal*) focus, as well as those with interdisciplinary (e.g., *Corporate Governance: An International Review*) and international (*Management and Organization Review*) emphases. And, given my background, the vast majority of papers that I review are empirical. Regardless of the focus, one question consistently surfaces when I read a new manuscript: "If I were to design a study to test these research questions, is this the ideal sample?" As the answer is most often "No," the second question is whether the sample is adequate. In some cases, the answer is still "No," other times it is the grudging acceptance of an imperfect, yet workable sample. In the majority of cases, though, the answer is "hard to tell," as authors may not provide sufficient information about the sampling process or characteristics of the data. Depending on the severity of the reviewer's concerns, sampling issues can be a "fatal flaw" that triggers a rejection, or enough of a problem to render an entire Results and Discussion section moot.

There are two sets of tactics available to authors (Table 14.1): The first is preventive, and aimed at keeping the sample questions from entering the reviewer's consciousness. The second set is reactive, such as responding to an editor's high risk revision invitation that emphasizes reviewer skepticism as to the validity of your data.

Table 14.1   Checklist for sample design preparation

Topic	Key Questions
What are the sampling norms for this type of research?	• Are the norms different depending on how I frame the point of comparison? For example, would there be different norms based on the methodology versus the topic? • Are the norms different based on the target journal? Consider that you will often not publish in your first choice outlet, but possibly second or third choice.
What are the relevant statistical power considerations?	• What are the effect sizes of relevant work – small, medium, or large? • Measurement error affects power. Do my power considerations include the effects of attenuation? • What are the method-specific power considerations? • If reviewers request alternate analyses, do I still have sufficient power?
Response rate	• What are the typical response rates for this topic? • What steps can I take to optimize the potential response? • When combining response rate, power issues, and attenuation, what is my target for data collection?
Response bias	• What analyses will I conduct to assess response bias?
Worst case scenario planning	• How much bias would be needed to skew my results? This can be explored empirically through simulation (Rogelberg and Stanton, 2007). • How feasible is it to replicate or create a different sample if required by reviewers?

PREVENTATIVE TACTICS

Benjamin Franklin is credited with the aphorism "An ounce of prevention is worth a pound of cure." Aguinis and Vandenberg (2014) drew on Franklin's wisdom to develop a checklist of research design considerations that authors should address well before collecting the first piece of data, some of which relate to sample issues. These ideas are also consistent with Toyota's Second Paradox (Ward et al., 1995): The notion that delaying the start of a project to spend more time on development and consideration of alternatives will actually lead to faster completion time, accompanied by better quality and lower cost. Consequently, the best approach that authors can take when considering their sample is to "hurry slowly."

To start, prospective authors should understand what the norms are for the research question of interest. This includes not only sample size, but data collection processes, sample characteristics, and so on. For example, if you are designing a new study of a strategic management topic, how large a sample size is needed? The answer is 4,523. This number is the mean sample size for a pool of roughly 500 empirical articles published in *Strategic Management Journal* in its first thirty years (Boyd et al., 2012). That number is an obvious straw man, for several reasons. First, sample sizes in this article pool vary widely for studies using survey data, where samples of 200–400 are common, versus archival studies, which have much larger samples. Additionally, the average sample size for archival-based studies in this pool has more than quadrupled from the early 1980s to more recent years. And, if your topic was strategic consensus, the sample size in prior work ranged between 19 and 252, with a mean sample size of 93, and a substantially higher mean of 151 in more recent papers (Gonzalez-Benito et al., 2012). Your goal as an author is to do more than convince reviewers that the sampling process is not weak, but rather that it is outstanding. For Gonzalez-Benito and colleagues, their sample of 102 observations was average for the overall pool of work on this topic, but smaller than the norm for more recent studies. Thus, a challenge for their manuscript was to convince reviewers that their sample was still sufficient for the research questions being posed.

Of course, sample size is not the only characteristic of a good sample. Other aspects, such as response rate and generalizability also are considerations. Again, norms may vary depending on the line of inquiry. For example, what is a good response rate? For a strategy study, the answer is 12 percent. This is based on the oft-cited Hambrick and colleagues (1993) article which suggested that response rates of 10–13 percent for executive surveys are typical. Again, this is an arbitrary guideline. Not only is this a dramatically different norm than employee surveys (which often yield 50 percent response rates), but content analyses of executive-based surveys reveal that the actual response rate is about one in three, and also that response rates are declining over time (Slater and Atuahene-Gima, 2004; Cycyota and Harrison, 2006). For Gonzalez-Benito and colleagues, their response rate was around 25 percent, but this was also based on multiple respondents per firm, which sets a higher bar. They also conducted comparisons of multiple archival variables as well as wave analysis (comparison of early and later respondents) to assess response bias. Additionally, they addressed social desirability bias, common method variance, and the similarity of key findings relative to prior work to infer generalizability. To sum up the first set of tactics, authors should present as much descriptive information as possible in the Methods and Results sections to benchmark the robustness of their sample. In addition to the topics mentioned here, other sample-related questions include statistical power, measurement precision, and implications for attenuation, as well as analytic considerations.

REACTIVE TACTICS

Possible response bias is often raised as a concern by reviewers, particularly if your response rate is low. This issue can be addressed by authors both before and after data collection. On the preventive side, factors such as survey length, endorsement of the project by opinion leaders, and other considerations can enhance the likelihood that senior executives will respond to survey invitations (Cycyota and Harrison, 2006; Bednar and Westphal, 2006). Research in other topic areas can help to provide best practices for a target audience. Subsequent to data collection, there are many options available to assess the generalizability of a respondent pool. Rogelberg and Stanton (2007) provide a review and an assessment of the main techniques. While in the design stage of your project, you should identify multiple avenues for analysis and be able to justify why you chose that tool. For example, Rogelberg and Stanton (2007) characterize wave analysis as a weaker tool. As a reviewer, I would ask for additional tests if wave analysis is the only test for response bias reported in a manuscript. If it were one of several tests, though, I would be less concerned.

Statistical power deserves special attention as a preventive measure. Unsupported hypothesis tests are common in management research. For instance, content analyses of transaction cost economics and the resource-based view each found that, on average, about half of hypotheses were supported (David and Han, 2004; Newbert, 2007). While many of the nonsignificant tests may actually reflect the absence of any substantive relationship, weak statistical power is a far more plausible explanation. Still, in the manuscripts that I review, authors very rarely rule out power issues when reporting a nonsignificant hypothesis test. Power is affected by many factors, including the underlying effect size, alpha levels, sample size, and statistical test being used. Power problems are also exacerbated by attenuation associated with imprecise measurement. While in the planning stages, prospective authors should conduct power analyses and report this information in the manuscript.

Despite these efforts, authors will still come under fire for their samples. What are some tactics for addressing these concerns in a revision? Following are a number of options.

Triangulating to Previous Studies

One way of demonstrating the suitability of your sample is to make formal comparisons to related work. There are two sets of tactics here. The first approach is to conduct a small-scale content analysis that compares aspects of your sample design to other studies. Following the earlier discussion of general tactics, a key step is to carefully articulate "related work" – this can be based on subject matter, methodology, or even by journal. For example, in an upper echelons study, reviewers questioned our sample size decision. We performed a content analysis focused on the target journal for a recent period and included all articles using the same methodology (structural equation modeling). We then compared sample size, model complexity (number of indicators), and the ratio of observations to indicators to benchmark our sample and model. To support these comparisons, we also ran additional models on our own data and re-ran some models using the published correlation matrix of another study. Together, the combination of comparisons and supplementary models provided a strong justification for our sample.

A second form of triangulation is to compare data or results to prior articles. These can be simply means of key statistics, or more substantive comparisons. For example, in a study of research norms among strategy faculty, reviewers were justifiably concerned as to whether a single discipline sample would be representative of the broader universe of management faculty. There was a prior *Academy of Management Journal* article that reported a mean of 1.2 (standard deviation of 2.39) articles per faculty member ten years post-Ph.D. We were able to replicate their coding scheme and came up with a corresponding estimate for our sample of 1.1 (standard deviation of 2.66) articles at the same time period. Thus, comparisons to norms in other studies, published statistics, or databases can be useful. A more powerful approach is to replicate findings in prior work. As another example, in one paper we tested a relationship which was not related to our hypotheses but had been studied in other settings and drew on variables used in our model. We then identified prior tests of this relationship, conducted a meta-analytic summary of these findings, and demonstrated how our result closely mirrored the entire stream of related work. Mechanisms to front-load these comparisons in your study include inclusion of consistently performing control variables in your model, and to include some relationships which are previously well established between the independent and outcome variables, and stating that they are included for purposes of replication and comparison.

A Second Sample

In many cases, no amount of triangulation will convince reviewers that your sample is meaningful. This situation is more common when using single-industry data, less mainstream international samples, rarely used databases, and other unique sources of data. Simply, what you might see as an "innovative" sample, reviewers might see as "suspect." For example, we used a sample of hospital executives to develop and validate a measure of strategic planning processes. Part of our rationale was that this setting offered strong comparison to prior work for our tests of predictive validity of the new measure. However, reviewers posed a critical question of whether strategic planning activities in this industry, which has many unique features, would be applicable to the Fortune 500, or other firms. In this case, the editor counseled us that a new sample was likely the only option that could satisfy reviewer concerns. Subsequently, we constructed a new survey based on a cross-industry sample of for-profit businesses, which strongly validated our original findings.

Holdout samples are often used as a preventive tool to forestall questions about generalizability. This entails collecting additional data using the same sampling process, and replicating results across the two subsets. However, there are many limitations with holdout samples, including inefficiency (i.e., they do not use all available data to test hypotheses), and they often fail to capture actual differences across subsets (Murphy, 1983). More critically, the holdout sample will have the same flaws and weaknesses as the primary sample. Thus, if reviewers are unsatisfied with the main sample, they will be equally nonplussed about the holdout sample. I have two main suggestions for this option: First, in the design stage, authors should brainstorm – and brainstorm widely, in the spirit of the Toyota Second Paradox – different ways that they might develop a second sample. Second, when reviewers push for a second sample, embrace the idea versus fight it. While the effort of a new dataset is substantial, it can add tremendous value to your manuscript.

CONCLUSION

In a review paper (Hitt et al., 2004), we compared empirical research to Porter's value chain, which is broken into primary and support activities. We characterized the research question and data as primary activities:

Given sufficient data at the outset, you can always redefine or refine measures, or try different statistical analyses. Without an appropriate sample and meaningful research question, though, every other aspect of the manuscript is suspect. Inter-rater reliability among reviewers is notoriously low (see Chapter 7 in this volume). Still, I hope that these suggestions will get you closer to a "Yes" when a reviewer asks "If I were to design a study to test these research questions, is this the ideal sample?"

REFERENCES

Aguinis, H., and R.J. Vandenberg (2014). 'An ounce of prevention is worth a pound of cure: Improving research quality before data collection', *Annual Review of Organizational Psychology and Organizational Behavior*, **1**, 569–595.

Bednar, M.K., and J.D. Westphal (2006). 'Surveying the corporate elite: Theoretical and practical guidance on improving response rates and response quality in top management team survey questionnaires', in D.J. Ketchen and D.D. Bergh (eds.), *Research Methodology in Strategy and Management (Volume 3)*, New York: Elsevier, pp. 37–55.

Boyd, B.K., K.T. Haynes, M.A., Hitt, D.D. Bergh, and D.J. Ketchen (2012). 'Contingency models in strategic management: Use, disuse, or misuse?', *Journal of Management*, **38**, 278–313.

Cycyota, C.S., and D.A. Harrison (2006). 'What (not) to expect when surveying executives: A meta-analysis of top manager response rates and techniques over time', *Organizational Research Methods*, **9**, 133–160.

David, R.J., and S.K. Han (2004). 'A systematic assessment of the empirical support for transaction cost economics', *Strategic Management Journal*, **25**, 39–58.

Gonzalez-Benito, J., H.A. Aguinis, B.K. Boyd, and I. Suarez-Gonzalez (2012). 'Coming to consensus on strategic consensus: A mediated moderation model of consensus and performance', *Journal of Management*, **38**, 1685–1714.

Hambrick, D.C., M.A. Geletkanycz, and J.W. Fredrickson (1993). 'Top executive commitment to the status quo: Some tests of its determinants', *Strategic Management Journal*, **14**, 401–418.

Hitt, M.A., B. Boyd, and D. Li (2004). 'The state of strategic management research: A view of the future', in D.J. Ketchen and D.D. Bergh (eds.), *Research Methodology in Strategy and Management (Volume 1)*, New York: Elsevier, pp. 1–31.

Murphy, K. (1983). 'Fooling yourself with cross-validation: Single-sample designs', *Personnel Psychology*, **36**, 111–118.

Newbert, S.L. (2007). 'Empirical research on the resource-based view of the firm: An assessment and suggestions for future research', *Strategic Management Journal*, **28**, 121–146.

Rogelberg, S.G., and J.M. Stanton (2007). 'Understanding and dealing with organizational survey nonresponse', *Organizational Research Methods*, **10**, 195–209.

Slater, S.F., and K. Atuahene-Gima (2004). 'Conducting survey research in strategic management', in D.J. Ketchen and D.D. Bergh (eds.), *Research Methodology in Strategy and Management (Volume 1)*, New York: Elsevier, pp. 227–249.

Ward, A., J.K. Liker, J.J. Christiano, and D.K. Sobeck (1995). 'The Second Toyota Paradox: How delaying decisions can make better cars faster', *Long Range Planning*, **36** (3), 43–61.

15. When being normal is not enough: a few thoughts about data, analyses, and (the storm of) re-analyses

Philip L. Roth and Wayne H. Stewart, Jr.

INTRODUCTION

Good research is hard to do. Getting accepted for publication is harder still. So, when the editors of this book asked us to contribute a short chapter, we turned to Pooh and asked, "What should we write about?" Pooh mumbled something about honey, ice cream and being the perfect weight for a bear a foot taller than he was, and then sort of wandered off to worry about more important issues in the world of bears. This left us with only a few other personalities in our own heads with which to brainstorm ideas. After talking amongst (all of) ourselves, we decided to extol the virtues of not being entirely normal when it comes to data and analyses.

A number of years ago, we published a meta-analysis (Stewart and Roth, 2001) on the relationship between entrepreneurial status and risk propensity (Pooh was not interested in that either). In short, we found that individuals who were entrepreneurs were more likely to have higher levels of risk propensity than were managers, a difference magnified if the entrepreneurs were growth-oriented. We were not terribly surprised when two researchers asked for our data (Eeyore did predict doom and gloom ...), but we were surprised when a rather "spirited" attack on our original meta-analysis appeared in the *Journal of Applied Psychology* (Miner and Raju, 2004). It was at this point that we were very glad that we were not entirely normal.

OBSESSIVE-COMPULSIVE AND PARANOID

We were thankful that we had been obsessive-compulsive and paranoid in several aspects of our research. Particularly, we were very glad that we had obsessed over the research question in which we clearly defined entrepreneurs (and operationalized our definitions of entrepreneurs in two ways) and contrasted their risk propensity to those of managers. We are also big proponents of drawing out research models to obsess on clarity and exactness of the research model when needed (even if you have to borrow a pencil from Piglet).

We were also obsessive about identifying primary studies and generating the meta-analytic data (we thought about this as creative paranoia). To be sure our data were of high quality: both authors coded every article in the meta-analysis. This is somewhat uncommon, as many meta-analyses have one author code all the data and a second author code a percentage of the data to establish some estimate of reliability. We are also big believers in getting your hands dirty in analysing the data (which is much better than washing your hands again and again ... we prefer getting them dirty again and again). So, we entered all the data ourselves, ran descriptive statistics on everything, and mulled over various aspects of the data, including large samples, influential cases, measurement, and watching for dependent data.

We were also paranoid about analyses. We literally thought about what someone else would think about how we ran the analyses (this is where multiple personalities come in handy as one can write and the other can question ...). So, we kept all of our original analyses, with notes on what we did and how we handled various cases. We felt like Owl setting up a detailed list for finding Roo.

Finally, we were careful to consider the "so what" question in our thinking and writing. We were sure we would get a reviewer like on some past papers. We were anxious to avoid reviewers like Dr. O.B. Tuse, as failing to answer the "so what" question can sink a manuscript. So, because we addressed a critical issue in entrepreneurship research, we thought our accepted original submission was on solid ground in terms of its relevance.

CONCLUSION

As Eeyore warned, a dark day came for us with the article by Miner and Raju (2004). It came with a vengeance, with a past president of the Academy of Management and an award-winning research methodologist teaming up against us. Fortunately, their arguments were not based on obsessive-compulsive and paranoid thinking. Instead, they engaged in fuzzy thinking in terms of the definition of entrepreneurs, use of unconventional measures of risk propensity, and use of dependent samples in their critique and re-analysis of our study (Stewart and Roth, 2004). The good news was that Miner and Raju discovered no errors in our analyses, but only added dubious data to the situation (mixing Heffalumps and Woozles can be very confusal).

We happened on an extremely well known meta-analyst at a professional meeting after our exchange in the literature. He said, "I read your reply to Miner and Raju ... devastating." At that point, we were extremely glad to have been far from normal. We were thankful for all the care we put into formulating the research question, extracting the data, and conducting the analyses. That is why we did everything we could to do the research right. At the end of the day, we heard the little voices in our heads saying "Are you paranoid if they really are out to get you?"

REFERENCES

Miner, J.B. and N.S. Raju (2004), 'Risk propensity differences between managers and entrepreneurs and between low- and high-growth entrepreneurs: A reply in a more conservative vein', *Journal of Applied Psychology*, **89**, 3–13.

Stewart, W.H. and P.L. Roth (2001), 'Risk taking propensity as a distinctive entrepreneurial characteristic: A meta-analysis', *Journal of Applied Psychology*, **86**, 145–153.

Stewart, W.H. and P.L. Roth (2004), 'Data quality affects meta-analytic conclusions: A response to Miner and Raju concerning entrepreneurial risk propensity', *Journal of Applied Psychology*, **89**, 14–21.

Section II.III

Navigating the review process

16. Selling your soul to the devil? Mistakes authors make when responding to reviewers

Pamela L. Perrewé[*]

The academic publication process is not for the faint of heart. First, as authors, we all need to cope with rejection occasionally (read: all too often). If you are not used to receiving decision letters that begin with "thank you for your submission, however … ," start steeling your nerves now. Second, many management scholars believe publishing involves unfair politics. We know that overcoming rejection and the perceptions of politics are part of the publication process, but more important than both is responding to reviewer/editor comments – here is how.

If you are responding to editor and reviewer comments, congratulations! This is great news! It means that the door is still open for a possible publication. Even if the decision to allow a revision is "high risk" (most editors and associate editors use this phrase), I encourage all researchers to work hard at their revision. As Jim Carrey remarked in the classic film, *Dumb and Dumber*, "So you're telling me there's a chance … . Yeah!"

First, it is a myth to believe you must agree with and make every suggested change made by reviewers. Often reviewers have excellent suggestions to help your research appeal to more scholars, to improve the rigor of your data analysis, to deepen your theoretical contributions, and so on. However, there are times when reviewers ask for changes that are simply not needed or that take away from the primary message of your research. For example, if a reviewer suggests changing the focus of the article to hone in on one specific finding rather than examining your entire conceptual model, it is appropriate to thank the reviewer but to politely argue that the meaningfulness of your message may be lost if the focus is specific to only one finding. Of course, it may be possible to discuss this "finding" that the reviewer found interesting in a bit more detail – everyone is happy. Also, it is a good idea to write to the editor or the action editor to explain why you are not accommodating every change.

Speaking of the role of editors and action editors, it is appropriate to ask for guidance if reviewers conflict in their suggested changes. However, try to read between the lines of the revision letter as good editors and action editors often offer suggestions to authors and, perhaps, tip their hat to one reviewer suggestion over another. Editors *always* have an opinion. Further, there may be times when it is clear you will *never* appease a reviewer (e.g., the reviewer finds your research topic uninspiring or not unique enough). If other reviewers find the topic interesting and offer suggestions to strengthen your article, you may want to contact the editor and/or action editors about the reviewer of concern.

I once had a second revision on a paper and it was very clear to me that one reviewer "did not think it made enough of a contribution." I contacted the editor stating I was inclined to withdraw the paper as, after two revisions of the paper, I was not able to convince this reviewer that my work made a significant contribution to the literature. The editor asked me not to withdraw the paper, but to focus on all of the comments I could address. The editor then told me that he has been known to go against a reviewer now and again. I thanked him, made the changes, and even though one reviewer was not satisfied, my research was eventually published.

A final note in regard to the role of the editor or action editor: editors often choose to become additional reviewers. Thus, authors may receive comments from two or three reviewers as well as additional comments from the editor or action editor. Editors vary in their involvement in the review process, but remember they do have a right as well as an obligation to try to make the research paper the best it can be. That being said, tensions can arise when the advice from an editor goes well beyond navigating the reviews and the editor becomes another reviewer (except with veto powers). Not long ago, I had an article that went through several reviews despite the editor's concern about my effect size. The editor allowed me to revise my research paper and I did my best to address the effect size issue. After three rounds of revisions and appeasing all of the reviewers (they all accepted the paper with no additional changes), the editor decided not to publish the article due to the effect size that was deemed too low. On the one hand, although ultimately this is the editor's call, I was disappointed that I was encouraged to continue to revise my paper if the effect size was a fatal flaw from the beginning.

On the other hand, I had another editor who saw something positive in my research and, even though the reviewers were brutal, he called me and helped me to reframe my research paper to make a more obvious contribution to the literature. The editor's insight helped me to reframe and better position my arguments for a wider audience and the paper was eventually published. To this day, I think about this editor's initiative, guidance, and care as he helped me navigate through the review process.

Another mistake authors make is to be overly emotional or defensive in their responses to reviewer comments. The anonymity of the review process can, at times, allow some rather caustic remarks to be made by reviewers about a research paper. Try not to take the negative reviews too personally. However, if a reviewer does get the better of me, I have no problem responding back with snide remarks initially (but privately – I never send these; it just allows me to vent and get rid of the emotion). After I calm down (it might take several days), I delete everything I wrote, and work on addressing the comments with kindness, political skill, and humility. It does absolutely no good to allow the tone of a reviewer's comments to affect the tenor of your responses to reviewer comments, as a negatively toned response to reviewers can anger them and result in them taking an even more critical view of your manuscript. Further, after my "defensiveness" goes away, I often find some good suggestions in the review (even though I could have done without the caustic tone).

Do not summarize reviewer comments or paraphrase their comments in an "easy to read" table with your responses. This annoys reviewers as their entire comment is not apparent in the response to the reviewers. I suggest you copy and paste the entire comment and then respond to this comment so that the reviewers see their entire comment as well as your response. For example, there might be an aspect of a comment that is important to a reviewer that you inadvertently omit in your paraphrasing. Even if you paraphrase perfectly, the reviewer might not trust that you did, in fact, paraphrase perfectly. Including the entire comment is the safest and easiest way to proceed.

Reviewers will often suggest new analyses to better flesh out some potentially intriguing findings in your research. Although the intent is good, this also has the potential of increasing the length of the paper as well as taking away from its main message. Clearly, conducting the suggested analyses may well be warranted; however, authors do not necessarily need to put the new analyses and results in the text of the paper. These new analyses and results can be included in the response to reviewer comments with the caveat that if the reviewer and the editor or action editor would like to see these additional post hoc analyses in the paper, the authors are happy to include them in a subsequent revision of the manuscript.

Including additional analyses, or working another suggested theory into your paper, is fine as long as you do not "sell your soul to the Devil"! Clearly, tweaking titles, bringing in additional theory, or even collecting additional data is all within the realm of a revision. However, be careful not to change the message you want to (and know you should) convey. I once heard another academic talking at a major management conference, who said that he would do anything a reviewer or editor wanted in order to get a publication. Yikes! There needs to be integrity in research such that even when the pressures of publishing to obtain promotions or raises are strong, research needs to be honest.

For example, a reviewer might want you to cut out part of your findings and conclusions for the sake of parsimony. Seldom should we be in favor of reducing the amount of information in a research article. However, if we are convinced this helps the message of the research, we may be amenable to the suggested changes. If the suggested changes affect the meaning of the research (e.g., taking out findings and conclusions), you might want to reconsider the reviewer comment. Sometimes reviewers will have a vested interest in *not* having something published that does not support their own research. This happens rarely, but be careful to convey the message you know you should convey. The integrity of our research is tied closely to our personal scholarly reputation and to our own integrity – no publication is worth risking that.

In conclusion, responding to reviewer comments is somewhat of an art form. First, even if the revision is "high risk," it is almost always worth the effort to revise your research paper as the door for publication has been left open. Second, be respectful in your tone and make all of the suggested changes or, at a minimum, explain why you did not make the change. Third, never hesitate to contact the editor or action editor for clarification; this is particularly important if reviewers seem to be at odds as to how best to frame the paper or reanalyse the data. Further, do not get overly emotional, arrogant, or defensive in your responses; there is no advantage in upsetting your reviewers. Finally, do not "sell your soul to the Devil" in your revision. Your scholarly reputation depends upon it and integrity is the key to meaningful research in our field.

NOTE

* The author would like to thank Jeremy D. Mackey, B.P. Ellen III, Charn P. McAllister, and D.J. Steffensen for their comments on this topic and chapter.

17. Respond to me – please!

James G. Combs

Dear Author,

I am a busy person. My spouse and kids want my time. My university places ever greater teaching and service demands on me. I believe in our profession and that what we do matters. As such, I am active in the Academy, and I serve as an editor, on editorial review boards, and as an ad hoc reviewer. Amidst all of this, I keep an active portfolio of research projects and I work hard to keep these projects moving toward publication. It is in this context that I sat down one evening to read your paper and spent much of the following day writing comments that I thought you needed to hear if you are to bring your research to a successful outcome. Your action editor read my comments and those of the other reviewers and gave you an opportunity to have your successful outcome at *this* journal: congratulations to you, more work for me!

When it came time for me to open your revised paper and response document, I did so with mixed feelings. On the one hand, the combined document is 90 pages – it's going to be a long night! On the other hand, I am invested in your paper and eager to see where it is going. We reviewers are not all alike in how we approach a revision, but I think that many are like me in that we start with your response document. I do this to remind me what your paper is about and what my concerns were. I also want to get a general feeling for how you changed the paper in response to the review team's comments.

At first, I am relieved to find that your formatting makes sense. You smartly put the review team's comments in bold italic with your responses in normal print following each comment. Some authors put their own responses in bold and the review team's comments in normal print, which signals that the authors think too highly of themselves. You also weren't afraid to split my comments when I brought up more than one issue in a single numbered comment. Reviewers sometimes ramble, and it is usually easier to split a comment than to have a long multi-part response. I should note that some journals now force response documents into web-based windows – where all the formatting goes out the window (pun intended). The only way to keep the reviewers on track is to use ALL CAPS (i.e., EDITOR COMMENT #1 ... RESPONSE TO EDITOR'S COMMENT #1). You can also use spacing to your advantage in these cases by double spacing between comments and responses, and triple spacing between responses and the next comment. Fortunately, that was not a problem here.

I am glad you got the formatting right because it goes downhill from there. I started with the editor's letter hoping to find a summary of the key issues and your solutions. Nope. Whereas the editor summarized the key issues raised by the reviewers and teed up a chance for you to summarize the changes, you ignored this opportunity by telling us to look for detailed responses below. Okay, I get it. These documents can get crazy long, and there is no need to be redundant, but can't you at least give me the broad strokes here while saving the details for the individual reviewer responses? I am frankly too lazy to go jumping around the response document. Another (perhaps better) approach is to simply start with an "Executive Summary." I have only seen a few of these and my heart leaps for joy when I see them. There it is: the three big issues raised by the review team summarized for me along with a brief overview of how these issues were dealt with in the revision. But, alas, you didn't do this either.

At this point, I am a little grumpy, but I am still eager to see how you responded to my comments. A good reviewer will list comments roughly in order of importance; my first comment was that your initial submission named three related theories in the introduction but you did not explain any of these or use them as the theoretical logic for your hypotheses. Also, none of these formed a theoretical frame dictating which hypotheses to include. What I was hoping for in your response was for you to tell me which theory you decided to use in the revision and to describe how you used that theory to ground your contribution and tie together all of your hypotheses. What I got was a two-page single-spaced review of the three theories (or perspectives, really) and how they relate to each other.

Now I am getting frustrated – big time. Yes, I want you to review the relevant theory in your paper. But in the responses, I just want you to make it clear that you heard me and to explain what you did in the revision. I am looking for phrases like "We made the following changes in the revision ..." or "We did not change ... in the revision as you suggested because ... ." What I don't want is a long diatribe on the history of a theory (or three theories) and all the prior research that pertains to this phenomenon. I plan to read your paper, and it's ultimately the paper I am going to judge – not the response document. When you either dump text from the paper into the response document (which is partially out of context for me) or try to engage me in a lengthy discussion of all of the issues related to my comment, what you *actually* did in the paper tends to get lost – and that's ultimately *all* I care about. This is subtle, but powerful. I want you to *describe* the changes in the revision as they pertain to each of my comments. I don't want you to actually give the changes to me here. Often, you will have details or analyses to justify the changes you made. This material can go after your succinct description (i.e., "the reason we went this direction is …") or in an appendix to the response document. Just be sure to first succinctly describe the changes. That way, *what* you did won't get lost in a long defense of *why* you did it – and I can skip the latter if I want.

Well, I'm done. I read your lengthy responses to my first two comments and found them overwhelming. I never got a clear sense of how you approached the problem. You buried me in detail and minutia. I learned not to expect much, so I am now going to read through the rest of my comments while skipping over your responses. I might also look at the other reviewers' main comments. Then it's on to your paper, sour mood and all. Even though you were unable to explain succinctly in the response document exactly how you responded to my concerns, with a little luck, perhaps you put all of your mental energies into the manuscript where you did indeed respond to my concerns. If so, all will be forgiven. Your paper will delight me and I will be pleased to see that the big issues from your initial submission are mostly resolved. If not, my frustration will grow as I see that your lack-of-response carries over into the actual paper.

Either way, I write you this letter because otherwise you will probably never know how frustrated I was by your response document, or how useless I found it for quickly digesting the changes that you made. All I really want is for you to acknowledge that you understand my comment, tell me briefly what you changed, and, if necessary, explain why. Don't waste my time trying to engage me in "interesting" discussions or making me re-read your paper in the response document. I truly hope that my advice here benefits those reviewers who will read your future response documents, of which I hope there will be many.

Sincerely,

M.A. Reviewer

PS. Stop with "thank you for this insightful comment" at the beginning of each response. Let's be honest; some of my comments made you angry, and you're not fooling anyone with false praise. If one of my comments helps you make real and significant improvements in your paper, thank me *after* telling me how. Then I will be gratified to see that some of my comments mattered.

PPS. Don't under-value Reviewer #3. Reviewers are NOT assigned numbers that represent their importance. Manuscript Central assigns numbers as the reviews come in. More often than not, I bet that the last review in is from a busy senior scholar, not from an eager junior scholar trying to win a seat on the editorial board.

18. Challenging the gods: circumstances justifying the protest of a journal rejection decision

Gerald R. Ferris

INTRODUCTION

Young scholars, new to the organizational sciences field, learn early on about the process through which their research gets published in scientific journals. It is called the "peer review process," it has been in operation for decades, and it is used in virtually all academic disciplines. Essentially, the publication fate of scholars' work typically rests at the hands of an associate editor and several anonymous reviewers, who presumably are knowledgeable about the subject matter of the scholars' work. It is their collective judgments about the quality of the work being reviewed, and perhaps its subsequent revisions, that determine whether the research is published in the journal or rejected. Therefore, it is fair to state that the field grants great deference to the evaluations of research by these "gatekeepers" in the peer review process.

So, given this process, and the esteem it is granted by the field, it might seem quite inappropriate to question or challenge/protest a decision to reject your paper. Indeed, I would agree that, in most cases, scholars need to accept the outcome of the peer review process concerning their research paper they submitted for review – whatever that decision might be. However, I am arguing in this article that there are situations or circumstances that arise where it is legitimate to challenge or protest a rejection decision by a journal editor or associate editor. I mention some of these circumstances, and then provide an example from my own experience over the past three and a half decades, an example of an associate editor's decision to reject my manuscript that I challenged.

A FEW HINTS ON WHEN TO CHALLENGE A REJECTION DECISION

In trying to better understand the peer review process, it is helpful to know a little about the context within which these decisions get made, and thus the mindset of the decision makers reviewing submitted manuscripts. With the ever-increasing volume of manuscript submissions to the top journals in our field, the mindset of reviewers is similar to that of employment interviewers – it is a search for negative information. That is, reviewers are not focused as much on the positive features of a manuscript that might lead to an acceptance, but rather a search for flaws and negative features that might result in rejection. Indeed, papers get accepted for publication less as a result of possessing many positive attributes, and more for reviewers' failure to detect a sufficient number of negative features to warrant rejection. That being said, rejection decisions in many if not most cases are warranted, but sometimes they are not, and it is appropriate to challenge or protest the decision. I see the following as some circumstances that might warrant the protest of a journal article rejection decision:

1. When decision makers get things factually wrong, due to their misinterpretation of the results or lack of understanding of the subject matter of the manuscript.
2. When decision makers render what appears to be a largely un-supported decision to reject after at least one or more rounds of revisions, when the reviewers appear to indicate that the authors responded acceptably to their concerns.
3. When there are large discrepancies between what you see the reviewers saying and what conclusion is reached by the associate editor or editor.

EXAMPLE OF A CHALLENGED REJECTION DECISION

Several years ago, I (and several co-authors) submitted a paper to a journal in our field (not one of the very top or A journals, but a solid, respectable A- or B+). The associate editor handling the review process sent us the evaluations and comments of three reviewers, and the decision was to invite us to submit a revision of our paper that responded to each of the reviewers' and the associate editor's comments. We did so, and on the next round, the associate editor and reviewers felt we still had some work to do in better addressing some of the comments, so we were given another revise-and-resubmit decision.

We prepared and submitted another revision of our manuscript, and the reply we received from the associate editor was an interesting one that presented somewhat of a dilemma for me. The reviewers felt that we had done a good job with almost all of their comments and concerns, and each only mentioned one or two points on which they still wanted a little more information, but they all were minor issues that could be dealt with easily. Thus, we expected that the associate editor was going to give us a "conditional acceptance," but instead the manuscript was rejected for what appeared to be no good reason at all, other than a statement that indicated that the associate editor didn't think we would be able to address the remaining concerns.

My co-authors were angry, but felt there was nothing to be done, so already were discussing what other journal we might consider sending our manuscript. After re-reading the reviewer comments and the associate editor's e-mail, I suggested to my co-authors that there were no fatal flaws in our paper, and the reviewers' remaining comments were all quite doable. Therefore, I suggested that we respectfully challenge the associate editor's decision and request another round of reviews where we would prepare another revision that responded to the remaining concerns. I was not confident that the request would be granted, so I was pleasantly surprised to hear back from the associate editor granting our request, and that they would evaluate another revision of our manuscript that was responsive to the remaining concerns. I must say that we took great care in our responses to this final set of reviewer concerns, and when we resubmitted the revision, the associate editor replied within just a few weeks accepting our manuscript for publication in the journal.

CONCLUSION

The ideas outlined in this chapter are meant to suggest situations when it might be appropriate to question, challenge, or protest a journal rejection decision. However, I would like to emphasize that these should be rare cases that come up where a protest is appropriate, and I think most scholars who have been in the field for many years would agree that it is indeed not a frequent occurrence. Although some scholars in our field might elevate journal editors and associate editors to "God-like status," the fact of the matter is that they are human beings, and sometimes make mistakes. When you feel mistakes have been made in the review of your manuscript, it is appropriate to question the process handled by those involved. Yet, whether we like it or not, the peer review process is the best system we have for determining publication status in our journals, until someone can come up with something better (which does not seem likely).

Section II.IV

Understanding the journals

19. Publishing in the top journals: the secrets for success

Michael A. Hitt

INTRODUCTION

Having your research published in top scholarly journals is one of the crowning achievements in our profession. It is exciting and satisfying to have your work published in one of these journals with other high-quality scholarly research. Most of the top scholarly journals accept 5 to 10 percent of the manuscripts submitted. So, they truly represent the crème de la crème of the research in the field. Yet, publishing work in these top journals is quite challenging, given the large amount of competition for journal space and high standards enforced by these journals (evidenced by the low acceptance rates). As such, the publication process can also be frustrating at times. Yet, there are actions that we can take to increase the probability that our work will be published in these journals.

First and perhaps foremost in my eyes is the *development of the capacity to excel*. Most of us believe that only the most talented people are able to publish their work in the top journals. These people have strong intellectual capabilities and are the well trained at the top research institutions. Yet, research across fields shows that individual talent (e.g., intellectual capability) and experience play only a small role in success. The research in such fields as medicine, science, sports and music shows that outstanding performance is based on intense, prolonged and highly focused efforts to improve one's current performance (Baron and Henry, 2010). Researchers refer to this as deliberate practice. Deliberate practice expands individuals' domain-specific knowledge and skills and enhances their basic cognitive capabilities. Perhaps the simplest analogy to understand is from sports. The top athletes often are quite talented but only those who practice tenaciously and are highly skilled because of that deliberate practice excel (David Beckham, Larry Bird and Pete Rose are three such athletes). This suggests that, in our field, people must practice deliberately to develop their skills in conducting research and in the development of manuscripts (especially the writing).

CONDUCTING THE RESEARCH

Publishing in top scholarly journals begins with the conduct of good research. That means developing a strong theoretical base and a strong research design with methodological rigor. Quality research, though, is catalyzed by a valuable research question. Obviously, the research question should be derived from a gap in the literature. However, while a void in the literature is necessary, it is also insufficient to qualify as a valuable research question. Answering the question must add value to our knowledge. Thus, it must also be an important research question.

The next concern is building a strong theoretical framework that leads to hypotheses, assuming the research is an empirical study. Kurt Lewin once said that "nothing is so practical as a good theory" (Van de Ven, 1989). Most empirical research is designed to add to our theoretical knowledge but focuses on extending current theory rather than creating new theory. Building new theory commonly involves development, feedback and refinement over a period of time (often years) (Smith and Hitt, 2005). Therefore, while there are studies, often qualitative, designed to develop new theory, most of us use existing theory. Yet, to publish research, most scholarly journals require a contribution to theory. This normally entails extending our knowledge of an existing theory. To do so requires considerable thought and care in developing the theoretical framework and in explaining how the research extends our understanding of that theory.

Concomitant to enriched theory is the need for methodological rigor in the design (e.g., sampling, measurement) and in the analytical process. One concern is the use of random samples. Yet, Short, Ketchen and Palmer (2002) found that only 20 percent of published research used random samples. It is difficult to select random samples because it is often challenging to identify the universe from which the sample is to be drawn. Therefore, most samples used in research are convenience samples. Sometimes this is absolutely necessary, but they must be justified to the editors and reviewers. Non-random samples create the potential for sampling biases that lead to potential errors in the results and interpretation (Heckman, 1979). A common concern often noted in strategic management research is that of endogeneity, for example.

Another potential concern is that of statistical power. Boyd, Gove and Hitt (2005) criticized much of the empirical research in strategic management because of the lack of attention to the statistical power in their studies (see Chapter 14 in this volume). They suggested that statistical power can affect both Type 1 and Type 2 errors. Interestingly, most of the top scholarly journals are more concerned about Type 1 errors (i.e., weeding out poor research designs). Yet in doing so, they often overlook potential Type 2 errors (Hitt, Boyd and Li, 2004), in which papers may be rejected when they contain valuable ideas that should be in the literature. Of course, authors may have excellent ideas but fail to follow through on some basic processes to assure the editors and reviewers that they have conducted quality research.

Boyd et al. (2005) also noted that macro researchers are often guilty of not paying adequate attention to measurement quality. In fact, they found that a significant number of studies used single-item indicators for constructs which are highly vulnerable to measurement error. Therefore, simply stated, researchers can increase the probability of publishing their work in top scholarly journals if they pay careful attention to sampling, avoiding Type 1 errors and avoiding (or constraining) measurement error.

DEVELOPING QUALITY RESEARCH

First, for quality empirical research, no shortcuts in the methodology should be taken. This is exceptionally important because almost any shortcut will be identified in the review process and will often serve as the reason that the manuscript is rejected. It is important to have a novel and valuable message. The manuscript should tell a story that explains the novelty and the value of the research done and its contributions. This explanation should be placed early in the manuscript and reiterated and reinforced in the discussion section. Key constructs should be defined early in the paper (the first time they are identified). Defining these constructs early avoids confusion on the part of the reader and even will reduce questions from the reviewers about the theoretical arguments, hypothesized relationships, construct measures and interpretation of the results.

As already noted, the hypotheses must be supported by strong theory-based arguments. This means that the theoretical underpinnings must be clearly and thoroughly (yet concisely) presented. The theory (or theories) being used and, hopefully, extended by this research needs to be clearly identified and well explained.

The methodology also requires thorough explication. If there are any weaknesses (and most assuredly there are no perfectly designed studies in our field), they should be acknowledged, justified and explained. For example, the authors should acknowledge a non-random sample and explain why the sample could not be randomly selected. Furthermore, the authors need to discuss (and likely test) the representativeness of their sample.

Normally, manuscripts should be developed over time using a patient refinement process. This process involves review by colleagues, who provide feedback to help further develop the manuscript. This feedback will help to avoid potential errors or lack of clarity in the critical areas noted earlier which could prohibit a positive decision. Thus, peer review and feedback is needed, even though it often requires extra time and delays submission to a journal. In addition, success requires clear and concise writing (and rewriting); there is no substitute for good writing. As such, deliberate practice can be quite helpful.

CONCLUSIONS

Everyone in our profession can publish their work in top scholarly journals if they develop the capacity to excel, identify a valuable research question, build a strong theoretical framework and ensure methodological rigor in the design of their research and in the development of the manuscript. When people engage in this process, there is a higher probability of having a long-term impact on the field. Scholars using this approach view their research with a longer-term lens. Therefore, rather than focusing on "low hanging fruit," these scholars will attempt to address important research questions that add value to our knowledge. Undoubtedly, the competition for journal space has increased considerably and likely will continue to do so. In fact, many scholars in other parts of the world, such as Asia, Latin America and other regions, are engaging in developing their capacity to excel. Thus, there is a greater balance in the research capabilities of scholars throughout the world.

REFERENCES

Baron, R.A. and R.A. Henry (2010). 'How entrepreneurs acquire the capacity to excel: Insights from research on expert performance', *Strategic Entrepreneurship Journal*, **4**, 49–65.

Boyd, B.K., S. Gove and M.A. Hitt (2005). 'Construct measurement in strategic management research: Illusion or reality?', *Strategic Management Journal*, **26**, 239–257.

Heckman, J.J. (1979). 'Sample selection bias as a specification error', *Econometrica*, **47**, 153–161.

Hitt, M.A., B.K. Boyd and D. Li (2004). 'The state of strategic management research and a vision of the future', in D.J. Ketchen and D.D. Bergh (eds.), *Research Methodology in Strategy and Management*. New York: Elsevier Publishing, pp. 1–31.

Short, J.C., D.J. Ketchen and T. Palmer (2002). 'The role of sampling in strategic management research on performance: A two-study analysis', *Journal of Management*, **28** (3), 363–385.

Smith, K.G. and M.A. Hitt (eds.). (2005). *Great Minds in Management: The Process of Theory Development*. Oxford: Oxford University Press.

Van de Ven, A.H. (1989). 'Nothing is quite so practical as a good theory', *Academy of Management Review*, **15**, 486–489.

20. Hitting your preferred target: positioning papers for different types of journals

Yehuda Baruch

INTRODUCTION

Our role as academic scholars is to generate (and disseminate) new knowledge. Knowledge is considered new if it is published in an academic outlet. And as a rule of thumb, the more prestigious the outlet, the more acclaimed is the scholar and contribution. Publish or perish is thus a cliché based on the true nature of academic work and careers (Baruch and Hall, 2004), and scholars aim to publish their work in the best possible outlet. When scholars write papers, they need to decide on their target outlets. Two questions then arise: which journal to target, and how to maximize the prospects of publication in the chosen journal.

In this chapter, I analyse this decision process, setting out a series of considerations to provide guidance to minimize costs (emotional, time and energy – clear outcomes of a misjudgement). The need for such a contribution is growing due to a significant acceleration in the number of academic scholars and their output (supply), and the limited set of quality journals (demand) (Edwards and Smith, 2010). There are very few so-called 'top journals', and there is a constant pressure to publish in them as a key factor for academic employability (during early career) and promotability (at a later stage).

What do academic scholars look for? Publications, and in particular, publications with impact. The expected impact would usually vary across types of writing. Those who wish to publish in *Harvard Business Review* aim at top executives, and in many cases, if successful, develop their articles into books, some of which are best sellers. The impact here would be measured in terms of business and management practice. Scholars who target *Academy of Management Review* aim at academics interested in theoretical developments. They may publish books, typically not best sellers, and their impact is confined to the research community. The target audience may be very specific, restricted to scholars with interests in a particular topic or a certain methodological approach. Further, not all journals are considered top journals, and subject to the strength of the message (contribution, relevance, etc.), scholars may better target a second tier journal to optimize the impact. In this case, it is better to publish in a second tier journal than receive rejection and suffer time lost (and emotional stress) by trying to shoot too high. The purpose of this chapter is to help scholars in optimizing such decisions.

The chapter considers three major issues: (a) which journal to opt for; (b) how to evaluate the fit between the manuscript and the journal and (c) practicalities, including dealing with an invitation for a revision, special issues, which arguments to avoid and how to gain insider knowledge. Finally, I return to the main point – publish or perish.

THE 'HOW TO' QUESTIONS FOR CHOOSING A TARGET JOURNAL

How to position a manuscript for the appropriate journal? The triad to decide:

- What is your target journal (and who is your target audience)?
- Fit of the manuscript to the target journal:
  - *Nature of the paper*, e.g. conceptual vs empirical, qualitative tendency vs quantitative; academic vs practitioners; general vs domain specific.
  - *The topic*, e.g. how closely does the paper relate to the core mission statement of the journal.
  - *Quality and reputation*, e.g. strength of the paper vs strength and reputation of the journal; how big is the message and how significant is the contribution.
- Practicalities, e.g. style (language, length, referencing); the audience – readership; past coverage of the topic in the journal; past experience with the journal (self and of others); costs (in time, money and emotion).

WHICH JOURNAL?

One of the issues to consider, as early as when you start writing your manuscript, is which journal(s) to target. Looking for a journal when the manuscript is ready for submission – or so you think – is far too late. No two journals are alike; no two editors are alike. The choice of your targeted journal (and the fall-back options) should guide your actual writing. Your first choice should be the best possible journal where it may realistically be accepted.

Yet, one may identify a 'cluster' of journals, and so the manuscript may fit more than one journal. Often a manuscript is rejected by the first choice journal – thus, it would be appropriate to consider in advance not merely your initial target journal, but also the possible one or two 'fall-back' options. In revising a paper that was rejected by your first choice, you need to be open to required changes, including revising the style and settings of the manuscript for the new target journal.

Choice of Journal and Desk Reject

A very strong indication that you have made the wrong choice is if you receive a desk rejection. Desk rejection rates have gone up as there are many submissions, few top journals, coupled with the challenge facing editors of identifying reviewers who will not decline invitations to review. Editors try to avoid burdening reviewers with manuscripts that are clearly off the mark. As a result, many submitted manuscripts do not make it even to the review process, and this can be around 50 per cent or more. There is a debate about how appropriate and ethical are reasons for desk rejections (Rupp, 2011), but it is a reality one should be aware of.

Why are papers being desk rejected? Apart from the poor quality of manuscripts, the most common reasons for editors to desk reject are lack of fit with the journal and poor preparation of manuscripts. The lack of fit may relate to the topic, field or discipline, the methodology, or even the style. The issue of poor preparation of manuscripts can be avoided through, to start with, rigorous attention to the particularities of the journal: its mission statement, target population, and requested style or presentation (use of headlines, section numbering and lack thereof, and in particular, referencing style). In addition, scholars should subject their final version to professional proof-reading and editing *before* submission, especially those for whom English is a second language.

FIT OF MANUSCRIPT

Nature of the Paper

There are many types of papers, and different papers will fit different journals. A paper may be conceptually or empirically oriented (empirical papers may offer a conceptual contribution too). Some journals will accept only non-empirical contributions – like *Academy of Management Review* or *International Journal of Management Reviews*. Others will consider only empirical, evidence-based contributions – like *Academy of Management Journal*, whereas some journals would accept both contributions, like *Journal of Management* or *Journal of Management Studies*.

As for empirical papers, the chosen methodology may also matter for the fit between the manuscript and journal. Studies may be qualitative or quantitative, or employ mixed methods. Authors should recognize that many journals have preferences with respect to methodology, whether qualitative or quantitative. Advice for scholars on this issue can be found in a number of editorial notes (e.g. *Academy of Management Journal*, amongst many). There are also books with specific advice for specific types of manuscripts. For example, Cooper and Burgoyne (2006) discuss qualitative submissions, Baugh, Hunt and Scandura (2006) discuss quantitative ones and Puffer, Quick and McCarthy (2006) give useful advice on scholarly practitioner journals. These authors provide useful indications of how your reviewers may evaluate your manuscript.

Another distinction is between academic and practitioner journals. Breakthroughs in the latter are particularly difficult, as these journals often have strong preferences for authors from particular institutions (e.g. papers by authors from Harvard University that publish in *Harvard Business Review* are out of proportion compared with their representation in the academic community or in other top management journals). Of course, belonging to a clique is one element – to make it into top journals authors must have the ability to articulate and present a paper that will attract executives to read it.

The prescription is simple: before submitting, check for fit. When there is not a 100 per cent fit, adjust the paper. Do not expect the journal to adjust to your work. But, the question remains: how should fit be evaluated? This is largely tacit knowledge, and asking learned colleagues, in particular your mentor, can provide good suggestions. You can also learn much from open material. What can you identify yourself? And what should you leave for others to point out? You can (and should) read the journal web page to learn its mission statement, aim(s) and scope.

Then, read some recent papers that were published in it. Can you see your manuscript sitting well with such papers? Do you cite papers published in the journal? This can be one indication that the manuscript fits the journal.

Still not sure? Editors are there to serve their community. You are entitled to consult editors when in doubt. When and how should you consult an editor? Both Feldman (2006) and Rynes (2008) write about it and provide general and specific advice for authors regarding the issue of how to communicate with editors. You should have a strong reason to approach an editor to inquire about whether or not to submit to their journal. But if you do have a good reason, do not hesitate. If it is an administrative issue (e.g. length, how long it typically takes for a decision, or the time from decision to print), it may be better to check with the managing editor or with the journal's secretary.

The Topic

Luckily, this point is usually straightforward. Does the topic of the manuscript correspond with the research area and mission statement of the journal? As a scholar, you should know your field and identify if related work has already featured in this journal. Sometimes, a paper combines two theoretical perspectives, so it is unclear if a paper should be sent to, for example, Human Resource Management or Industrial Psychology journals. Also, there are journals that are general in nature and open to a wide variety of contributions (like *Academy of Management Journal, Journal of Management, Journal of Management Studies*), whereas others are specific to their field (e.g. *Strategic Management Journal* or *Journal of Finance*). Authors need to decide whether to opt for a general or specific journal. The guiding line is the fit for the audience – the readership.

Quality and Reputation

How can you know the quality, strength and status of a journal? How can you know the quality of your manuscript? Both evaluations are needed to match the right manuscript with an appropriate journal.

Knowledge of the quality of a journal is both tacit and explicit. There are several journal rankings that can provide some guidance. But, any such ranking can, at best, offer only a proxy for the relative importance and relevance of a journal within a specific field. One is the Institute for Scientific Information (ISI) Impact Factor ranking, which uses a formula related to citation levels. Currently, there are close to 200 journals in the

ISI Management and Business rankings, and even these comprise just a fraction of all available journals in the field. More exclusive is the *Financial Times* 45 Ranking that lists only 45 major journals, whereas a more inclusive list is the Vienna List with some thousand journals. There are national rankings, like the ABS UK list (labelled as The International Guide to Academic Journal Quality) or the CNRS French list, and there are many other rankings offered by various institutions (for detailed current lists see http://www.harzing.com/jql.htm).

The problem is that any such ranking is politically influenced by various factors, such as who decides to include the journals listed or evaluates their 'worth'. Having said that, most of these various rankings tend to be strongly correlated. Thus, the recommendation here would be to become acquainted with more than one ranking, with the journals of interest and with the preferences of your institution.

The next question is how to judge the strength of the manuscript. The main factor that should determine the worth of the manuscript is its contribution – to theory and to practice (or to both). Having said that, self-evaluations are often biased – positively, if you are a strong believer in yourself, or negatively, if you are truly humble and tend to under-estimate your own work.

When in doubt, feedback can help. For example, whether an earlier version was accepted for a prestigious conference (and what feedback the audience gave), what trusted colleagues say about it, along with your own estimation – the authors should know, for example, if the empirical results are robust. In empirical studies, for example, cross-sectional data structure may be less well regarded than longitudinal data, or data collected from multiple sources (avoiding Common Method Bias); sample type and size are also important indicators. Of course, data is not enough. How did you analyse the data? Did you compare means? Did you test correlations? ANOVA? Regression? Structural equation modelling (SEM)? Bayesian analysis? Did you use the latest software (e.g. for SEM, one can use LISREL, AMOS or MPlus). How significant are the results (statistically, for quantitative work; reaching saturation, for quali-tative studies)? Going beyond the data and analysis, you should know if this is a confirmation of existing theory, refinement of theory, or a major theoretical breakthrough. There is a difference between an evolutionary refinement to theory and a revolutionary conceptual breakthrough.

When in Doubt

Here my advice is aim at the right level. I would say: '*Aim high, be sensible.*' Well, it is true that one should aim high, but one has to be realistic too. Submitting a problematic paper to a top journal is a futile exercise. It will cost you time, in particular if the editor invites a review. You would need to wait a number of months just to have a rejection decision. The feedback might be useful, but the price is high. It is not just the costs in time. There is also reputation. You do not wish editors to consider you a time-waster or someone that typically submits substandard work.

On the other hand, aiming too low may gain you a quick journal publication, but you would waste a valuable opportunity to publish well. If a manuscript submission was accepted very fast and with minor corrections, it might be that you 'shot too low'.

Practicalities

While academic competence and rigour are the critical factors, some exogenous factors can hinder the process. Authors must pay attention to style (language, length, referencing). Match the style, the language, the spelling, in particular US versus UK (e.g. organization, labor or organisation, labour). It is unfair on institutions with low resources, but paying for professional proof-reading can be the best practice in terms of return on investment.

Consider the readership. Check for your own and others' past experience with the journal (time to respond, quality of feedback). And lastly, consider the costs (in time, money and emotion).

OTHER ISSUES AND SPECIFIC TIPS

Resource Optimization

It is good to have several papers in the 'pipeline', but this means a need for an optimization of submissions, as resources are limited. Authors may need to juggle manuscripts that are at different stages of the publishing process (in writing, under revise and resubmit, rejected and revising for another journal). It is important to know when to invest in a new project, when to abandon a failed manuscript, what to do in cases of invitation to revise and resubmit, and whether it is worth considering special issue calls, to mention a few opportunities.

Great News: Revise and Resubmit: What Now?

It is very rare for a high-quality journal to accept a submission 'as is' – the best one can hope for is an invitation to 'revise and resubmit'. What should you do if this is the case? The normal custom, and usually the appropriate action, is to revise and submit it to the journal which invited you to do so. But, there can be exceptions, such as trying other journals, of higher or lower quality, with or without revising first (Altman and Baruch, 2008). It might be that the reviewers are asking for too much (in your opinion) or for something you cannot do (e.g. collect more data or run an analysis for which you are technically unqualified). Even if this is the case, it would make more sense, and show integrity, to consult the editor (with whom the decision ultimately lies). The editor can suggest, for example, what is essential, what is 'nice to have' or even something more specific – 'I am open to a revision based on the current data' or 'you will definitely need to increase the sample size'. They will also provide a time limit for resubmission, which is another consideration to bear in mind (though such a time limit can be negotiated if you cannot make it within the suggested date). Then you can make an informed decision about your next step. Again, in most cases, the best option would be to revise and resubmit to the original target journal, in particular because your chances of acceptance are probably reasonable.

Opportunities

Special issues – should you try?
Special issues can be a great opportunity. However, at the same time, there is a dilemma – one can never know if this is a 'stitched' system (see Chapter 23 in this volume). There have been rumours that guest editors know in advance which papers they are going to accept, so it would be futile for others to try. However, my experience suggests that such a phenomenon is not prevalent, but one should read between the lines – how inviting is the 'call'? Is it based on papers presented in a certain conference track, and do they expect you to attend a special seminar (possibly costly) before approving it? In leading journals, this gaming is rare or non-existent. On the positive side, the odds of acceptance in special issues are typically (though not always) better than in regular issues.

Personal connections
You (think) that you know the editor (or the associate editor ...), or even you consider him or her as a friend or colleague. This is not a good reason to target the journal. Do not think it will help – it might backfire too, though such contacts can be a good source of sincere feedback. A good friend, be it an editor or any colleague, may help you direct your

manuscript to an appropriate journal (and, indeed, perhaps to the journal where your friend is the editor).

How to gain insider knowledge about your target journals?
When you go to conferences, attend 'Meet the editors' sessions and network with people who are involved with the journal or published there. When you correspond with an editor (see Feldman, 2006 or Rynes, 2008), you may learn things that are not official open knowledge. For example, that the journal is trying to enter a new field, or that the editor is tired of too many articles in a certain field. It is legitimate to use this knowledge as a further input for the decision to submit (or refrain from submission).

Another great way to learn about journals is by reviewing for them. As a reviewer, you learn from the experience of others (Sullivan, Baruch and Schepmyer, 2010; Tjosvold, 2014). You see both why certain manuscripts do not make it, and why others are more successful. Typically you will be sent the comments of the other reviewers to compare with your own and gain further learning experience. Learning from the failure of others can help you to avoid similar mistakes. Just learning from successes (papers that were published) would not give you the full picture.

Rejection
Rejection is not the end of the world, it is part of life, and academic life in particular. In fact, there is no such a thing as 'rejection'. I would advise to take a 'reject' decision as an invitation to revise and resubmit to another journal. The first thing to consider when receiving a rejection letter is not to take it as a personal insult – the reviewers and the editor do not dislike you, they just do not agree with your ideas, methods or conclusions. See what you may learn from the commentary and start from the beginning: which journal to try next. Read the comments and respond by revising the paper appropriately – if not, the same criticism may come from the second (and third) journal. If you are upset by the rejection, I recommend reading the suggestions of Nancy Day (2011). Remember, Barney's (1991) theoretical study on the resource-based view was rejected from several journals before making it to print, and so was the case for many fine contributions, including Nobel Prize winning contributions. Thus, persistency and self-belief are critical ingredients for successful publication.

Table 20.1 summarizes the main messages of this chapter.

Table 20.1   Takeaways

Advice	Rationale
Consider target journal early in the process of writing	Improve the fit, less work in revising or re-writing to fit the journal later
Have in mind one fall-back option or more	The chance of straight acceptance in the first journal is fairly low
Consult colleagues and editors when needed	Use their experience and knowledge
Know your target journals and their level of prestige as reflected in your own 'community'	Different schools, different countries, different scholarly communities have divergent views on the prestige of journals
Consider new journals backed by prestigious professional associations and/or edited by leading scholars	You may have better chances at such journals, which may later become high-flier journals (e.g. *Academy of Management Annals* or *Strategic Entrepreneurship Journal*)
Fit for manuscript	
Be attentive to the respective natures of your manuscript and the journals in your field	So you can identify a successful match
Be honest when evaluating your manuscript: (a) subject prominence, (b) strength of theoretical contribution, (c) strength of data	Over-estimating your manuscript may lead to disappointment and loss of time when the inevitable rejection arrives
Consider specialist journals, even if not ranked as high as other outlets	Specialist journals might grant better fit and have high appeal to particular audiences
Aim high, be reasonable	Use logic, not wishful thinking
Practicalities	
Submit when you feel that the manuscript is ready	Perfectionism will lead you to never submitting. Remember, the enemy of the 'good' is the 'better'
Don't trust your own proof-reading	This is a separate professional job, even when English is your mother tongue – certainly if it is not
Check journal web page for style; use the latest edition of the guidelines	If not, expect a desk rejection

Table 20.1 (continued)

Advice	Rationale
Consider both journal and publisher reputation	In particular, journal reputation is a major factor
If rejected, revise and readjust before trying alternative journal	Benefit from the free advice of reviewers – they might have had good reasons for recommending rejection
Do not submit prematurely if you believe that the manuscript may be publishable in a better journal	Good ideas might not receive due attention if published in lower ranked journals
Do not let one or two rejections discourage you	There is always an element of luck in the process
But sometimes, it is appropriate to bin a manuscript. Give up if you get the thumbs down from too many	Some manuscripts are just not good enough for publication. Beware of the trap of emotional sunk costs
Miscellaneous	
Review for your target journals	Gain insider knowledge
Have more than one manuscript in the pipeline	With a high rate of rejection, this is advisable
Look for 'special issue' calls	The acceptance odds may be better than in a regular issue, if there is a good fit
Be resilient: rejection decision is not a catastrophic outcome	Better to expect the worst and hope for the better
Ask practitioners to read your manuscript	They can often have a clearer judgement, reflect on managerial implications and be less tolerant of academic jargon

FINAL NOTE

Do not be afraid – but be reasonable. When you write a paper, you want it to be published and become part of contemporary knowledge. Do not keep your papers for yourself, make them public knowledge by publishing them. But choose wisely and effectively. Learn from others – from both successes and failures.

Think: why am I here? What is my 'calling' (Hall and Chandler, 2005)? How will this be translated into my quest of progressing academic knowledge? Then, follow your heart, but apply a measure of logic before submission.

Good luck in this quest!

REFERENCES

Altman, Y. and Y. Baruch (2008), 'Strategies for revising and resubmitting papers to refereed journals', *British Journal of Management*, **19** (1), 89–101.
Barney, J. (1991), 'Firm resources and sustained competitive advantage', *Journal of Management*, **17** (1), 99–120.
Baruch, Y. and D.T. Hall (2004), 'The academic career: A model for future careers in other sectors?', *Journal of Vocational Behavior*, **64** (2), 241–262.
Baugh, S.G., J.G. Hunt and T.A. Scandura (2006), 'Reviewing by numbers: Evaluating quantitative research', in Y. Baruch, S.E. Sullivan and H.N. Schepmyer (eds), *Winning Reviews: A Guide for Evaluating Scholarly Writing*, Basingstoke: Palgrave Macmillan, pp. 156–172.
Cooper, C.L. and J. Burgoyne (2006), 'Reviewing for academic journals: Qualitative-based manuscripts', in Y. Baruch, S.E. Sullivan and H.N. Schepmyer (eds), *Winning Reviews: A Guide for Evaluating Scholarly Writing*, Basingstoke: Palgrave Macmillan, pp. 143–155.
Day, N.E. (2011), 'The silent majority: Manuscript rejection and its impact on scholars', *Academy of Management Learning and Education*, **10** (4), 704–718.
Edwards, D. and T.F. Smith (2010), 'Supply issues for science academics in Australia: Now and in the future', *Higher Education*, **60** (1), 19–32.
Feldman, D.C. (2006), 'Communicating more effectively with editors: Strategies for authors and reviewers', in Y. Baruch, S.E. Sullivan and H.N. Schepmyer (eds), *Winning Reviews: A Guide for Evaluating Scholarly Writing*, Basingstoke: Palgrave Macmillan, pp. 236–250.
Hall, D.T. and D.E. Chandler (2005), 'Psychological success: When the career is a calling', *Journal of Organizational Behavior*, **26** (2), 155–176.
Puffer, S.M., J.C. Quick and D.J. McCarthy (2006), 'Reviewing for scholarly practitioner journals', in Y. Baruch, S.E. Sullivan and H.N. Schepmyer (eds), *Winning Reviews: A Guide for Evaluating Scholarly Writing*, Basingstoke: Palgrave Macmillan, pp. 173–195.
Rupp, D.E. (2011), 'Ethical issues faced by editors and reviewers', *Management and Organization Review*, **7** (3), 481–493.
Rynes, S.L. (2008), 'Communicating with authors', in Y. Baruch, A. Konrad, H. Aguinis and W.H. Starbuck (eds), *Opening the Black Box of Editorship*, Basingstoke: Palgrave Macmillan, pp. 56–67.
Sullivan, S.E., Y. Baruch and H. Schepmyer (2010), 'The why, what, and how of reviewer education: A human capital approach', *Journal of Management Education*, **34** (3), 393–429.
Tjosvold, D. (2014), 'Reflecting on reviewing: Applying conflict management research', *Journal of Organizational Behavior*, **35** (8), 1079–1092.

21. Targeting journals: a personal journey

Franz W. Kellermanns

INTRODUCTION

When asked by the editors to contribute a chapter to their book on how I position family business research in targeting different types of journals, I thought that this would be a simple task. Codifying intangible knowledge, however, is easier said than done. Thus, I searched my memory to find where this intangible knowledge comes from and how I have established my publication pattern.

When I was a doctoral student at the University of Connecticut, I was interested (and still am) in both strategy process research and family business research and have tried to thread these passions throughout my work. At the time, I was exposed to and strongly influenced by the work of my dissertation chair, Steven Floyd, and by the groundbreaking work on family firm research by Michael Lubatkin and Bill Schulze. A series of papers (i.e., Schulze, Lubatkin, and Dino, 2003a; Schulze, Lubatkin, and Dino, 2003b; Schulze, Lubatkin, Dino, and Buchholtz, 2001), as well as the establishment of the theory of family firm conference (Chrisman, Chua, and Steier, 2003), led me and the field of management (and finance) to develop a strong interest in family firm research. Specifically, studies by Schulze et al. highlighted that classical agency theory assumptions (e.g., Eisenhardt, 1989; Jensen and Meckling, 1976) did not hold for the family firm context. The fact that some papers were published in mainstream journals (Lubatkin, Schulze, Ling, and Dino, 2005; Schulze et al., 2003a; Schulze et al., 2001) as opposed to family business journals (e.g., *Family Business Review*) or entrepreneurship journals (e.g., *Entrepreneurship Theory and Practice, Journal of Business Venturing, Journal of Small Business Management*) drew substantial attention to family business research, which had been minimal up to this point (Debicki, Matherne, Kellermanns, and Chrisman, 2009).

My first academic position was at Mississippi State, one of the leading family firm research universities (Debicki et al., 2009), where I met Jim Chrisman, who became a mentor and friend. Mississippi State had a clearly defined journal list; it was clear that publishing in mainstream management journals was not necessarily required to gain tenure. However, advice given to me early in my career by Gregory Dess influenced me then and influences me still. He suggested trying to establish a record of publications aimed not at obtaining tenure at one's current institution, but at allowing movement to other institutions. In my case, this meant that I needed to target both entrepreneurship/family business and general management journals. With this in mind, my comments are based on three themes: publishing for tenure, assessing contribution, and learning from co-authors and reviewers. I conclude with specific examples of the positioning of three of my papers to illustrate some of the points made throughout the chapter.

PUBLISHING FOR TENURE

While many of us deeply love research, we ultimately need to be employable and tenureable. Although elite institutions may require multiple top-notch publications in general management journals, most institutions are satisfied with a mix of journal articles at various levels published in both general and niche journals. For faculty not at an elite institution, focusing only on top-notch publications is a dangerous proposition. As a general rule, higher level journals have more stringent standards and the publication process takes longer. Publishing in a few such journals presents the opportunity to move to other institutions. More often than not, however, this strategy seems to result in a portfolio that is insufficient for tenure and often insufficient to pursue other academic positions at another comparable institution. Therefore (as reflected in my record), I am a proponent of the "shotgun" approach, which targets both general and specialty journals at different levels and allows papers rejected by higher level journals to move to lower level journals. I am a firm believer that investing significant time in a paper should lead to publication. This approach allows that papers are published at lower levels and the effort put into the paper is not entirely wasted. The shotgun approach also increases the likelihood (at non-elite institutions) of achieving tenure or of moving to a different school. Below, I approach the question of how to target journals by their varying level of contribution in more detail.

ASSESSING CONTRIBUTION

What constitutes a contribution has been widely discussed (for a more family firm specific guide see Reay and Whetten, 2011; most notable Whetten, 1989). Generally speaking, in order to publish a niche topic in a general management field, the contribution needs to be substantial and of general interest; that is, it needs to add more than incrementally to the topic and speak to the wider management audience. This is most easily accomplished if the article also advances a theory that is already well accepted. For example, Schulze et al.'s work (2003a; 2001) not only contributes to the family firm literature, but also to agency theory. Although a contribution to mainstream theory is required, it does not have to be dominant. For example, a previous paper (Eddleston, Keller-manns, and Sarathy, 2008) makes a contribution to both the family firm and resource based view literature, yet is clearly focused on a family firm contribution. Publication in general management journals is also possible, but frankly less likely to occur if the paper develops a new theory (e.g., Gómez-Mejía, Haynes, Núñez-Nickel, Jacobson, and Moyano-Fuentes, 2007) or makes a substantial contribution to the literature in this particular niche (e.g., Zellweger, Kellermanns, Chrisman, and Chua, 2012). The latter is often a difficult sell, as the editor/reviewer will have to judge whether the topic is of interest to the wider journal audience in addition to making a strong contribution. Even substantial contributions to a sub-discipline, however, are often published in more specialized journals (e.g., Astrachan, Klein, and Smyrnios, 2002; Habbershon and Williams, 1999; Klein, Astrachan, and Smyrnios, 2005).

If a paper meets wider journal quality assumptions (e.g., sample size, study design) but reviewers fail to see a substantial contribution, the likelihood of publication in higher level general management journals decreases; therefore, more niche specific journals should be targeted. As a general rule, a paper targeted at a general management journal may be considered by a more niche specific journal, but one that was initially written for a niche journal is almost impossible to place at a general management journal. Targeting a niche journal does not imply that the paper is not important; it simply indicates that the interested audience is likely to be more narrowly defined (e.g., see Eddleston and Kellermanns, 2007; Kellermanns and Eddleston, 2004). On the bright side, however, papers in these specialized journals may receive much more attention from interested scholars since they have higher visibility in the niche area (e.g., the following papers I co-authored illustrate this: Kellermanns,

Eddleston, Barnett, and Pearson, 2008; Zellweger, Eddleston, and Keller-manns, 2010).

CO-AUTHORS AND REVIEWERS

The more papers one gets published, the more papers one gets rejected. If this relationship is not true for you, then you need to target higher quality journals. While we want every paper to hit with the first attempt, it should not. If you hit every *Academy of Management Journal* (*AMJ*) or *Administrative Science Quarterly* (*ASQ*) you submit to, your time is better spent writing another article rather than reading this chapter.

Taking the assessment of the paper's contribution into account, the journal should be targeted based on the impact of the paper and in relation to journal quality. In general management, particularly in the United States, a publication in *Organization Science* or *Journal of Management* is more highly regarded than a publication in *Journal of Management Studies*, which, in turn, is more highly regarded than *Journal of Business Research*. Yet, there are some contextual exceptions to this rule; in the United Kingdom, *Journal of Management Studies*, due to a stronger focus on the *Financial Times* 45 list, may be a more highly regarded publication than the *Journal of Management*, which is not on the list. Similarly, in entrepreneurship, *Journal of Business Venturing* and *Entrepreneurship Theory and Practice* are considered higher level jour-nals than *Journal of Small Business Management* or *Small Business Economics*, and *Family Business Review* is higher regarded than *Journal of Family Business Strategy*. Although publication in any of these journals (and many others) constitutes an excellent publication, the truth is that the field values certain journals more than others and the submission process needs to reflect this reality. When in doubt, the Social Science impact factor is a good, albeit not flawless, guide, as are journal rankings (e.g., Chrisman, Chua, Kellermanns, Matherne, and Debicki, 2008; Harzing, 2015).

Journal submission decisions should also be guided by the input of co-authors and (friendly) reviewers. Although more experienced co-authors may have a better feeling for the level of journal that the paper might hit, they are not always right in their assessment of where the paper will ultimately get published. There is an element of luck in the submission decision (for a general discussion of luck see Barney, 1986), as the blind review process relies on reviewers who have different knowledge sets and preferences. If working with less experienced co-authors, asking for feedback from other authors in the field helps to assess the contribution of a paper and the level of journal. The article on which I obtained the most feedback from a large number of senior scholars and which I consider one of my strongest papers was also my most rejected paper before acceptance. Unfortunately, it is not among my most cited works (Kemmerer, Kellermanns, Walter, and Narayanan, 2007). Thus, this approach does not necessarily guarantee the desired outcomes.

Last, while a negative review (and a rejection from a journal) does not mean that the paper cannot hit at another same-level journal, consistent (negative) feedback indicates that lower level journals or more niche specific journals should be targeted.

POSITIONING EXAMPLES

The first paper I published on family firm research (Kellermanns and Eddleston, 2004) focused on conflict among family members. It took established constructs from conflict theory and used this literature to provide a theoretical foundation to the abundant conflict often observed in family firms. Yet, to that date, the discussion about conflict in family firms was void of theory and mostly anecdotal. We then supplemented the conflict theory with family firm specific constructs and grounded the paper in the family firm literature. This positioning was clearly intended to make a contribution to the family firm literature. While it showed that conflict theory has unique moderators in a family firm context, this contribution would likely have been insufficient for a general management journal and the paper was thus targeted for and published in *Entrepreneurship Theory and Practice*.

Another family firm paper of mine (Eddleston et al., 2008) was targeted at a general management journal. If one reads the contribution section in the introduction, the first contribution targets the resource based view. We suggest that in addition to just having resources (Newbert, 2007), it is how these are leveraged that is important. At the same time, we apply this theory to the realm of family firms and make a family firm contribution. Thus, this paper was of interest to both the general management audience as well as family firm researchers and was published in *Journal of Management Studies*.

Lastly, let me comment on a paper of mine that extents the notion of familiness (Zellweger et al., 2010). This paper was specifically written for the *Journal of Family Business Strategy*. As a theoretical paper that focuses on a family firm specific construct (i.e., familiness), such a paper would be very difficult if not impossible to publish in a general management journal. Yet, the contribution to this family firm specific construct by introducing the importance of identity in the development of familiness was important for the field and the paper is widely read and cited.

CONCLUSION

Similar to my suggestion to use a shotgun approach in the publication process, I recommend mixing ambition (junior faculty) with experience (senior faculty). Articles written with other junior faculty members firmly establish your contribution to the field (for an early publication of mine with at the time a junior faculty member see Kellermanns and Eddleston, 2004). Articles written with senior faculty members, although providing exposure to great skill sets and increasing your overall ability to publish, do not allow you to establish an independent identity. I was fortunate to publish (and continue to do so) with Kim Eddleston, another junior scholar, as well as with senior scholars (most notably, Steven Floyd and Jim Chrisman). By focusing on a research area and working with a variety of co-authors, one will acquire tacit knowledge about article positioning over time, which will increase chances to publish. Rejections, however, are part of the publication process. While extremely frustrating, particularly early in an author's career, it happens to the best authors and papers. If a paper is rejected, take the reviewers' advice that you find useful and try to resubmit quickly again. Unlike good wine, most papers do not get better with age.

REFERENCES

Astrachan, J.H., S.B. Klein, and K.X. Smyrnios (2002). 'The F-PEC scale of family influence: A proposal for solving the family business definition problem', *Family Business Review*, **15** (1), 45–58.

Barney, J.B. (1986). 'Strategic factor markets: Expectations, luck, and business strategy', *Management Science*, **32** (10), 1512–1514.

Chrisman, J.J., J.H.Chua, F.W. Kellermanns, C.F. Matherne, and B.J. Debicki (2008). 'Management journals as venues for publication of family business research', *Entrepreneurship Theory and Practice*, **32** (5), 927–934.

Chrisman, J.J., J.H. Chua, and L.P. Steier (2003). 'An introduction to theories of family business', *Journal of Business Venturing*, **18**, 441–448.

Debicki, B.J., C.F. Matherne, F.W. Kellermanns, and J.J. Chrisman (2009). 'Family business research in the new millennium: An overview of the who, the where, the what, and the why', *Family Business Review*, **22** (2), 151–166.

Eddleston, K., and F.W. Kellermanns (2007). 'Destructive and productive family relationships: A stewardship theory perspective', *Journal of Business Venturing*, **22** (4), 545–565.

Eddleston, K., F.W. Kellermanns, and R. Sarathy (2008). 'Resource configuration in family firms: Linking resources, strategic planning and technological opportunities to performance', *Journal of Management Studies*, **45** (1), 26–50.

Eisenhardt, K.M. (1989). 'Agency theory: An assessment and review', *Academy of Management Review*, **14** (1), 57–74.

Gómez-Mejía, L.R., K.T. Haynes, M. Núñez-Nickel, K.J.L. Jacobson and H. Moyano-Fuentes (2007). 'Socioemotional wealth and business risk in family-controlled firms: Evidence from Spanish olive oil mills', *Administrative Science Quarterly*, **52** (1), 106–137.

Habbershon, T.G., and M. Williams (1999). 'A resource-based framework for assessing the strategic advantage of family firms', *Family Business Review*, **12**, 1–25.

Harzing, A.-W. (2015). 'Journal quality list', http://www.harzing.com/jql.htm. Retrieved March 21, 2015.

Jensen, M.C., and W.H. Meckling (1976). 'Theory of the firm: Managerial behavior, agency costs and ownership structure', *Journal of Financial Economics*, **3**, 305–360.

Kellermanns, F.W., and K. Eddleston (2004). 'Feuding families: When conflict does a family firm good', *Entrepreneurship Theory and Practice*, **28** (3), 209–228.

Kellermanns, F.W., K. Eddleston, T. Barnett, and A.W. Pearson (2008). 'An exploratory study of family member characteristics and involvement: Effects on entrepreneurial behavior in the family firm', *Family Business Review*, **21** (1), 1–14.

Kemmerer, B., F.W. Kellermanns, J. Walter, and V.K. Narayanan (2007). 'Empirical validation of resource-evaluation frameworks: A judgment analysis perspective', Working Paper.

Klein, S.B., J.H. Astrachan, and K.X. Smyrnios (2005). 'The F-PEC scale of family influence: Construction, validation, and further implication for theory', *Entrepreneurship Theory and Practice*, **29** (3), 321–339.

Lubatkin, M.H., W.S. Schulze, Y. Ling, and R.N. Dino (2005). 'The effects of parental altruism on the governance of family-managed firms', *Journal of Organizational Behavior*, **26** (3), 313–330.

Newbert, S.L. (2007). 'Empirical research on the resource-based view of the firm: An assessment and suggestions for future research', *Strategic Management Journal*, **28**, 121–146.

Reay, T., and D.A. Whetten (2011). 'What constitutes a theoretical contribution in family business', *Family Business Review*, **24** (2), 105–110.

Schulze, W.S., M.H. Lubatkin, and R.N. Dino (2003a). 'Exploring the agency consequences of ownership dispersion among the directors of private family firms', *Academy of Management Journal*, **46** (2), 179–194.

Schulze, W.S., M.H. Lubatkin, and R.N. Dino (2003b). 'Toward a theory of agency and altruism in family firms', *Journal of Business Venturing*, **18** (4), 473–490.

Schulze, W.S., M.H. Lubatkin, R.N. Dino, and A.K. Buchholtz (2001). 'Agency relationships in family firms: Theory and evidence', *Organization Science*, **12** (2), 99–116.

Whetten, D.A. (1989). 'What constitutes a theoretical contribution?', *Academy of Management Review*, **14**, 490–495.

Zellweger, T.M., K.A. Eddleston, and F.W. Kellermanns (2010). 'Exploring the concept of familiness: Introducing family firm identity', *Journal of Family Business Strategy*, **1** (1), 54–63.

Zellweger, T.M., F.W. Kellermanns, J.J. Chrisman, and J.H. Chua (2012). 'Family control and family firm valuation by family CEOs: The importance of intentions for transgenerational control', *Organization Science*, **23** (3), 851–868.

22. Read the damn article: the appropriate place of journal lists in organizational science scholarship

M. Ronald Buckley

Recently, I received a call from a colleague whom I could best describe as crestfallen. I had known this professor for well over ten years as he had completed his PhD with one of my dearest friends. The reason he was feeling this way was due to a recent conversation he had with an administrator (i.e., dean, associate dean, or department chair in business schools in the United States) in his business school in which he was told "you don't publish in journals we value around here." I asked where this had come from and was told by my colleague that it was due to the notion that he did not publish in the journals that were at the top of the journal list of his college. I tried to assuage his negative emotions by telling him he had a fine record and some really well-cited publications. I hoped he felt better after we spoke, and it forced me to think of that most recent shibboleth that we are increasingly witnessing in business schools around the world today, that is, the dreaded *journal list*, which outlines the quality of publications in the absence of reading said publications. Journal lists have been with us for a number of years but their importance has increased more recently.

Let me share with you my bias. In his farewell address to the nation, President Ronald Reagan said something that really spoke to me: "It is as true as a law of physics – when government expands liberty contracts." My opinion on journal lists, with apologies to President Reagan, is this: "When our reliance on journal lists expands, scholarship contracts." It is ridiculous that these journal lists, which have come to frequently be the sole indicator of scholarly activities, seem to only serve administrative purposes (so no one has to actually read the article), and facilitate a situation whereby nascent scholars are forced to follow local college norms; norms which often do not align with the norms of our profession. In doing so, we fall into the system that we internally mock.

This reminds me of a presentation of a well-known scholar in which he proudly proclaimed: "I have five of those and six of those and three of those ..." I have no idea what his scholarly contribution was, only that he had a lot more of the "baseball cards" than many of our colleagues. (Do you remember saying "Got 'em, got 'em, need 'em" when we were collecting baseball cards as children? That is what he was doing – collecting top publications, as defined as being on "the journal list.") Obviously he was not acquainted with the quote often attributed to Einstein: "not everything that can be counted counts, and not everything that counts can be counted." And, please don't get me started on the bounty system implemented in many business schools today – isn't publishing in high-quality journals the reason why we are paid these fortunate base salaries and provided research expense accounts?

Let me give you an example of how the journal list mentality might fail to recognize high-quality scholarship. The article written by Jay Barney (1991) where he outlines the tenants of the resource based view was published in the *Journal of Management*. At the moment, this article has 38,533 Google Scholar hits. According to these "journal lists" being developed today, in many business schools, this would not have been treated as a premiere journal article, nor would it have been ranked as a premier journal article in Professor Barney's annual review. As such, it would have deprived Professor Barney of the global recognition he has achieved from the impact demonstrated by this fine piece of work.

In spite of this, my own graduate work at the wonderful Auburn University, and the outstanding scholars who trained me (e.g., Achilles Armenakis, Art Bedeian, and Kevin Mossholder), impressed upon me the high quality of the *Journal of Management*, and that it is a premiere journal in the organizational science field. In fact, those 38,533 Google Scholar hits for that one *Journal of Management* article are more than the aggregated Google Scholar hits of a high percentage of entire business schools around the world (I know this for a fact, as I have looked it up). Likewise, Baron and Kenny's (1986) fundamental work outlining the standard procedures for testing mediation and moderation has 48,983 Google citations. While the *Journal of Personality and Social Psychology* is a fine journal, would these authors be recognized for their exceptional work that has probably influenced a majority of our field more than most others or would it still not be considered a "top-tier pub"? Furthermore, according to the journal lists, Peter Drucker, one of the seminal thinkers in our field, would have had low research evaluations during his tenure as a professor. Most of his contributions were made through his books, which would be devalued by the "keepers of the journal lists," yet, no one can seriously doubt Drucker's gargantuan influence on our profession and practice.

One of my students was on the job market this year, and we discussed the journal lists of his potential employers as he received campus visit invitations. What I quickly realized is that there is a wide range of positions that universities today seem to be taking on this issue of "journal lists." At one extreme, a university with a doctoral program reported that they didn't have a journal list, but that when it comes to tenure, "you tell us what the good journals in your field are." Alternatively, we saw that some journal lists were older and less current, and thus failed to appreciate the advancement of certain journals to elite levels in our field.

Other journal lists were obviously so politically charged that they were undoubtedly created by neither the norms of the field nor the scholarly impact of the journals. Instead, such lists seemed to be motivated and created by where certain list creators or political players were able to publish and then, subsequently, successfully lobbied for those journals to be included on "the list" for their institution. Over the years, I have witnessed this phenomenon first hand, and I have also heard similar stories from some of my colleagues, who related stories of the "annual lobbying for journal quality" process. How can one observe such a process and then regard "journal quality" as an objective reality when it clearly is a socially constructed reality?

OK, so is there any type of rational or logical pattern developing here with regard to these journal lists, and if so, what is it? Quite interestingly, and perhaps even rather perplexing, some widely established top-tier journals were not reflected in many of the journal lists, and on other lists, many high-quality journals were omitted, whereas significantly lower-level scholarly journals were well represented. I hope you're picking up my confusion here, because I am laying it on pretty thick! My student and I then had the local norms versus national norms of our profession discussion, and I am confident he will produce high-quality research, according to the norms of our profession.

Unfortunately, many of the journal lists imply that only premier journal articles are acceptable (i.e., "counted" in your favor for promotions, tenure, etc.), and anything else is categorized under the "journals we don't value around here" category, relegating such publications to such inferior status as to sometimes even be regarded as "worthless." Personally, I categorically reject this position that many in the field seem to be taking today as they promote their "distinguished and selective lists of journals." The aforementioned is far afield from the trunk (i.e., premier publications) and branches (i.e., other quality publications) strategy impressed upon me by my fine mentors at Auburn University. I am partial toward the advice of my old Auburn faculty members (i.e.,

Achilles, Art, and Kevin), as it has served me well in my pursuits, and I am confident that same advice will serve my students very well in their career progress and achievement.

So, I say to my administrative colleagues (and, yes, these "journal lists" typically are the creations of deans and department chairs, who are trying to convince their constituencies that they are running an elite, high-quality business school, represented by premier scholarly faculty who publish only in select, high-quality journals): Give yourself some credit, because you are intelligent, and can understand research; indeed, research elicited your interest in our field. ***Read the damn article*** before you judge it according to any journal list. I would wager that the administrator in the example presented in the introduction to this chapter would have found some value if he had read the articles of the crestfallen colleague. Furthermore, where does such an administrator derive the chutzpah to say such a thing? If Jay Barney, Peter Drucker, Achilles, Art, or Kevin made such a statement to me, I would be worried. If an administrator lacking in research bones says that to me, I will treat it in accordance with those research bones. We all need to understand that not everything is destined for a premier journal, but also that publications in journals not appearing on the "journal lists" are still of value in your overall research program and development as a contributor to our scholarly pursuits.

To my junior colleagues in business schools around the world, I leave you with the following advice:

- Do high-quality research that you find interesting and it will find an appropriate publication outlet. Don't ever apologize for any of your publications – they each fill an important niche in your overall program of research.
- National professional norms should be followed, not local norms (i.e., "the journal list"), you know what the premiere journals are!; the market for our services does not reside in the town in which you are now located, but rather, it is in the national and international profession within which we operate.
- Find good colleagues with whom you enjoy working and discussing your ideas, and work with them. Good training, scholarly, fecund collegial interactions, and hard work are your friends, and will yield success.
- Every successful researcher I know understands the concept of "chair time" (i.e., you have to spend time in your desk chair writing articles), so I suggest you follow their lead!

- Don't let a socially constructed local list be your guide. Make scholarly contributions that incrementally advance what we know about the management discipline.

REFERENCES

Barney, J. (1991). 'Firm resources and sustained competitive advantage', *Journal of Management*, **17** (1), 99–120.
Baron, R.M. and D.A. Kenny (1986). 'The moderator–mediator variable distinction in social psychological research: Conceptual, strategic, and statistical considerations', *Journal of Personality and Social Psychology*, **51** (6), 73–82.

23. Publishing in special issues

Timothy Clark

INTRODUCTION

This chapter focuses on exploring a range of issues concerned with submitting to special issues. As a number of contributors to this volume have alluded to (see Chapters 5 and 20), special issues are associated with a number of dark practices. It is often not clear how a special issue was commissioned, how the editors were chosen, how papers were reviewed and so forth. Many people comment on the closed and opaque nature of special issues. As an author I have experienced some of these frustrations. Similarly, many colleagues have voiced their annoyance and anger following their perceived mistreatment by special issue editors. Whilst grumbles about rejection from journals are not uncommon, indeed, they are the stuff of everyday corridor conversations, they seem more intense in relation to special issues. I have witnessed colleagues hunt down special issue editors at conferences to vent their ire. That said, anyone who has edited a journal will know that occasionally hiding you name badge gives you a moment of peace at a conference. On one occasion a very frustrated collaborator dragged me to the publishers' exhibition at a leading international conference. They thrust the latest edition of a journal into my hands and asked if I was aware of this special issue. I was not. It focused on an area of research in which we had a joint interest. To us and others we spoke to it seemed to have emerged via some secretive process.

Special issues, because of their thematic nature, perhaps intensify the issues that attach to journal publishing more generally because they appeal to a defined subset of the academic community. If your article is not included in a special issue a rejection may hurt more than normal because your work is being evaluated within a tighter field. Your work is not only being evaluated in relation to similar work but also the operation of cliques and their biases becomes more apparent. This is in turn intensified by the review process. Given their focused nature, special issues draw on a narrower pool of reviewers, some of whom will know your work well. It can be difficult to maintain an anonymous review process in these circumstances. From a journal editor point of view, the journal invests its reputation with a theme that may not generate the requisite number of quality articles and in editors who may be untested in relation to the management of manuscripts.

In an attempt to partly demystify the process I am going to address a series of questions that relate to different points in the lifecycle of a special issue. The chapter thus begins by considering how special issues and their editorial teams are chosen and then proceeds to consider different approaches to reviewing and decision-making.

HOW DO SPECIAL ISSUES BECOME COMMISSIONED?

This question is at the heart of the vignette I recounted above. Many people in the field were unaware of the special issue to which I referred until it was published. It was an apparently closed special issue both in terms of submission and reviewing. The work published was therefore drawn from a pre-selected group and not subject to the normal reviewing conventions in that people who usually review in the area of interest for the journal in question were not contacted.

As a former journal editor, I have experienced on many occasions approaches at conferences and emails from people who have a ready-made collection of papers from a conference, seminar or workshop that they believe will make a themed special issue. Indeed, the promise of a special issue may be what brought people to that event in the first place. The people who push these journals are like barrow sellers in markets. They metaphorically wheel their barrows up to editors and tip the contents onto the floor in front of them and say 'will you publish my lovely papers', which more often than not are past their sell-by date and have been previously dropped in the front of three other editors prior to their 'fortuitous' meeting with me.

In my experience, special issues derived from such approaches tend to serve the interests of those involved rather than significantly advance the state of knowledge in a particular area. On taking up an editorial role I have inherited a number of special issues that appeared to have been commissioned on this basis. In these cases, the special issue editors proceeded on the assumption that the publication of the issue was guaranteed. Consequently, the standards of reviewing fell below those for a normal issue and they did not result in a sufficient number of quality papers to justify a special issue. Indeed, on several occasions, in consultation with the other editors of a journal, I have had to inform the special issue editors that there is either insufficient quality in the papers for a themed issue and so it is cancelled or a few papers may be publishable and have to be refashioned as a smaller themed section within a normal issue. This has resulted in very problematic correspondence.[1]

To avoid such issues, increasingly journals are adopting open commissioning processes in which they advertise that they are seeking special issue proposals. These are then reviewed by subject specialists or the editorial board and a small number selected. Alternatively the editors of a journal may identify an emergent area to give it a push or an established area that they think requires detailed critical examination. Again these ideas may be reviewed by the editorial board and individuals with more specialist knowledge before being approved. Regardless of the manner used to select special issues, calls for papers are commonly advertised in issues of journals, on their websites, distributed at conferences and circulated to relevant email lists in order to ensure that the community of relevant scholars is fully informed about a forthcoming special issue and has an opportunity to submit a paper for possible publication.

IS THE NORMAL REVIEWING PROCESS FOLLOWED?

The extent to which the reviewing process conforms to that used for normal issues varies. In large part, it depends on the degree of discretion afforded to the special issue editors. As a journal editor, I have been very conscious that one has to establish and consistently enforce a clear threshold for acceptance in order to secure a reputation as a leading management journal. This has meant not acting as a 'post box', simply accepting and rejecting papers based on the balance of reviewers' recommendations, but rather actively reading papers and coming to a judgement that usually is consistent with that of the reviewers but occasionally is not. Trusting special issue editors to understand the threshold of publication is therefore critical in determining where control of the reviewing process lies.

This places a critical emphasis on selecting the right team of special issue editors. Experience of the editorial process is a critical issue. Do they understand the manuscript review process? Have they experience of making editorial judgements? Do they understand the threshold for publication? In relation to these issues, prior experience of editing special issues in equivalent journals or other forms of editorial experience are key indicators. Do they have links to the journal (e.g., published in it, acted as reviewer and so forth) that would suggest they understand its ethos and mission? How open are they to submissions from different areas? Do they have sufficient credibility as a team to attract a sufficient number of potentially publishable submissions? What is their strategy to engage the community and publicise the special issues as well as help develop submissions? These are all key questions that are asked to ascertain the competence of the proposed editorial team.

With respect to the review process, I have operated two approaches both as a journal editor and as an editor of special issues for other journals. The first process is simply to put special issue papers through the same reviewing process as papers submitted to normal issues. When the reviews are returned, these papers are sent to the special issue editors for an initial revise and resubmit decision. These preliminary decision letters are then sent to the editors/associate editors of the journal to ensure the quality of decision-making and feedback is consistent with normal papers. Under this approach, special issue editors are typically only able to recommend a paper for publication, so authors would receive a conditional acceptance. An action editor from the journal is responsible for making the final decision. Apart from ensuring consistency between normal and special issues of a journal, this also overcomes the difficulties special editors find themselves in when rejecting papers of people known to them (see also endnote one). The second option is to delegate the whole reviewing process to the special issue editors including decision-making on acceptance and rejection of papers. Some journal editors adopt this approach but ask to see the list of reviewers to assure themselves that an appropriate group is being contacted. Apart from heightening the potential inconsistency in reviewing standards and decision-making, this approach can result in poorer feedback to authors and accusations of favouritism.

Understanding which reviewing process is being adopted is important because as an author you need to know who will make the final decision to accept or reject your paper. I have experienced situations both as an author and editor where a special issue editor has written an acceptance letter only for the journal editor (me in some cases) to require further work to get the paper to the point of publication. In a very small number of instances, my fellow editors and I have disagreed with the decision of the special issue editors and rejected papers that subsequently were unable to address the issues raised. Unless the decision-making process is clearly communicated, this can lead to confusion and resentment.

Who controls the reviewing process has important consequences of which many contributing authors may be unaware. Although journals increasingly make their content available digitally, and many journals are reducing their dependence on paper issues, publishers still establish a page quota for their journals each year. This governs the paper and print costs of a journal and is a key element of a journal's financial budget. Critically, the page quota determines how many papers can be published annually and therefore the number in each issue. The journals with which I have been involved have published an average of six to eight papers per issue.[2]

This means that to be commissioned, a special issue has to be seen to have the potential to publish five to seven papers in addition to an introduction. The special issue editors will therefore feel pressure to generate the requisite number of papers to ensure an issue is filled. Given that top journals have acceptance rates of 5 per cent to 10 per cent, this would imply that special issues need in the region of fifty or more submissions. That level of submission is very rare. In my experience, special issues rarely receive over thirty submissions and more usually around twenty.[3] Few of these submissions (especially those to narrowly focused topics) will have the potential to be of sufficient quality to meet the threshold for normal publication. As a consequence, if the incentive to publish the special issue is greater than ensuring quality, a small number of papers that fall below the publication threshold for inclusion in normal issues may be accepted to ensure publication. In these circumstances, the acceptance rate is higher than for a normal issue of a journal.[4] Your odds of acceptance can therefore be many times better in a special issue. The key point here is to ask at the outset where the authority to finally accept your paper lies.

CAN I RESUBMIT MY PAPER TO A NORMAL ISSUE OF THE SAME JOURNAL?

Again this varies between journals and is a question you should ask at the outset (of course, not wanting to undermine the strengths of your paper at the point of submission). It is important to ask in part because you may have written the paper for that journal and remain committed to publication in that outlet regardless of the special issue. It is also important to ask because given my earlier point about the number of papers per issue, there are occasions when there are five slots but six papers of similar quality. In these circumstances one paper has to be rejected for inclusion in the special issue. Usually the decision is made on the degree of fit with the theme. Where this occurs what happens to the sixth paper varies between journals. Also, as I have indicated above, special issues can collapse because not enough papers are deemed publishable. On a few occasions I have seen papers completely rejected by the journal since they do not accept the overflow from a special issue. This can lead to a huge sense of disappointment and resentment with repercussions that may never fully heal. More commonly, journals will publish the papers that did not fit in a regular issue.

CONCLUSION

In this short chapter I have sought to highlight a number of issues that can relate to submitting to special issues. Publishing a paper in a journal is a very gratifying experience. Publishing in a special issue can sometimes be even more pleasing because you are both contributing to a focal area of research and your work is appearing alongside that of a number of peers. In my experience, special issue papers are picked up more quickly by other researchers. However, I have suggested that you need to clarify who is going to oversee the review process, who will make the final decision on your paper and whether you can resubmit your paper to the same journal should it be rejected or a special issue collapse. Doing this will avoid potential future frustration.

NOTES

1. Dealing with 'big names' and the correspondence that can follow a rejection led me to develop a second level of anonymity when I was a General Editor of *Journal of Management Studies*. Mike Wright and I did not know the identities of the authors submitting the papers. We were thus not influenced by prior encounters with authors.
2. Publication backlogs in the printed issue of a journal are often caused by acceptance rates exceeding the number of papers that can be published in a year.
3. This might suggest that they are frequently too tightly framed with the consequence that there is not the volume of potentially publishable work in relevant communities to be submitted. Editors also have to keep a close eye on other journals in their field to ensure that they are not commissioning special issues that potentially overlap with those either being commissioned or published.
4. The reverse is also true. The number of submissions to a special issue can be too low to sustain the publication of the issue.

24. Using new media to promote and extend published work

Aija Leiponen and Will Mitchell

INTRODUCTION

On-line media and other media innovations are providing increasingly powerful ways to promote our work and to develop and extend our ideas. This contribution addresses ways of stimulating discussion around our scholarly work, including building a base, leveraging institutions, and engaging social media. Our core premise is that research will have the strongest conceptual and applied impact if, rather than ending a project after being accepted by a journal or other outlet, we instead engage with a wide range of audiences before and after publication.

BUILD YOUR BASE

- **Conferences and seminars**: Research impact begins long before publication. Actively seek opportunities to present and discuss your work in large-scale meetings, smaller conferences, and research seminars. Highlight the links between your ideas and the work of your colleagues – and encourage, or even help, them to build on and refer to your work when they present their research.
- **Pre-publication and publication links**: Once your article is accepted, post a link to a pre-publication working paper on your own website and/or on professional websites such as the Social Science Research Network (SSRN), ResearchGate, Kudos, and Academia.edu, so long as this is permitted by your publisher's copyright agreement. In turn, once your article is published, update the sites with links to the formal article, including pre-publication posting such that many journals now offer (e.g., the "Early View" links on Wiley's Online Library). You can find the URL for your article by signing on to your publisher's website.

- **Email signature**: Add the publications page on your website to your email signature – and add a direct link to a recent publication as an easy way to tell colleagues about your new work.
- **Your research community**: Send links to your article to scholars who are likely to be interested in your work. At a minimum, send links to people whose work you have cited in the research, to help them see the connection with their work. "Table of Content" alerts from your core journals offer useful ways to follow the evolving discussion around your topic. Several publishers also have relevant mobile apps that include journal abstracts, book recommendations, and conference information that help track the discussion.
- **Wikipedia**: People commonly start their research about a topic by searching Wikipedia. Look for relevant Wikipedia pages about your research topics and add a link to your work.

LEVERAGE YOUR INSTITUTIONS

- **Media relations**: In addition to posting on your own website, send the URL to your school and/or university's Media Relations office with a description of your work so they can include the information in their promotional activities. Develop the skill to prepare short, clear descriptions of your work, which will help the media relations staff provide cogent summaries or press releases. Media offices often work with these "tip sheets," which they then circulate to their relevant external media contacts, such as journalists in related outlets. If your tip sheet offers a timely and intriguing viewpoint, reporters may approach you for an interview. The two-part abstracts that the Strategic Management Society journals have recently adopted – including both "academic summaries" and "managerial summaries" – provide a model for concise descriptions. As always, the core point here is to take the point of view of the audience you want to connect with – and use the language that they find compelling.
- **Publisher services**: Several publishers now offer publication support services such as tracking your accepted articles through production, nominating colleagues for free access, optimizing search engines, and other activities. The links at "Wiley Author Services" provide an example of such services.
- **Media**: If you know of upcoming news coverage and have a chance to weigh in, prepare a tip sheet and make sure that outlet has the article URL. The university Media Relations office may have

contacts with business and economics writers in major media outlets to whom you or the media office can reach out.

- **Your journal**: Your journal has an incentive to promote your work. Let your editor know if your article is mentioned on blogs, websites, and listservs in your field or is included in major media outlets. You can track media mentions of your work on services such as Altmetrics.

ENGAGE SOCIAL MEDIA

- **Post**: Share your work with a link on Twitter, Facebook, LinkedIn, and other social networks. The Strategic Management Society groups on Facebook and LinkedIn are active sites to discuss the research, teaching, and management implications of your research.
- **Twitter**: Many scholars use Twitter to follow people whose ideas they are interested in and to spread their own ideas. It is useful to build a following on Twitter with an ongoing stream of thoughtful comments about your work and related ideas.
- **Video abstracts**: Several journals and academic societies are now posting "video abstracts" of published work, typically with links to the published article. Discuss this opportunity to prepare brief video summaries with your editors. You can gain ideas for how to frame your work with a video abstract by watching the videos on the Strategic Management Society's YouTube channel. In addition to postings on your journal's and publisher's sites, the videos are useful for your institution's Media Relations office and potentially for your own video channel on YouTube, Vimeo, or elsewhere.
- **Blogs**: Many scholars are experimenting with research blogs.[1] It is useful to search for discussions that are relevant to your research activities and thoughtfully tie your ideas to the discussions. Consider starting your own blog – ideally with focused discussions of important ideas that are relevant to your research. Blogs work best when they are updated regularly, though – take on this activity only if you are prepared to keep the discussions fresh and regular. If you only wish to blog occasionally, you may be able to write for commercial management blogs, such as for Forbes[2] or Bloomberg Businessweek.[3]
- **Lead a discussion**: Once you have posted an item, whether on a social media group or your own blog, encourage active discussions of the ideas. You can prompt ideas with questions, responses to comments from members of the group, links to relevant ideas, and

ongoing summaries of the discussion. One-off threads tend to fall below the radar in social media groups – you can keep the discussion alive with thoughtful refreshment and new relevant ideas.

- **Social media style**: The attention span of scholars and practitioners reading social media tends to be very short. Therefore your writing style should be clearer and more pointed than in regular scholarly writing. Think about the "hook" to engage the reader's interest. Positive humor often works well to capture attention, as do thought-provoking questions (but sarcasm can be difficult to interpret!). Although you will want to be perceived as a thoughtful and professional contributor to intellectual debates, social media necessitates a sharper communication style than many academics are used to both in terms of the core ideas and their areas of potential application – how the ideas matter.

These are only a few of the many ways that we can use on-line media to expand the reach of our research. The core point to all these ideas – and for many other venues – is that our opportunities and responsibilities as scholars do not end with publication. Research impact does not occur by "counting coup" with an entry on our CV. Rather, the impact of our research comes from active, wide-ranging discussion with as many people as possible. The power of social media is that it engages scholars and practitioners globally, 24/7. This engagement has risks – misinterpretation and flame wars are too common, even in academic settings. But rather than ignore or run from the risks, we will have the most impact and take the greatest control of our ideas by finding ways to engage, in ways that suit our personal preferences and skills.

NOTES

1. e.g., organizationsandmarkets.com and www.digitopoly.org.
2. Forbes.com.
3. http://www.businessweek.com/bw/blogs/the-management-blog.

25. Should you publish in an open access journal?

Charles C. Snow

INTRODUCTION

Young scholars in the organizational sciences are trained and advised to publish in the top academic journals. Often, a department's promotion and tenure committee identifies a specific set of journals as top quality, and reward systems are structured to encourage if not demand that junior faculty focus their attention on publishing in those journals. Moreover, articles published in the top journals tend to be cited more frequently than articles in lesser-quality journals, so publishing in the top journals is widely viewed as the best way to build your professional reputation and create visibility for your research program.

All of the top journals in the organizational sciences are so-called "subscription" journals. Subscription journals are owned by publishing companies or professional associations, they have a defined amount of space per issue that is set contractually, and they charge readers in one form or another to gain access to the knowledge contained in their pages.[1] Top journals are also difficult to publish in, with acceptance rates for submitted papers running at approximately 10 percent.

In recent years, a new type of academic journal has emerged called "open access." Open access journals offer a publishing alternative to subscription journals, but as yet no open access journal in the organizational sciences has been judged to be a top journal. Therefore, it is reasonable to ask, should you try to publish papers in open access journals?

In my role as founding co-editor of the *Journal of Organization Design* (JOD), an open access journal (www.jorgdesign.springeropen.com), I want to take this opportunity to build a case for publishing in JOD and other legitimate open access journals. The journal is published by the Organizational Design Community (www.orgdesigncomm.com), an international community of scholars, executives, and organizations dedicated to advancing the theory and practice of organization design. The mission of the journal is to publish theoretically sound and practically relevant articles on all aspects of organization design. JOD has a distinguished editorial board and a double-blind review process, ensuring that the journal maintains rigorous scientific standards and publishes high-quality work. JOD has an impact factor and is covered by the major abstracting and indexing services. The editorial team of JOD is committed to conducting a prompt review and editorial process so that authors are able to publish their ideas and findings in a timely fashion. JOD publishes certain types of articles that the traditional academic journals will not. Consequently, you may be able to make a contribution to the literature on organizations and management that might not be possible if you submitted your paper to a traditional journal.

OPEN ACCESS PUBLISHING

Open access means unrestricted online access to, and reuse of, peer-reviewed scholarly research (Wikipedia, 2014; Craig et al., 2007). Building on the early self-archiving practices of computer scientists and physicists, the initial concept of open access was primarily intended for scholarly journal articles. The term "open access" itself was first formulated in three public statements: the Budapest Open Access Initiative (2002), the Bethesda Statement on Open Access Publishing (2003), and the Berlin Declaration on Open Access to Knowledge in the Sciences and Humanities (2003). The Budapest statement discusses open access as follows:

> By "open access" to this literature, we mean its free availability on the public internet, permitting any users to read, download, copy, distribute, print, search, or link to the full texts of these articles, crawl them for indexing, pass them as data to software, or use them for any other lawful purpose, without financial, legal, or technical barriers other than those inseparable from gaining access to the internet itself. The only constraint on reproduction and distribution, and the only role for copyright in this domain, should be to give authors control over the integrity of their work and the right to be properly acknowledged and cited. (http://www.budapestopenaccessinitiative.org/read)

The benefits of open access publishing over traditional (subscription) publishing include the following:

- Open access journal articles are free to read and reuse (even though each journal must have a sustainable cost-recovery business model).

With open access, researchers anywhere can read and build on the findings of others without restriction.

- Much scientific research is paid for with public funds. Open access allows taxpayers and funding agencies to see the results of their investment.
- Researchers, teachers, and students around the world have free and quick access to the growing stock of information and knowledge in a scientific discipline. Free access is particularly valuable in emerging economies that cannot afford to pay for the high cost of many subscription journals.
- Open access helps to diffuse knowledge by breaking down some of the barriers associated with academic fields. An open access article can be read by anyone – a professional in the field, a researcher in another field, a journalist, a politician or civil servant, or an interested layperson.
- Although the evidence is not definitive, all else being equal, open access articles may get cited more frequently than articles published in subscription journals (Craig et al., 2007; Hamad and Brody, 2004; Lawrence, 2001; Pringle, 2004). In any case, combining open access and traditional publishing allows authors to maximize their research impact by reaching different audiences.

Currently, there are almost 10,000 open access journals listed in the Directory of Open Access Journals (DOAJ, 2014), only a few of which focus on organizations and management. Unfortunately, some open access journals – no one knows for certain how many and which ones – are not legitimate academic journals. An illegitimate open access journal can be spotted if it has an undistinguished editorial board, irregular publication rates, unrealistic time frames for peer reviews and author revisions/resubmissions of their papers, and large article-processing fees charged to authors. Most would agree that journals of this sort are not publishing properly vetted studies, and authors should shy away from such journals.

REASONS TO PUBLISH IN LEGITIMATE OPEN ACCESS JOURNALS

The flexibility provided by the open access format has led the creators of open access journals to attract submissions that most traditional journals do not embrace. In the case of JOD, it can be distinguished from traditional journals in three main ways. The first is the journal's objectives and audience. Authors are always advised to carefully investigate a target journal, as well as other candidate journals, before deciding where to submit their paper (Day, 2007). JOD seeks to publish any paper that has implications for how organizations are or should be designed and managed. The journal is concerned with both theory and practice, unlike traditional journals that tend to focus on one or the other. Moreover, JOD will publish any paper that, in the judgment of its reviewers, contributes to the scientific record. Authors are not required to contribute to theory, present empirical evidence, or otherwise conform to criteria set by the journal. They must simply convince the experts on JOD's editorial board that their ideas and findings contribute to the literature on organization design.

A second differentiator involves JOD's focus on the future. JOD seeks papers that explicitly focus on the future and its impact on the present. It welcomes papers that include the future as a theoretical variable and its effects on organizational strategy, decision-making, and behavior. As a result, JOD welcomes papers based on research methodologies such as computational modeling, thought experiments, scenario planning, and Delphi studies. Traditional top journals seldom publish articles based on these methodologies.

Lastly, JOD offers authors multiple formats in which to submit their papers. The traditional format for a theoretical or empirical research article is available, but there are also four other formats from which authors can choose. A translational article, for example, is one in which an organizational concept or study is translated for practitioners or researchers, with clear implications for organization design. A point of view article allows the author to analyse the design and/or management of organizations from a particular theoretical or practical perspective. An urgent issue article is one that brings an important organizational design issue to the attention of scholars or executives. Lastly, a case study article can take a variety of forms such as the illustration of a new theoretical framework, description of a new type of organization or management approach, demonstration of a need for a new concept, and so on. The primary evaluation criterion for a paper in any of these formats is that it advances organization design theory or practice.

CONCLUSION

Open access publishing in the organizational sciences may increase in the future, offering authors even more opportunities to publish their work. The *Journal of Organization Design* is a forerunner in this domain as it gives both scholars and practitioners a variety of ways to contribute to the literature on organization design. There are distinctive advantages to publishing in such journals.

NOTE

1. See http://sasconfidential.com/2015/11/06/obsolete/ for an insightful critique of the business model underlying most subscription journals.

REFERENCES

Berlin Declaration on Open Access to Knowledge in the Sciences and Humanities (2003). Retrieved on 09/29/2014 from openaccess.mpg.de/Berlin-Declaration.

Bethesda Statement on Open Access Publishing (2003). Retrieved on 09/29/2014 from legacy.earlham.edu/-peters/fos/Bethesda.htm.

Budapest Open Access Initiative (2002). Retrieved on 09/29/2014 from www.budapestopenaccessinitiative.org/.

Craig I.D., A.M. Plume, M.E. McVeigh, J. Pringle, and M. Amin (2007). 'Do open access articles have greater citation impact? A critical review of the literature', *Journal of Informetrics*, **1** (3), 239–248.

Day A. (2007). *How to Get Research Published in Journals (2nd edition)*, Aldershot: Gower Publishing.

Directory of Open Access Journals (DOAJ) (2014). www.doaj.org.

Hamad S. and T. Brody (2004). 'Comparing the impact of open access (OA) vs. non-OA articles in the same journals', *D-Lib Magazine*, **10** (6).

Lawrence S. (2001). 'Online or invisible?', *Nature*, **411** (6837), 521. Retrieved on 09/22/2014 from http://citeseer.ist.psu.edu/online-nature01/.

Pringle J. (2004). 'Do open access journals have impact?', *Nature* (Web Focus). Retrieved on 09/26/2014 from http://www.nature.com/nature/focus/access debate/19.html.

Wikipedia (2014). Open access. Retrieved on 09/22/2014 from en.wikipedia. org/wiki/Open_access.

PART III

Publishing across disciplinary boundaries

26. Publishing in finance versus entrepreneurship/management journals

Douglas Cumming

INTRODUCTION

I was pleased to be invited by the editors to write a brief chapter on my experiences publishing in finance versus entrepreneurship/management journals. I am sure there are better folks than me for this job (including but not limited to the editors of this book), but I do think I have a few things I can share. I do so with the hopes that I do not overly offend someone (to be a nerd and put it in economics terms, I hope that this chapter is Pareto optimal), and if I do, then at least I hope the harm I cause to some will be outweighed by the benefit I will do for others by sharing my experiences (back to being a nerd, if Pareto optimality is not possible, I nevertheless hope that this chapter is Kaldor–Hicks optimal). Also, although I express concerns with some reviewers through anecdotes herein, overall I hope to convey that I have greatly benefited from feedback from colleagues and through the review process. While my experiences that I share here of course reflect my personal biases, I nevertheless hope they are helpful for others in the future. In this chapter I address two questions that I am often asked by other professors: the first is often asked by junior professors – "how do I publish in different fields?" – while the second is more often asked by both junior and senior professors – "why do I publish in different fields?"

To begin, I briefly explain what my experience has been to date so that you the reader can deem whether or not I am qualified to write anything on this topic. I have experience publishing in leading journals in finance (*Review of Financial Studies, Journal of Financial Economics*), management and international business (*Academy of Management Journal, Journal of International Business Studies*), entrepreneurship and innovation (*Research Policy, Entrepreneurship Theory and Practice*), and economics and law (*Economic Journal, Journal of Empirical Legal Studies*). Since 2000, I have published over a dozen books and over 125 refereed journal papers, including many sole-authored papers. In the last ten years, I published on average more than ten papers per year. I am the founding editor of *Annals of Corporate Governance* and a current co-editor of *Entrepreneurship Theory and Practice, Finance Research Letters,* and *Eurasian Business Review.* I have guest edited a number of special issues of different types of leading journals, including the *Journal of Corporate Finance, European Financial Management, European Journal of Finance, Journal of Business Ethics, Journal of International Business Studies,* and *Strategic Entrepreneurship Journal.*

DIFFERENCES BETWEEN FINANCE AND ENTREPRENEURSHIP/MANAGEMENT JOURNALS

The differences between orientating a paper towards a management journal or a finance journal are straightforward, if you allow me to overgeneralize. Finance journals typically do not want a verbal theory section, and if there is a section that speculates a few [reverse engineered] "hypotheses" then it needs to be rather short and to the point. Formal mathematical models are occasionally appropriate in finance journals but rarely used in management journals. Finance papers want the best and most up-to-date data and most rigorous robustness checks. Management papers prefer to focus on longer verbal theory sections. I am aware that many finance folks view these long verbal theory sections as being superfluous because they do not involve math. In my experience, counter to what I have heard many finance professors claim, not everyone is capable of writing theory sections in management papers, and a tremendous effort is needed to do so. The section needs to be very well reasoned with consideration to alternative explanations. Empirical tests in management papers are often less concerned about the quality of the data and/or whether there is a complete set of robustness checks as long as the research question is new and interesting, while finance papers, by contrast, are extremely resolute about demonstrating robustness even when (at times, in the view of some folks) the research question is not terribly new or interesting.

PUBLISHING HOME BIAS IN DIFFERENT DISCIPLINES

Why would someone ever want to publish in a journal that is not in the field of their home department? I begin by explaining that there is "home bias" among faculty in different departments to prefer their own journals, and this home bias is particularly strong in finance. Finance professors like finance journals, and do not pay much respect to non-finance journals. Finance faculty members are more inclined to think that finance journals are substantially harder to publish in than management journals (despite the fact that acceptance rates at many top journals in both fields tend to be in the neighborhood of 5 percent). Management faculty likewise prefer their own journals, but in my experience management faculty are more inclined to acknowledge that it is difficult to publish in top journals in all fields.

My home department has been "finance" in each of the universities where I have worked (currently I am at a university where my home is "finance" and I am cross-appointed to "entrepreneurship"). For those that are not familiar with finance departments, it may be helpful to share a few stories about the typically very strong and negative sentiment that finance professors have for the research done by non-finance professors. Two of my stories are as follows. First, one day, shortly after joining a new university, a finance colleague walked into my office – uninvited – and proceeded to tell me that I am "cheating by publishing in crappy management and entrepreneurship journals as a way to artificially inflate my publication numbers." Second, a finance professor indicated to everyone at a visiting speaker department seminar that "publishing in *any* finance journal would be better than stooping so low as to publish in a management journal." The people involved in these stories may not be completely representative. And to be fair, my son's middle name is "Jedi" and I like to joke that these episodes are "disturbances in the force," so perhaps I too am not perfectly representative of finance faculty.

Nevertheless, I believe that these stories are quite representative. I have worked either as a regular finance faculty or as an extended visitor at different universities around the world, including universities in Australia, Canada, China, England, France, Germany, the Netherlands, and the U.S. I have experienced this negative sentiment by finance faculty towards management journals at most of the universities where I have had the opportunity to work and visit. I have spoken with countless others at different universities and have been told about a similar sentiment universally held at other institutions that I am aware of. Most finance faculty I have spoken with even contend that B- and C-level finance journals are substantially superior to A* management journals even though the impact factors of the B- and C-level finance journals are substantially lower. Finance faculty counter that their journals tend to have lower impact factors than management journals because reference lists are longer on average in management journals than finance journals. Possibly ... but I have no basis to confirm whether or not this is true and know of no other objective or quantifiable measure to compare these journals.

What does this home bias mean for authors contemplating sending their paper to a journal outside of their own area? It means that referees and editors will likely be suspicious that your paper was rejected by one or more journals in your own area. As such, if you drift to a journal outside of your home area, you have to take extra care to ensure that the paper has been written with the journal and target audience in mind. Make sure that the paper has been properly formatted to the target journal requirements and that all relevant literature has been cited. Minimize cites to your home area. Finance referees tend to not like cites to management papers, and likewise management referees tend to not like cites to finance papers, unless they are directly on point (typically, management referees are more open to cross-cites to other disciplines than finance referees).

Despite a negative sentiment to publishing outside your own area, sometimes you have a good reason to do so, and it should be made clear to your target journal editors and referees. For example, I have recently become more interested in the topic of fraud, and have a paper relating gender to fraud. I do not like to tell my finance colleagues that I have worked on such a paper (I mentioned it to one finance colleague and he looked at me like I was crazy, so I stopped telling other finance folks that I have such a paper). I confess that this paper was desk rejected very quickly at a finance journal (the editor merely said the paper was obviously incorrect). But thankfully, many fields other than finance are interested in the topic of fraud, and the paper was published in the *Academy of Management Journal* and featured in a *New York Times* column. I am aware that the paper has been referenced by those that work on legislative reform, such as the Ontario Securities Commission in their work on minimum standards for the proportion of women on boards. In short, I feel lucky to have had the opportunity to look outside the normal range of finance journals to publish on topics that are industry relevant but not within the normal range of topics considered by finance journals. Moreover, the advice and helpful comments from the three referees and editor at the *Academy of Management Journal* were extremely detailed, helpful, and constructive.

PAPERS THAT ARE INCONSISTENT WITH PRIOR WORK

It is very hard to publish a paper that is inconsistent with something that has been written by one of your potential referees. In that case, there is a massive probability that your referee will reject you. Moreover, if you write a paper that is inconsistent with the leading professor(s) in your area of research, you may reasonably expect that person to have a long memory about how you dared to challenge his or her authority on the topic. There is an inherent problem in some disciplines where those that are first on a topic and become other folks' referees can distort the evolution of an area in ways that favor their own interests, possibly even after their views have been discredited. Your options to avoid such a referee are: (1) seek a lower tier journal in your same field, or (2) switch fields. Switches are possible with some topics, albeit not all (e.g., corporate governance and corporate finance topics are more often transferable across fields, while asset pricing topics are scantly transferable across fields).

To shed further light here, at the risk of sounding disgruntled, let me refer to a personal example. One of the original topics from my 1999 JD/PhD thesis at the University of Toronto was venture capital (VC) contracting. There are many papers (over 100) in the literature that all say the same thing – convertible preferred equity is the optimal security in VC contracts (with the only evidence coming from small samples in the U.S. with up to 213 observations) – and this view is most strongly expressed in finance journals. As a Canadian, I discovered that venture capitalists (VCs) often do not use convertible preferred equity in Canada (I first learned this fact in January, 1997 – it was a moment of "eureka" for me!). I subsequently discovered the same thing when visiting Europe in 2001 and 2002 – that European VCs use different securities, not just convertible preferred equity. After more travel around the world that decade, I discovered that the only country in the world (of the countries where data have been collected) where convertible preferred equity is the most commonly used form of VC finance is the U.S. The narrow set of finance VC referees in the late 1990s and early 2000s – all of whom published papers on the optimality of convertible preferred equity or had working papers on the topic – were apparently not particularly welcoming of the idea that VCs might do something other than what they say they do. So, after receiving rejection letters from a massive number of finance journals saying I am a complete idiot (and/or that Canadians and European VCs are not as sophisticated as U.S. VCs, and that the Canadian VC data collected by the Canadian VC Association involving over 10,000 deals was not as accurate as the proprietary hand-collected data of 213 deals by U.S. academics, and more generally that non-U.S. data are clearly wrong unlike the U.S. data, etc.) I contemplated the idea that I should look to publishing in journals in other disciplines such as entrepreneurship and management, and even law. Fortunately, I had enough success doing so insofar as it helped save my career from oblivion (surprisingly I am now a tenured professor, even with a Chair!) Luckily for me back then, two well-known law professors (Ronald Gilson and David Schizer) wrote a paper (my favorite paper!) in the 2003 *Harvard Law Review* that shows that the U.S. VC contracting evidence is distorted by tax biases particular to the U.S., which has helped me to gain credibility, by showing that my non-U.S. data were worth looking at, and enabled me to finally get published on this topic. But I am aware of a couple of finance folks that were not so lucky and were forced out of academia where they could not get around a small set of hostile referees for daring to challenge their work, and I would guess the senior guys that are responsible could not care less about what they did to these folks and are simply content to protect their turf.

Given the time I invested in a topic where the international data showed the opposite of what prior U.S. academic work had shown, without the option of publishing in different fields I would never have obtained a tenured position and would most likely be working some-where in industry right now. It took seven years to finally find a home for my first international VC contracting paper in 2005. I eventually pub-lished papers on this topic in the *Review of Financial Studies*, *Journal of Corporate Finance*, *Entrepreneurship Theory and Practice*, *Journal of Business Venturing*, and *European Economic Review*, among others. But it has been a long haul after a million rejection letters … okay, maybe not a million, but at least a thousand. Indeed, maybe my earlier work was the "crap" folks said it was. But the time lag certainly enabled others to publish on the topic before me, without proper referencing of prior work, despite very wide dissemination of the work on the topic on SSRN (Social Science Research Network) and numerous conferences over many years. In one case, the paper was published in a journal where the editor and author were at the same university … and it appears to have been accepted within a year of it being released as a working paper, and if you are not familiar with the literature you would think that this paper is the original paper on the topic, particularly due to the timing of securing a spot in a journal. I've heard a joke repeated many times that some journals are the working paper series for the faculty within the same university as the journal's editor, particularly when there is competition on a topic.

SHOULD YOU POST YOUR WORK ON SSRN OR OTHER PUBLIC WEBPAGES?

Short answer: for finance, YES (typically); for management, NO (typically). In today's world, it is hard not to have working papers or their titles widely disseminated on the Internet or at least searchable on the Internet. It is substantially more prevalent in finance than management to see papers online at finance conference webpages and venues such as SSRN.com, and so much so that many finance journals do not keep the author's identity blinded as it would be a fiction to pretend the referee does not know the identity of the author.

Finance is somewhat distinct from management and entrepreneurship in that almost all working papers are available online long before the work appears in a journal. In management and entrepreneurship, editors prefer that the paper not be online and prefer that the paper is truly hidden. Management journals may even desk reject you if they see your paper has been widely disseminated on the Internet (or at a minimum the editor will ask that you remove the paper from any webpages before they review the submission). Personally, I find the practice of dissemination online to be appropriate because the posting "time-dates" your work. Also, posting online facilitates or enables others to provide feedback on your drafts before it appears in print. Further, it enables folks to gain traction with citations as a measure of the paper's quality and as a signal to editors.

If you don't post online, be careful. I am aware of a sentiment that is often repeated in some academic circles that senior faculty that control different areas would gladly kill a junior professor's paper, at a massive cost to the junior in terms of the junior's career, in order to protect their turf with the trivial benefit to them of securing an additional paper which has no bearing on their career whatsoever (or possibly no bearing, as unfortunately there are research awards, and folks that engage in this type of behavior too often receive research rewards). Even among senior faculty there have been well-publicized fights (where complaint letters were posted online and sent to their competitor's deans) about who was first on a topic. For example, there was a dispute in 2014 between two chaired professors at two of the leading universities in California, and this dispute was a huge topic of discussion (hundreds of postings and thousands of views) on the online forum "Finance Job Market Rumours." Fights such as this one may in part be resolved by looking at who posted first on SSRN.

SHOULD YOU GET A BIG NAME CO-AUTHOR?

In finance, normally the top four journals (those on the *Financial Times* list of 45 journals) use only one referee (although recently, the *Journal of Finance* often seeks two reports). Finance departments are particularly prone to a growing trend that rewards faculty, particularly junior faculty, only for publishing in the top four finance journals. Senior professors that control the top four journals reinforce their oligopoly by stipulating that faculty must send their best work to their journals. The set of referees at these journals will be especially narrow in some fields, which serves to increase the "rents" earned by those that "rise to the top" and control specific sub-fields.

There are "rents" earned by academics that rise to the top in certain fields and control what does and does not end up being published in the leading journals. Many junior finance faculty members invest their time in doing anything to gain favor with the folks that control their area of interest. Instead of working on their own papers, many junior faculty members merely strive to become co-authors with senior folks that control an area. Junior faculty members appear to spend enormous time and money attending conferences to meet top authors with the objective of securing a top author as a co-author. I have even seen junior faculty members that secure a big co-author become incredibly arrogant about their new academic status and importance, with the expectation that in the future they will be the person that junior folks will "bow down to." In some cases, there are even rumors of junior faculty doing things that are "unethical" to be affiliated with senior faculty (yes, I am intentionally not elaborating here, at the suggestion of some helpful colleagues!). The "by association" benefits to the junior author are very large (by analogy, think of the weakling in jail and a big bully that acts as the protectorate). Editors at journals appear to be more likely to pay attention to securing suitable referees for papers where there is an established co-author on the paper.

In short, it can help to have a "big name" co-author. But if as a junior faculty member you can get into a top journal with a solo-authored paper, there may be long-term benefits in terms of the respect you will have earned among your peers and your ability to get tenure and be promoted.

GETTING PUBLISHED: THINGS TO DO

Regardless of where you publish, it is helpful to be a "good citizen" in order to get published and cited. Being a good citizen includes offering comments on your colleagues' papers, attending seminars, serving on external review committees, refereeing papers, writing book chapters that may not get as many cites as you would like, making sure you are fair in your own citation practices, being friendly to people that you meet at conferences, and acting as a reviewer for other people's conferences even when you know that the conference organizers are likely to reject your own work. In regard to journal review requests, I [almost] never turn down requests [the exception is from journals that ask for reviews within two weeks – sometimes that just is not feasible when you are away from the office]. In a typical year I review dozens of papers, and I never tell an editor that I am "too busy" to help with a referee report (despite often feeling too busy – please see the second paragraph of this chapter). I simply agree to do it and, in fact, get it done. I likewise don't think it is appropriate to selectively review for some journals and turn down requests from others (academics talk, and people quickly figure out what you do, and the person that you are too important for today may subsequently become the person you are "bowing down to" tomorrow). How likely do you think it is that someone cites you or gives you a good referee report if you are not a good citizen and do not act as a fair and diligent reviewer yourself? More generally, good work is not limited to a small number of journals, counter to the claims I've too often heard from others.

Sometimes, even when you have the best intentions and are a good citizen, someone may try to label you as a bad citizen, especially if they are exposed as having done something inappropriate. As an example related to some of my earlier work when I had merely a few publications, a practitioner colleague asked me to work with him on a topic that came to him from his business interests (and if I did not, he would simply do it himself or find another colleague to do it with him). Around the same time, a senior professor mentioned to me at a conference that he was doing something along this line of research. I thought it would be okay to go ahead anyway and work on this topic with my practitioner colleague (who had no knowledge of what other academics were doing), but apparently not. As I failed to appreciate, the senior professor was reputed to be extremely hostile to folks that stepped on his turf, and apparently I did, which appears to have been at a long-term cost to me (at least in some senses, but a benefit in other senses). For readers not familiar with these types of "academic eraser fights," match the famous line "every-thing I needed to know in life I learned in elementary school" with the other famous line "academics fight so hard because the pie is so small." If you inadvertently get caught up in some sort of conflict, just brush it off, say too bad and oh well, don't sweat the small stuff, as life goes on and you can't please everyone. Keep doing the things that you do and keep being a good citizen regardless. Keep writing good papers, and if you get a few rejections from folks that you have upset then just move on and try elsewhere (remember the old adage, "God grant me the serenity to accept the things I cannot change, the courage to change the things I can, and the wisdom to know the difference"). There is always a home in a good journal for a good paper.

GETTING PUBLISHED: THINGS TO NOT DO

Academic dishonesty can come in a variety of forms, and the presence of different fields can facilitate that dishonesty. If you do things that are dishonest, it can make it difficult to publish later on. Think of a short-term benefit at a long-term expense.

Misconduct is sometimes observed among editors and referees. For example, I have encountered editors and referees that have not kept submissions confidential and/or borrow ideas from a paper or a confer-ence and use it for their own benefit in their other work. I have also encountered editors that do not fully pass along complete referee reports to authors – including cases of hiding negative comments to support publication, cases of hiding helpful comments to be unfriendly to authors, and cases of hiding comments to distort what a referee has said to create conflict between a not-so-blind referee (it is easy to guess the identity of a referee in many cases) and the authors. There can be short-term benefits to borrowing ideas, or disclosing such information to help a colleague's competing papers (or other benefits), but at a longer-term cost if other people find out that about the misconduct or breach of confidentiality. I have also encountered editors that "go on the offensive" so to speak when you inadvertently get caught up in misconduct by another editor, co-editor, guest editor, or referee. The best response is for you to try to distance yourself from the misconduct. The returns to whistleblowing are more often than not negative.

Misconduct is perhaps more often observed among authors. For example, in working as an associate editor and a co-editor at a number of different journals, I became aware of a junior faculty member submitting the same paper to at least two journals at the same time. It is possible that this person thought that he would get away with it, because the referees would normally be quite different in different fields. As another example, I have seen firsthand folks borrow ideas from one field and introduce it in another field, claiming to be innovative and not referencing the proper source. This type of activity can happen across management and finance. It can even happen within a field such as finance, where I've seen ideas from work on private firms applied to studies of publicly traded firms without acknowledging that the same work was previously done on privately held firms. I have also encountered authors that knowingly publish work that is wrong and remove tables from working papers to hide their mistakes.

Misconduct is sometimes observed among co-authors and colleagues. For example, I've heard of co-authors removing names of colleagues from drafts of work. Also, I've heard of colleagues spreading false rumors as a result of a perceived need to cover up misconduct and/or for retaliation. Further, I have heard of misconduct among deans and acting deans. For example, I have seen evidence of an acting dean changing the terms of someone's contract after that person gave up a job at another university to protect himself from a complaint. The acting dean initiated a full blown investigation into the character of the person harmed and spread false rumors about that person's character.

As another somewhat funny example of misconduct (based on hearsay), it is rumored that a well-known chaired professor was not happy about a working paper that was inconsistent with their work. They were so unhappy that apparently they called the data provider to stop the distribution of the competing working paper with the rationale that the data was being used to the detriment of the industry in which the data provider represents. The data vendor apparently indicated that the agreement was not being violated, and the working paper was not inconsistent with the use of the data, and that the working paper did not make the industry look bad, but instead only made them look bad. I can't verify the accuracy of this story, but I can say that I've heard it repeated more than once. To be fair, the apparent source of the story is someone who deleted a reference to one of my own papers on the exact same topic as one of their papers (with a main difference being the unit of observation) at the page proof stage, despite the fact that my working paper appeared over 12 months before their working paper (first presented at the same annual conference a year later). This person emailed me and my co-author within a day of the journal posting their accepted paper online, showing us that their paper was now accepted and asked us to update our reference to their paper as forthcoming. Our paper was accepted a few months after his was accepted. Unfortunately you can't control the speed

222   *How to get published in the best management journals*

of reviews. If you have upset someone in the past, or just happen to be dealing with an unethical person, then that person can hold up on your paper to enable a follow-on paper to come out first in a journal, thereby making you lose credit for originating the idea and giving that credit to someone else where it is not due.

In short, there are many rumors of misconduct, and many cases of actual misconduct, and neither the rumor nor the actual misconduct is helpful for getting your work published or cited. It is just distracting for everyone. And it makes you and everyone else involved look bad. Avoid this at all costs, and try to minimize contact with unethical folks. There are plenty of highly ethical people in academia; if you surround yourself with those folks then you can reasonably hope for the best long-term outcomes.

TAKEAWAYS

To wrap up, many business academic topics can be researched and published in various journals. For example, corporate governance and corporate finance topics can be published in finance journals and management journals. In this short chapter, I've offered some anecdotes and advice about the opportunities and pitfalls that different fields offer to researchers. I hope these stories help scholars in the future decide how to position their work and to manage their careers.

Finally, let me say a warm thanks to Sofia Johan, David Robinson, Armin Schwienbacher, and Ralph Winter for helping me to edit this chapter and take out any details that could possibly lead to any person or journal being identified in any of my stories. Also, I owe many thanks to the editors Tim Clark, Mike Wright, and Dave Ketchen for their helpful comments and suggestions.

27. Publishing in management journals: how is it different from economics journals?

Saul Estrin and Sumon Kumar Bhaumik

INTRODUCTION

This chapter will try to identify the key differences between reporting empirical research in journals belonging to the fields of Economics and of Management. Our focus will be restricted to empirical papers; we will not consider purely theoretical research in either field. In the case of theory papers, the differences are equally pronounced, but are somewhat different. We also focus attention on top journals in Economics and Management respectively, by which we mean either leading general journals or top field journals. The differences are similar in more lowly ranked journals but less sharply drawn.

The structure of this chapter is as follows. We will first outline the principal differences between the expectations of the two types of journal for submitted papers in terms of structure and content, at a general level. We will then illustrate these arguments with reference to several of our own works published in both Economics and Management journals.

KEY DIFFERENCES: THE STRUCTURE AND CONTENT OF PAPERS

Differences in Structure of Papers

There is, of course, considerable latitude in how papers are organized and structured in both Economics and Management. However, in practice many papers in each field follow a fairly standard format, and many of the differences in expectations about the papers follow from this difference in structure. In this section, we will compare a stylized form of the standard structure in Management and Economics papers respectively, before going into greater detail as to differences in content within each section.

The structure for standard empirical papers in Economics and Management journals is shown in Table 27.1. The key differences are that Management papers will usually contain new theoretical insights, formulate explicit hypotheses and discuss in an independent section (Discussion) whether the findings are consistent with the hypotheses.

Table 27.1   Structures of standard empirical papers in Economics and Management

	Economics	Management
Introduction	√	√
Literature survey/theory	√	√
Hypotheses (sometimes merged with theory)		√
Data and methods	√	√
Results/findings	√	√
Discussion		√
Conclusion	√	√

The stylized strategy with respect to formulating hypotheses is strikingly different in the two literatures. Consider, for example, the following two papers: Bhaumik and Estrin (2007), which was published in the *Journal of Development Economics*, and Meyer et al. (2009), which was published in *Strategic Management Journal*. As we discuss in more detail later, Bhaumik and Estrin (2007) de facto hypothesize that if market-supporting institutions exist the relationship between a firm's output/performance and inputs would follow a predictable pattern, for example output change would be positively associated with changes in labour and capital. They use this implicit hypothesis to discuss the wider issue of development of market institutions in China and Russia. The central hypothesis in Meyer et al. (2009) is that the choice of entry mode of multinational enterprises when they enter emerging markets is dependent on the interaction between their resource needs and the quality of local institutions. However, they explicitly tease out the implications of this meta-hypothesis for specific combinations of resource needs and institutional quality such that the paper has a series of explicit hypotheses. We shall discuss the empirical implications of this difference later in this chapter.

Difference in Contents of Papers

These differences in structure underlie much more substantial differences in content, even within sections within similar titles. In this subsection, we compare the typical content within each section of the two types of journal.

Introduction: This section would typically be rather short in both Management and Economics journals. The Economics journal paper would probably lay out the research question, explaining its importance or significance, and explain the dataset. There would probably be a summary of the key literature on the topic and of the principal findings of the paper. The contents would be similar in a Management journal paper, but one expects to find more emphasis on the research contribution, relative to the literature. Indeed, there is an increasing emphasis on highlighting the contribution(s) of the paper up front, in the first couple of pages of the text of the manuscript. There could also be more explicit explanation of how this work builds on research that had been done recently, with reference to 'calls' in previous papers for research of this sort to be undertaken.

Literature Survey/Theory Section (Economics journal) as against Theory Section (Management journal): The Economics journal would probably summarize in some detail what has been found in the literature to date, as well as the data employed, methods and methodological weaknesses. It is generally good practice to clearly outline a heuristic 'model' (see Bhaumik and Estrin, 2007) on which the subsequent empirical analysis is based. But once the broad strand of the literature – neoclassical, agency theory and so on – has been identified, references are generally made to key theoretical and empirical contributions in the literature. Since Economics is based on a single discipline, there is little or no debate about the underlying conceptual lens through which issues are addressed.

In contrast, it would be extremely difficult for a paper to be published in a leading Management journal without a well-defined contribution to the theory, in addition to supporting empirical evidence. This is true, even for primarily empirical papers. Further, the Management field is multi-disciplinary and hence theoretical contributions have to be couched within a particular framework, for example, the resource based view, or transactions costs theory (see Meyer et al., 2009).[1] For example, this framework could be used to identify a class of outcomes which previously appeared to be only ambiguously related to a set of independent variables but because of the theoretical development, a new set of subclasses can be identified. Increasingly the theoretical development would take the form of a new construct whose effect would not be additive (as is the norm in Economics) but is multiplicative – a so-called moderating effect which works through other independent variables.

Hypotheses Section (usually only in Management journals): The theory section would lay out general cases about the relationship between phenomena. However, to move to applications there would be specific hypotheses linking particular dependent variables to independent ones. This section might be combined with the theory section if there are no sharp distinctions between the new concepts being considered and the manner in which they might be tested in practice. The development of explicit hypotheses aligns these hypotheses with specific aspects of the empirical analysis. For example, if regression analysis is used to test the hypotheses, each hypothesis is generally associated with a single co-efficient in the regression model (see Bhaumik, Driffield and Pal, 2010, p. 443).

In the absence of explicit hypotheses, the nature of the discussion of empirical results in Economics papers can be significantly different. It would be wrong to surmise, however, that in the absence of explicit hypotheses up front, it is acceptable to use ex post justification of results in Economics papers. Even though Economics papers rarely have explicit hypotheses, as in the Bhaumik and Estrin (2007) paper, subsequent analyses of results have to flow from the underlying theories in an ex ante consistent manner.

Data and Methods Section: In Economics journals, datasets are usually secondary sources and have been used before, often quite frequently. Hence there is little discussion about the quality of data. However, there is considerable emphasis on empirical methodology. Thus one, for example, might expect stress on how the paper is going to address issues of stationarity, endogeneity, collinearity and reverse causality. Such focus leads naturally to an emphasis on strategies to address instrumentation. A major concern of the Economics journal will be to ensure that the results themselves are highly robust in terms of causality and specification.

However, Management journals would typically place relatively more emphasis on the data itself and how it was constructed. This is because many Management datasets are developed for the research in question while economists tend to use data which is in the public domain. Hence Management readers will want to understand the research judgements made in building the dataset. Also, there is the issue of whether the data used actually capture the ideas in the hypotheses; the theory will contain constructs which the data are seeking to measure, and it is an issue as to how well this has been achieved. Variables would be categorized into dependent variables, independent variables and control variables (derived from the previous literature); a distinction which is rare in Economics papers. However, there might be typically rather less importance attached to pure methods in Management papers, and the expectations about econometric methodology might be relatively less exacting, although this is changing.

Results: This would typically be a very long section in Economics papers with reports about the key results using a basic equation, and numerous further tests and specifications, for example addressing questions of collinearity and especially endogeneity. A wide range of cutting edge econometric methods would be expected and emphasis would be placed on test statistics and implications of differences in results, for example between regressions which have and have not been instrumented. In contrast, in an empirical Economics paper, this section involves long discussions of the results and plethora of tests to establish the robustness of the results. In Management journals, this section instead would often be rather short, simply enquiring whether hypotheses are confirmed or rejected by the data in the regressions reported. However, there might also be a number of robustness checks of the results to make sure that they hold with different specifications or methods or measures of the hypothesized concept.

Discussion Section (usually in Management journals only): The discussion section is typically merged with the results and/or concluding sections in Economics journals and has a less formalistic flavour because the analysis is not usually framed in terms of hypothesis testing. In Management journals, this is quite a long section in which the results of the previous section would be considered in terms of contribution to the literature (from the introduction) and in which the theoretical ideas outlined in section 2 and the hypotheses in section 3 would be evaluated. This section would also contain a serious discussion of limitations of the study; for example, that the measured concepts did not quite measure what the theory was trying to capture, or that the dataset was small or weak in some way.

Conclusions: This section would be similar in Economics and Management journals, considering the implications of the research and the findings for future research. However, in Economics journals there might be a concern also to draw out the implications for policy makers, while in

Management journals the audience might include practitioners in the business community.

EXAMPLES OF ECONOMICS AND MANAGEMENT PAPERS

Let us first consider papers targeted at Economics journals. To recapitulate, good Economics journals prefer empirical papers that have a firm theoretical basis, whose results are generalizable (and thereby have implications for the conceptual discussions in the literature), and that demonstrate the robustness of the results using rigorous empirical analysis. However, the relative emphases on these characteristics of empirical papers can vary considerably both across journals and also among papers published in the same journal. In this section, we shall discuss three papers as illustrations of these points, the first two are in Economics and the third is in Management.

Examples of Economics Papers

To begin with, we consider the Bhaumik and Estrin (2007) paper that has been mentioned above. The paper addressed a question that is rooted in traditional microeconomic theory but which has interesting implications for the conceptual discussion about the evolution of market capitalism in transition (and, by extension, developing) economies. Specifically, the paper proposes that if market capitalism works in an economy, then the relationship between a firm's output, and tangible inputs (such as capital and labour) and other characteristics such as ownership, should be predictable on the basis of stylized firm and agency theories. There is already a huge literature about the forms of that stylization. If, on the other hand, economic reforms fail to develop market institutions then these predictable relationships may not be observed.

It is easy to see that the paper is rooted in economic theory – its empirical basis is the extended production function that captures the relationship between a firm's output and tangible and intangible inputs – and that its results and conclusions have implications for the discussion about conceptual issues that link development and transition Economics to new institutional Economics. In other words, the conclusions are generalizable and not specific to the Sino-Russian contexts. Specifically, the results have bearing on whether there are optimal approaches to developing market based economic systems, and the contrasting experiences of China (which emphasized the development of market institutions over private ownership of resources) and Russia (which emphasized rapid privatization over establishment of market institutions) provided a natural experiment to address the aforementioned question. Further, the paper paves the way for a discussion about the 'deep' institutions and political economy of economic reforms that results in a choice of alternative pathways for reforms, some of which may be suboptimal.

This brings us to the robustness of the results, which makes them attractive to the referees and journal editors. The Bhaumik and Estrin (2007) paper uses data from separate primary firm-level surveys in China and Russia that use slightly different, but comparable, survey instruments. This is a little unusual in that most papers in this field use data generated from national surveys such as the census of production; however, information of this sort is not in the public domain for either China or Russia, hence the use of surveys. The data are for a comparable period: 1995–2000 for China and 1997–2000 for Russia. The nature of the data (including missing observations) permits simple difference-in-difference estimation but not panel data estimation and corresponding econometric methods such as the generalized method of moments (GMM) that can address potential problems with endogeneity and other econometric issues. The paper, therefore, addresses the robustness issue in a different way.

First, it starts with a simple specification of the production function, where the change in output depends only on changes in labour and capital, and thereafter incrementally adds other firm characteristics, and controls for industry and location to demonstrate that the key results are unaffected by this expansion of the model specification (see Table 27.2). Second, given the incident of the Russian sovereign default and associated crisis in 1998, which has implications for formal institutions but is exogenous to individual firms, it examines the aforementioned relationship between firm output, and inputs and other firm characteristics in the Russian context for the pre- and post-1998 periods. Third, it unpacks the dummy variables for the regional controls and replaces these dummies with economic and institutional characteristics of regions such as the initial levels of per capita gross regional product and legislative quality. The basic results for Russia, for which the aforementioned relationship did not hold, and hence required careful explanation, stood up to these exercises, thereby highlighting their reliability.

Table 27.2 Empirical analysis for Economics journals: an example

Determinates of sales growth in China

Explanatory variables	Spec 1	Spec 2	Spec 3	Spec 4	Spec 5	Spec 6	Spec 7	Spec 6a	Spec 7a
Changes in (logarithm of) quantity of labour	0.81***	0.78***	0.78***	0.77***	0.78***	0.75***	0.79***	0.78***	0.83***
	(0.27)	(0.28)	(0.28)	(0.28)	(0.28)	(0.27)	(0.28)	(0.28)	(0.29)
Changes in (logarithm of) quantity of capital	0.49***	0.49***	0.49***	0.49***	0.42***	0.44***	0.41***	0.42***	0.39***
	(0.12)	(0.12)	(0.13)	(0.13)	(0.14)	(0.13)	(0.14)	(0.13)	(0.14)
Logarithm of sales in 1995				-0.01	-0.02	-0.04	-0.04	-0.02	-0.03
				(0.04)	(0.04)	(0.04)	(0.05)	(0.04)	(0.04)
Percentage of capital stock that is less than 5 years old					0.006	0.006	0.006	0.006	0.006
					(0.004)	(0.004)	(0.005)	(0.004)	(0.004)
Index of firm-level restructuring						0.008*	0.006	-0.001	-0.01
						(0.005)	(0.005)	(0.05)	(0.05)
Dummy variable for change from full state ownership to corporatized status							-0.31		0.38*
							(0.21)		(0.21)
Constant	-0.45***	-0.43***	-0.42**	-0.31	-0.32	-0.71	-0.52	-0.32	-0.17
	(0.08)	(0.15)	(0.19)	(0.43)	(0.44)	(0.43)	(0.44)	(0.41)	(0.42)
Industry controls	No	Yes	Yes	Yes	Yes	Yes	Yes	Yes	Yes
Regional controls	No	No	Yes	Yes	Yes	Yes	Yes	Yes	Yes
Adjusted R-square	0.22	0.19	0.17	0.17	0.18	0.19	0.19	0.18	0.19
F-statistic (Prob>[F])	18.44	7.91	5.98	5.31	5.03	5.22	4.67	4.71	4.26
	(0.00)	(0.00)	(0.00)	(0.00)	(0.00)	(0.00)	(0.00)	(0.00)	(0.00)
N	138	138	138	138	138	138	137	138	138

Notes:
1. The values within parentheses are standard errors
2. ***, ** and * indicate significance at the 1%, 5% and 10% levels, respectively.
3. Specifications 6 and 7 use the broader measure of index of firm-level restructuring, with a range of 32-160.
4. Specifications 6a and 7a use the more restrictive measure of firm level restructuring, with a range of 0-15, that is comparable with the corresponding index for Russia.

Source: Bhaumik and Estrin (2007), Table 2, p. 383.

Our second example of an Economics paper, published in the *Review of Economics and Statistics*, is by Bruno, Estrin and Bytchkova (2013) and is about a similar topic, namely the effects of institutions on economic behaviour. Once again a fairly standard Economics concept is being investigated, namely the effects of entry barriers on the rate of entry of new firms into different industries. It would typically be argued that entry rates would be lower when barriers are higher, and there is strong evidence to that effect from around the world. However, especially in developing countries, political processes may also play a role in new firm entry, though the impact is quite hard to identify in cross-country studies because so many phenomena other than political processes may also be changing. The main contribution of the paper is therefore to move beyond standard cross-country modelling to analyse cross-regional and cross-sector entry rates within a single economy: Russia. This gives the work the character of a quasi-natural experiment, because other sources of heterogeneity in the data are controlled for. The data is derived from different publicly available sources on entry, institutions and political change respectively.

However, to address problems of spurious correlation or endogeneity, the paper exploits the concept of 'natural' entry rates in the context of difference-in-difference methods, using the rate of entry by industry in developed countries as a proxy for a sector's 'natural' entry propensity. These natural entry rates are taken to reflect, for example, technological barriers in the industry caused by economies of scale or organizational efficiencies gained by incumbents. The emphasis in the paper is on econometric method, and the results are clear: that heterogeneity in Russian regional institutions over time does affect entry rates relative to the levels that pertain in developed market economies. In particular, it finds that political change has a negative effect on entry rates in industries in which the barriers to entry are lower. Thus, industries characterized by higher entry rates in Western economies experience comparatively less entry in those Russians regions which suffer from greater political change. Once again, the analysis is set up in such a way that the findings are generalizable from the Russian context.

Example of a Management Paper

We now turn to the Management literature, where there is more emphasis on theory development and data, and less on the econometric methodology. To recapitulate, theory development in this literature, which unlike in the Economics literature does not have widely accepted paradigms, refers to the development of postulates or hypotheses based on critical analyses of the extant literature. While this requires a very different way of approaching research questions relative to Economics, it nevertheless allows interesting innovations, in some cases by synthesizing two or more different strands of literature.

Consider, for example, the aforementioned paper by Meyer et al. (2009). It addresses a much discussed question in the international business literature, namely the determinants of the choice of entry mode by a multinational enterprise (MNE) that enters a developing country (or emerging market) economy. However, much of the literature on entry mode choice is based on the logic of transactions cost, and thereby focuses on the institutional context of foreign firm entry. The Meyer et al. (2009) paper facilitates a much more fine-grained analysis by bringing together two frameworks that dominate the international business litera-ture: the transactions cost and resource based views. Specifically, it argues that while institutional improvements in developing countries reduce the likelihood of entry by way of joint venture (JV), the intensity of an MNE's needs for tangible and intangible resources is positively correlated with choice of JV and acquisition based entry modes. The interaction between quality of host country institutions and resource needs of MNEs, which is the key contribution of the paper towards theory development, is summarized in Figure 27.1.[2]

This figure is the basis for the following hypotheses:

H1. The stronger the market-supporting institutions in an emerging economy, the less likely foreign entrants are to enter by joint venture (as opposed to greenfield or acquisition).

H2a. The stronger the need to rely on local resources to enhance competiveness, the less likely foreign entrants are to enter an emerging economy by greenfield (as opposed to acquisition or joint venture).

H2b. The effects of Hypothesis 2a are stronger when requiring intangible assets compared to tangible assets.

Note that the hypotheses indicate a clear direction for the nature of the expected relationship between the outcome (i.e., entry mode) and the relevant explanatory variables. Correspondingly, as we have mentioned above, there is a clear match between each of the hypotheses and an estimated coefficient in the regression model.

Aside from the nature of theory, the characterizations of the explicit hypotheses in Management papers, which we have discussed above, are also evident from this example. We should also note that while regression results in Economics papers rely on the so-called two-tailed test (against the

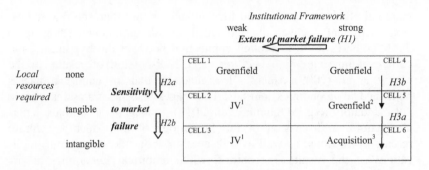

Notes:
1 In rare cases acquisition may be feasible (e.g., acquiring subsidiary of another MNE).
2 Except when asset specificity is high, when acquisition or JV may be appropriate.
3 Except when market failure is bilateral and takeover is infeasible (e.g., due to scale issues), when JV may be appropriate.

Source: Meyer et al. (2009), Figure 1, p. 66.

Figure 27.1   Theory and hypotheses development for management journals: an example

null hypothesis of non-significance), and thereafter discuss the sign and economic significance of coefficient estimates in the light of theory and the relevant literature, the explicit hypotheses of papers in Management journals require one-tailed tests (of positive or negative coefficients).

Thereafter, given the emphasis of Management journals on data (including measurement issues), the Meyer et al. (2009) paper explains in a fair amount of detail the choice of measure(s) for institutional strength (or quality) and resource needs of firms. While the former is based on the five items of the *economic freedom* index developed by the Heritage Foundation, the latter is based on data collected specifically for this study in four emerging markets using a survey instrument. Next, the paper addresses the issue of multicollinearity, which is a major concern of referees of Management journals. While this paper allays concerns about potential multicollinearity by reporting the correlation matrix for the explanatory variables, other Management papers often also do so with reference to the variance inflation factor (VIF).[3] In fact, the correlation matrix is usually reported in Management journals as a matter of course, as a basis for discussion of multicollinearity, but this is less common in Economics journals.

Following the rigorous discussion of the data, however, the empirical strategy of the paper is simple, as with most papers published in Management journals, and involves the use of the multinomial logit model. (It is virtually standard in the Management literature to report the marginal effects for probit and logit models, rather than the raw regression coefficients.) Given the detailed theory development leading up to the hypotheses and the explicit connection between the hypotheses and corresponding regression coefficients, the discussion of results in the Meyer et al. (2009) paper is less nuanced than in empirical papers published in Economics journals. This paper also illustrates that, while not mandatory (e.g., Bhaumik et al., 2010), Management journals generally require a discussion of the limitations of the paper and future research directions, as well as a discussion about the managerial implications of the results. In contrast, while empirical Economics papers sometimes have discussions about the policy implications of the results, they more rarely include explicit discussions about limitations of the papers themselves.

CONCLUSIONS

We have argued and illustrated that there are significant differences in the way that papers in Economics journals as against those in Management journals are constructed and written. For example, in the former there is more emphasis on econometric method and robustness of empirical results; in the latter on theory development (in the Management sense) and hypothesis testing. However, that does not mean that with appropriate fine-tuning a given project can be simply written up for either a Management or an Economics journal. In practice, the differences reach back to the nature of the research question and to the methodologies developed in order to test that question. Management research is more deeply rooted in the need for theoretical development and explicit hypothesis testing, perhaps using datasets specifically developed for the purpose. Economics journals which rely on a common intellectual paradigm expect less conceptual novelty and data originality but are more demanding in terms of the use of econometric methodology.

A final illustration will help to solidify these differences. If you are writing a paper for a Management journal, it is best to start with the research idea, linked to a literature/intellectual framework. For example, if the phenomenon of interest is multinational firms from emerging markets, for a Management journal one has to start by choosing the theoretical framework with which the question will be addressed. One then has to identify the ways in which emerging market multinationals might differ from the types of firm that have been analysed already in the literature. This indicates that the differences are likely to relate to 'home country effects'; after all, the most obvious thing that is new theoretically about such multinationals is that they are based in less developed economies. However, the reasons why they internationalize their activities, and the impact of their internationalization, have already been studied extensively, and it would be hard to publish a replication study of this phenomenon, even if the source economies under consideration were different. From here, one might conceptualize about how being based in less sophisticated business environments might affect the capabilities that such firms have developed, giving them advantages, for example, in expanding their operations to other emerging markets but disadvantages in more developed economies. This could form the basis for hypothesis development and testing, using a dataset perhaps gathered for precisely that purpose. The empirical work would represent a counterpart to test the theoretical development, and not necessarily represent a large proportion of the written paper.

In contrast, Economics journals might well be interested in new empirical findings from a new database which covered a different sample of firms and source countries, without expecting any systematic theoretical originality or the use of a proprietorial dataset. Indeed, it might be hard to develop an original theoretical insight; the concepts in this field are well established in Economics but their application to new countries would be original. Thus, the issue would be whether the paper had interesting findings and whether these were econometrically robust. In this sense, 'interesting' would include facts or relationships not hitherto identified, or indeed the converse – relationships which have traditionally held in developed economies but which do not seem to pertain in emerging market multinationals. However, the standards of proof for the robustness of the new relationship identified would be very high.

NOTES

1. For a summary of the frameworks used most frequently in strategic management research, see Kenworthy and Verbeke (2015).
2. Similarly, the theory development in the Bhaumik et al. (2010) paper is based on the reconciliation between the agency theoretic and resource based views of family firms and the stylized international business literature about a firm's decision to invest in overseas locations.
3. See, for example, Bhaumik et al. (2010). The rule of thumb is that a VIF test statistic value of 5 or less is acceptable from the multicollinearity perspective.

REFERENCES

Bruno, R., S. Estrin and M. Bytchkova (2013). 'Institutional determinants of new firm entry in Russia', *Review of Economics and Statistics*, **95** (5), 1740–1749.

Bhaumik, S. and S. Estrin (2007). 'How transition paths differ: Enterprise performance in Russia and China', *Journal of Development Economics*, **82** (2), 374–392.

Bhaumik, S., N. Driffield and S. Pal (2010). 'Does ownership structure of emerging market firms affect their outward FDI? The case of Indian automotive and pharmaceutical sectors', *Journal of International Business Studies*, **41**, 437–450.

Kenworthy, T. and A.Verbeke (2015). 'The future of strategic Management research: Assessing the quality of theory borrowing', *European Management Journal*, **33** (3), 179–190.

Meyer, K., S. Bhaumik, S. Estrin and M. Peng (2009). 'Institutions, resources and entry strategies in emerging economies', *Strategic Management Journal*, **30** (1), 61–80.

28. Publishing in management journals as a social psychologist

Rolf van Dick

INTRODUCTION

One of the main fields of social psychology is the study of stereotypes and prejudice. Prejudice is the unfounded generalization of (mostly negative) characteristics to every single member of a certain group and, as a result, unjust discrimination against the individual as a member of that group. I was trained as a social psychologist in my postgraduate education. I completed my PhD at Philipps University's social psychology department where I taught social psychology courses in the undergraduate psychology program. After a spell in a U.K. business school at Aston University I returned to Germany, and for almost ten years now I have been a chair of social psychology. Therefore, I think I know what I am talking about when (self-)stereotyping social psychologists as a bunch of 2x2 researchers. I am, of course, exaggerating greatly, and there are certainly as many social psychologists who have never conducted a lab experiment as there are management scholars with backgrounds in economics, marketing, or sociology who run experiments within and outside the laboratory. But I think the following example is a good way to illustrate the challenges a social psychologist may face when trying to publish in management journals.

THE SOCIAL PSYCHOLOGIST AT WORK

The stereotype of a social psychologist is that they sit in their office all day thinking about a clever way to manipulate some variables (normally two, then called a 2x2 experiment) and then run an experiment with first year psychology students to test whether the manipulation has any effect. To keep the number of participants manageable, each of the two manipulated variables comes in two levels: high and low. So, a typical

experiment may want to test the hypothesis that poor academic performance has a negative effect on one's self-esteem but that this is the case
only when the performance dimension is seen as important. The
researcher invites participants to the lab, asks them to perform a math test
which is introduced to half of the (randomly assigned) participants as
very established, highly reliable, and valid for the prediction of academic
performance. The other half is told that this is just some test that needs to
be pilot tested for use in future lab studies on people's endurance in lab
experiments. So, this makes the first "2" of the first manipulated factor –
in this case importance of the test high versus low. Then (again randomly
assigned) each half of the participants who have taken the important test
and half of those who have taken the unimportant one are told that they
have performed below average, whereas the other participants are
informed that they have performed above average. So, this makes our 2x2
design complete with the second factor being poor versus good performance. Finally, participants are asked to complete a standard self-esteem
scale with items such as "I feel I do not have much to be proud of" and
then are rewarded for participation (usually with course credits) and fully
debriefed, that is told that they have been subject to some manipulation
(or deception) that in no way reflects their true abilities and so on. The
measure of self-esteem then makes the dependent variable, test performance and importance of the test comprise the independent variables, and
the researcher may predict one main effect (when test performance is
above average, self-esteem is higher than in the other condition) and an
interaction effect (e.g., that the main effect is enhanced when the test is
seen as more important). An analysis of variance between the four
groups of participants with self-esteem as the dependent variable is then
performed and means in the four conditions compared against the
predictions.

Sounds like a plausible theory of practical relevance and an appropriate
way to test it, doesn't it? If the researcher – given that the ANOVA
produces significant results – writes up her results and sends them to a
classic top-tier social psychology outlet (*Journal of Personality and
Social Psychology*, *Personality and Social Psychology Bulletin*, *European
Journal of Social Psychology*, or *Journal of Experimental Social Psychology* to name but a few), she will probably receive some good feedback
from reviewers and may have a good chance of being invited for a
resubmission. Often, the decision letter asks for an additional experiment
ruling out an alternative explanation, but rarely are social psychologists
asked to replicate their results in a longitudinal design or with external
(or even objective) data sources.

PUBLISHING SOCIAL PSYCHOLOGY RESEARCH IN MANAGEMENT JOURNALS: ISSUES WITH EXPERIMENTAL WORK AND STUDENT SAMPLES

But let us assume that the social psychologist thinks she should submit to a management journal because she works in a business school. Her school may have a relatively narrow list of journals that are considered top outlets – some schools, for instance, use the *Financial Times* list of 45 journals as a basis for promotion or reward pay decisions. Social psychology outlets are not included in this and similar lists and they would thus not help our colleague much with her career. She may therefore think, for instance, of the *British Journal of Management* (BJM). For over a dozen years, I was involved in several work and organizational and management journals, including three years as Editor-in-Chief of the BJM. From my experiences there and with many other journals – as author, reviewer, or board member – I estimate the chances of getting such an article published in BJM or any other decent management journal are very close to zero. She may rather receive a desk reject letter without her paper even being reviewed. Why? Firstly, because reviewers and editors of management outlets typically do not like purely laboratory research with its completely artificial settings and relatively artificial manipulations and measured variables. And secondly, because reviewers and editors will certainly ask whether the findings would, in any meaningful way, generalize to a non-student (translate: practitioner) population.

Some of these problems are due to misunderstandings and stereotypes and may be overcome. Firstly, the experimental researcher when conducting experiments such as the above, for instance, is interested less in generalizability but in cause and effect. Or, in other words, she is less concerned with external (or ecological) validity but more with internal validity. She puts in a lot of effort to develop nice manipulations, realistic cover stories, and to get the random assignment of participants to experimental conditions right. If this is achieved, the experiment is able to answer the one question it was designed to answer: whether variable A influences variable B. This may sound simple but is, in practice, not always easy to translate into a study design and often goes well beyond a purely correlational study that shows a relation between the two variables. Moreover, it is highly relevant for any practical application – only when I have proof of a *causal* relationship can I start devising interventions that help increase (or reduce) the variable that causes the effect.

Secondly, the experimental social psychologist does not care whether his participants are psychology students or not. And rightly so! Why should students of theology, chemistry, or business administration be better or worse as participants? Also, business school students (certainly in MBA and EMBA programs) have working experience. However, even if an experiment were to be run with students from many different academic disciplines it would still not be generalizable to the general public. And this is not a big problem because an experiment's main purpose is not to generalize (see above)! But if we look at management research, do we see much difference? Almost every published study has been conducted in either one organization or (often a convenience sample of) several organizations. But can I generalize from a single study conducted, for instance, in a bank to other working populations, for example in the health industry or in the blue collar sector? Or can I draw serious inferences from a sample of employees in manufacturing organizations to populations of school teachers, nurses, or call center agents? Probably not, even if we talk about an excellent study with a good response rate of all employees and a very decent sample size of a several hundred participants! These arguments have been made by prestigious research methods experts such as Highhouse and Gillespie (2009), but they are hardly heard by editors and reviewers. One reason for the ignorance of such arguments may be the extreme scarcity of journal space – when 90 percent (and sometimes more) of all submitted papers are rejected, editors use heuristics that fit their respective journal's mission and scope statements, and these often explicitly reject student-based studies.

One way I got around this problem in my own work was to combine experimental research with laboratory studies. In some of our papers which found their homes in top-tier applied journals, we even used this as a key selling point. For instance, in a paper with Johannes Ullrich and Oliver Christ (2009) published in the *Journal of Applied Psychology*, we combined two studies: First an experimental scenario study with 127 students as participants in which we manipulated leader prototypicality and leader fairness as two independent variables and then tested the manipulations' effects on student reports of how much they would support the leader. Then, as a second study, we added a survey with a heterogeneous sample of the working population, spread across industries and sectors, in which we measured the above variables. We stated in the general discussion: "Our findings demonstrate that this moderator effect can be generalized from distributive to procedural fairness and from the lab to applied contexts when personally relevant outcomes are at stake" (p. 243).

Sometimes, student samples are also perfectly acceptable in a single study paper for other types of research such as studies with student project teams in settings where students work together on real projects and the outcomes of their joint work are important to them (e.g., for their marks or when they can earn real money). The journal *Academy of Management of Learning and Education*, for instance, frequently publishes research based on student samples. In management journals, this is, however, the exception rather than the rule. For example, we conducted a study on the moderating role of students' beliefs that team diversity was good or bad for their teams' performance on the relation between ethnic diversity in team composition and their level of identification with their teams. This paper eventually got published in *Human Relations* (van Dick et al., 2008). During the review process we had a really hard time convincing one reviewer that our work was suitable for this (applied) journal. We could not, of course, easily change our sample, nor did we want to collect new data in an organization as it was already a rather lengthy paper reporting two studies, but we were successful by adding the following paragraph which included appropriate references to groundbreaking books and research in other top-tier management journals:

> One might also consider the use of student samples a limitation. Note however, that our main aim was to provide a first test of a new theoretical proposition. In accordance with Cook and Campbell (1979; see also Calder et al., 1982) we therefore think that external validity, which pertains to generalization of established findings, is a secondary concern. Nevertheless, it is important to note that the context and setting in which the groups operated closely resemble work environments of project teams in organizations. As in many organizational settings, tasks were often complex. They required a variety of activities such as the identification of problems, decision-making, generation of solutions, generation and implementation of action plans and the generation of presentations and reports. Thus, although these student teams are not the same as teams in organizations, they do rely on the same processes and mechanisms (such as communication, or active management of time and other resources) to succeed on their tasks (see, for similar arguments for the validity of student project teams as research subjects, Taggar, 2002). Based on the nature of our sample and setting of the research, we therefore believe that our findings can be generalized to other work and organizational contexts. (p. 1484)

DESIGN ISSUES AND THE RESEARCH GAP

Sometimes it is the nature of the samples used to test one's hypotheses which makes it more difficult to get into management journals. But sometimes it is also the study design which prevents (easy) acceptance in such outlets. Management researchers are in principle also often using a 2x2 framework, but instead of manipulating two factors (in the lab or in the field), they measure the two variables on continuous scales and use moderated regression analysis instead of ANOVA. Both designs have advantages and disadvantages. As mentioned above, the manipulation of independent variables helps answer the causal direction of relations but the measurement of continuous variables allows depicting the relation in a more complex way. Reality often is more complex than just the "all or nothing" of a manipulated variable – and measuring them allows, for instance, to test for curvilinear relations.

Finally, a good strategy to start a paper in the management and marketing literature is to identify the research gap early on and to include a statement about why filling the gap is important for the journal's readers. In a paper in the *Journal of Marketing* with Jan Wieseke and colleagues (2009) we obviously hit the right buttons with editors and reviewers by illustrating the research gap in a figure combining existing research in the three fields of identity, leadership, and marketing research and literally presenting the gap as a hole in the center of these three areas. We also clearly stated the research gap in the following paragraph:

> In light of its definition and nomological validity, the construct of OI [organizational identification] is undoubtedly relevant to research on internal marketing and should be the ultimate goal of internal marketing. However, the three research streams – leadership, internal marketing, and OI – have yet to be systematically integrated. This discussion reveals important gaps in the internal marketing and OI literature. First, the role of leaders' OI in building followers' OI remains unexplored. Second, previous research has largely ignored the link between OI and important firm outcomes. To the best of our knowledge, no previous research on OI has directly examined financial performance as a consequence of OI, especially at the business unit (BU) level. This void deserves close attention because such a link would not only provide for external validation of the effects of OI but also help managers evaluate the effectiveness of their firms' internal marketing efforts. Methodologically, OI researchers have exclusively focused on a single level, leaving much of the rich phenomenon of how OI can be developed across levels of leader–follower interaction uncharted. (Wieseke et al., 2009, pp. 123–124)

Usually, social psychologists are a little less concerned with making the contribution of their work obvious so early on – as far as it concerns applicability or organizational relevance.

As I have said elsewhere, good research will eventually find its home somewhere (van Dick, 2011), but it is important to not only target the specific journal carefully but also to think about the general audience early on when planning one's research and when writing the paper. Some of my early work that was ultimately published in an organizational psychology journal (van Dick et al., 2005) comprised two organizational surveys, one with a small experimental manipulation. Because of this manipulation, because of the social psychology theory I used (social identity theory), and certainly because I was working in a social psychology department when writing the paper (and in which social psychology journals were seen as "better" than management journals), I submitted it to two prestigious social psychology journals first. The editor of the first journal (with "experimental" and "social" in its title) came back to me several weeks after submission with the following letter:

> Dear Dr Van Dick, after carefully reading your paper myself, I have decided not to send it out for review. My main reason for rejecting the paper is that I think it is a poor fit with [name of journal] and would be better suited for an organizational psychology journal ...

Because of the above reasons, I did not listen and submitted to a second social psychology journal. This time, I made a step forward and the paper was sent out for review – which in the end was more a curse because it took almost half a year before I received another letter:

> Dear Rolf, ... most of all that the paper is not suited to be of interest to [name of journal]'s readership ... lead me to reject the paper.

So, all in all, I only lost considerable time and had to learn the hard way that the paper was better submitted to a more applied journal, which in this case was the *Journal of Occupational and Organizational Psychology* (published as van Dick et al., 2005) – not too bad a journal I guess and one to which I submitted many times thereafter and several times with success.

CONCLUSIONS

To find a home for his or her paper faster, the social psychologist who wants to publish in management journals should carefully target the journal even before designing the study and analysing the data so that it fits the management literature's readerships' expectations. Targeting the right journal means, for instance, reading the respective outlet's mission and scope statement, screening the past issues for potential papers that the author can refer to, or even sending a brief email to the editor prior to submission inquiring whether he or she thinks that the paper might be of interest (although I would use this approach sparingly and only when having serious doubts about fit with the journal). Social psychologists have interesting theories to offer, and they normally have an excellent grasp of the state-of-the-art tools to analyse their data. Getting their work published is not only rewarding for the individual but will also enrich management both as an academic discipline and an organizational practice.

REFERENCES

Calder, B.J., W. Phillips, and A.M. Tybout (1982). 'The concept of external validity', *Journal of Consumer Research*, **9**, 240–244.

Cook, T.D. and D.T. Campbell (1979). *Quasi-experimentation: Design and Analysis Issues for Field Settings*, Boston, MA: Houghton Mifflin.

Highhouse, S. and J.Z. Gillespie (2009). 'Do samples really matter that much?', in C.E. Lance and R.J. Vandenberg (eds.), *Statistical and Methodological Myths and Urban Legends: Doctrine, Verity and Fable in the Organizational and Social Sciences*, New York: Routledge, pp. 249–268.

Taggar, S. (2002). 'Individual creativity and group ability to utilize individual creative resources: A multilevel model', *Academy of Management Journal*, **45**, 315–330.

Ullrich, J., O. Christ, and R. van Dick (2009). 'Substitutes for procedural fairness: Prototypical leaders are endorsed whether they are fair or not', *Journal of Applied Psychology*, **94**, 235–244.

Van Dick, R. (2011). 'Publishing management research', in C. Cassell and B. Lee (eds.), *Challenges and Controversies in Management Research*, London: Routledge, pp. 138–151.

Van Dick, R., D. van Knippenberg, S. Hägele, Y.R.F. Guillaume, and F. Brodbeck (2008). 'Group diversity and group identification: The moderating role of diversity beliefs', *Human Relations*, **61**, 1463–1492.

Van Dick, R., U. Wagner, J. Stellmacher, and O. Christ (2005). 'Category salience and organisational identification', *Journal of Occupational and Organizational Psychology*, **78**, 273–285.

Wieseke, J., M. Ahearne, S.K. Lam, and R. van Dick (2009). 'The role of leaders in internal marketing', *Journal of Marketing*, **73**, 123–145.

29. Publishing historical papers in management journals and in business history journals

Steven Toms

Business history and management research have, until quite recently, evolved as separate disciplines. At first sight this divergence seems surprising, but it has important implications for management researchers publishing in business history journals and for business historians publishing in management journals. Business history emerged originally as a branch of microeconomics and economic history (Supple, 1977) and quickly developed methodologies founded on the traditional tools of historical research based on the investigation of archives. Such methods typically do not feature in social science research methods texts (Gunn and Faire, 2012), and by the same virtue in business and management research methods texts. Notwithstanding the divergent origins of business history, opportunities for historical research in business and management have subsequently widened. From the 1980s, reflecting increasing involvement in the discipline of business history by Business and Management School academics (Kipping and Üsdiken, 2008), new areas of historical investigation have included management strategy themes such as networks, family capitalism, corporate governance, human resource management, marketing and brands, and multi-national organisations. To make the most of these new opportunities requires careful consideration of suitable research questions, bearing in mind the still influential differences between publishing in business history and mainstream management journals. This chapter will outline these opportunities, whilst providing advice on how to accommodate the differences. There are many possible approaches to historical writing that might be considered by management scholars. For convenience, three specific ones are considered here. A fourth, reflecting the purist business history tradition, is also explained for the purpose of contrast.

The first approach available to management scholars is to use business history to test, or augment, existing management theories. In general, management theories may use static approaches, and the introduction of a time-based dynamic creates the opportunity for historical analysis. The possibilities include building on the work of Nelson and Winter (1982), Chandler (1977) and Teece (2010) to develop a dynamic capabilities view of business history (Edwards, 2011). The value of this approach was recognised recently in a special issue of the *Journal of Management Studies* devoted to business history themes. Accordingly, Bucheli, Mahoney and Vaaler (2010) follow a similar approach to examine time-specific circumstances where vertical integration fails in the absence of certain transaction cost considerations. In a similar vein Jenkins (2010) enhances the existing view that incumbent firms have difficulty adapting to discontinuities by showing that firms can develop sustainable resource configurations to deal with such discontinuities. In parallel, there have been recent moves in the business history field to develop a 'new business history', which utilises a range of methodologies with the objective of obtaining generalisable results (de Jong and Higgins, 2015).

The second approach is to use historical anomalies to develop new theories. For example, Williamson noticed that forward integration occurred in some industries in the late nineteenth century but not in others and attributed the differential response to transaction costs arising from asset specificity and opportunistic behaviour in the value chain close to the point of sale (Williamson, 1981, pp. 561–562). In a recent application of such an approach, Reveley and Ville (2010) use counter-factual analysis to complement the comparative method of organisation studies, to suggest new theoretical approaches to the investigation of trade associations.

The third approach is to use management theory to test generalisations using historical data. Chandler's (1977) contention that structure follows strategy would be an important example, which he put to convincing effect in his subsequent (Chandler, 1990) work on scale and scope. Such an approach can be used to illustrate contrasting publishing opportunities in the two types of journal. Writing in a management journal, Filatotchev and Toms (2003, 2006) take the strategic management literature as their point of departure, building on the theoretical model developed by Robbins and Pearce (1992), to examine declining industries and opportunities for turnaround contingent on corporate governance factors. More specifically, Filatotchev and Toms identify a gap in the management literature (2006, p. 409) to suggest that 'managerial ... inaction may not in itself be the product of poor management, particularly where financial constraints operate', whilst also noting that the finance literature does not address the impact of such constraints on the process of strategic decision making. To scrutinise the process and dynamic interaction of strategy and finance, their paper uses historical evidence to suggest that governance changes are an important precondition to strategic action and subsequent restructuring. By way of contrast, writing in a business history journal, Toms and Wright (2002, 2005) use a historical approach to examine the evolution of the British and United States corporate economies since 1950. Their point of departure from the business history literature is the incompleteness of Chandler's explanation, with the need to extend economies of scale and scope to incorporate external economies and to incorporate variations in corporate governance. By taking a historical approach from the outset, they add a dynamic element to two established theories in the management literature, the resource based view (Barney, 1991) and resource dependency theory (Pffefer and Salancik, 2003), which are shown to interact, thereby explaining patterns of corporate growth and restructuring. Their approach (Toms and Wright, 2002, pp. 93–95) recognises knowledge as a common ingredient in both theoretical approaches, as a basis for competitive advantage on the one hand and as a monitoring mechanism on the other. Based on this conceptualisation, information cost is utilised as an empirical variable to investigate its role historically as a determinant of corporate change. In summary, both these approaches use history to address conceptual gaps or integrate mainstream management theories. The important difference is how they are rooted in the separate literatures, and this underlines the importance of reading the literature in both disciplines.

The three approaches outlined so far are increasingly welcomed in mainstream management journals and indeed business history journals. A fourth possibility would be the 'history for history's sake' approach, which is an avenue open exclusively for the latter type of journal. Because the typical managerial scholar is not a trained historian, this approach is to be treated with some caution.

The enormous growth of business history over recent decades has established it as a *sui generis* discipline, and crucially, created its own literature. The impetus for the rapid growth of business history literature has come from the discipline's three core journals, *Business History*, *Business History Review* and *Enterprise and Society*, which have published around 120 papers per year between them, in addition to the journals specialising in management (as opposed to business) history, numerous non-English language journals with the same objective, and further specialist journals in fields such as accounting history and marketing history. The literature in the business history journals covers familiar managerial themes, with an agenda that is often empirical, and a focus on filling gaps in historical knowledge or challenging generalis-ations. For example, business historians (Toms and Wilson, 2003) have challenged and adapted the earlier conclusions of Chandler and others on the performance of the British economy. Where the pure historical approach is not intended, it nonetheless performs a useful function for present purposes in terms of specifying the delimitations of management research using historical methods.

In general, management scholars who are not historians first and foremost will be more interested in the three approaches outlined above than this more empirical agenda. Moreover, the history journals increas-ingly welcome such contributions as the discipline continues to grow and integrate with the mainstream literature. Even so, the methodological traditions of business history remain important, and the traditional scope of these journals is suggestive of mistakes to avoid. One such mistake would be to assume that an old dataset would, of necessity, be of interest to the editors of a history journal. Datasets, which have become old as a result of previously failed attempts at publication in mainstream journals, are particularly inappropriate. If they have failed in their original task of investigating a contemporary problem, there is nothing to suggest that they will become any more useful for testing the same problem as it recedes into the historical record. Datasets, unlike port wine, do not simply improve with age. Recycling datasets from successful mainstream projects into historical journals is similarly to be guarded against. Understandably, in both these cases, business history journal editors will be determined to ensure the relevance of the research for their core audience, which means, in practice, identifying an appropriate research question based on the ex ante business history literature. Generating such a research question on the basis of a dataset that has already been created for another purpose is, in general, not to be recommended as the basis for a successful publishing strategy.

At the opposite end of the spectrum is the purely empirical approach. Business history is highly resistant to antiquarianism (Hannah, 1983), and autobiographical musings, which although no doubt of interest to the individual involved, do nothing to engage a wider audience concerned with questions of historical significance. The single company case study, in some respects the traditional bedrock of the Chandlerian and Harvard approaches to business history, is likewise discouraged. In part, this is because extreme specialisation can often easily guarantee some empirical originality in historical research, without necessarily contributing much to knowledge. Where the researcher, for example, notes a previously undiscovered fact about fish processing in the nineteenth century, unless they can also show how the wider literature should be modified in consequence, the research will be unsuitable for publication.

Even so, and of necessity, there is extensive and often extreme specialisation in the business history field. Expertise ranges from the role of entrepreneurs in medieval England (Casson and Casson, 2014) to systems of innovation in the late twentieth and early twenty-first century Japanese pharmaceutical industry (Umemura, 2014). Perhaps more so than in mainstream journals, it is easier to speculate about the identity of the likely reviewers, as the editor may have only a small group of expert specialists to draw upon. However, a balance is needed. The more specialised your submission, the less likely it is to have a wider impact and therefore the more likely it is to be rejected. Drawing the lessons of the paper out for a wider audience is therefore an important requirement, but at the same time increases the likelihood of involvement by non-specialised but highly experienced reviewers. It is these reviewers that it is best to have in mind when preparing your manuscript, whilst also keeping in mind that a more specialist second reviewer is likely, whose expertise can still lead to the enhancement or rejection of your paper.

Stylistically, the business history tradition reflects important differences. These can best be described by explaining the role of footnotes in business history journals. In the management literature, footnotes provide some embellishment of the main argument, but are treated as otherwise marginal and are actively discouraged by many journals. In business history, on the other hand, footnotes are of methodological significance. They indicate the data sources used, most commonly from the archive, revealing the process of investigation for future researchers. Specification of the scope, location, type of document and so on, with respect to archival evidence, provides the basis for judgement by the reader and reviewer as to its adequacy, and for replication by future researchers.

Although such considerations seem to emphasise that business history is steeped in empiricism, many of its leading advocates nonetheless place strong emphasis on theory. Organisation theorists increasingly agree 'history matters', adding that a theoretical stance is essential (Rowlinson, Hassard and Decker, 2014, p. 250). This 'historical turn' in organisational studies (Clark and Rowlinson, 2004) was based in part on 'some of the newer and influential research programmes within organization theory' such as neo-institutionalism and population ecology (Üsdiken and Kieser, 2004, p. 321). Lamoreaux, Raff and Temin (2008) have meanwhile argued for a reconsideration of the value of economics for business history. Lazonick (2005), for example, favours using business history to investigate the fundamentally historical characteristics of capitalism, as described by Marx and Schumpeter, rejecting the apparently timeless characteristics of behaviour that feature so strongly in mainstream economics (O'Sullivan and Graham, 2010). In the spirit of this approach, a recent special issue of *Business History* features a series of parallel papers using the evolutionary theory of Nelson and Winter (1982) in step with business history style approaches to triangulate specific themes of investigation. For example, evolutionary and business history approaches to the history of financial services (respectively Jacobides, 2015, and Toms, Wilson and Wright, 2015) are contrasted and evaluated (Nelson, 2015).

These examples form part of a wider trend, likely to promote further integration of management research with business history as both disciplines reach maturity. As this develops, the divergent traditions of the disciplines will become less relevant and the opportunities to publish historical papers for a business and management audience will increase, certainly along the lines of the three approaches suggested earlier. They illustrate a tendency to relate history to our understanding of the present and show how management research can move 'forward by looking backwards' (O'Sullivan and Graham, 2010). In a similar vein, the discipline of business history aims to learn the lessons of the past to inform present day agendas.

To take advantage of the publication opportunities set out in the different approaches sketched above, several general points are worth bearing in mind. Joint authorship between business history and management scholars can be especially productive, as each can provide the relevant expertise for dealing with the literature. Such collaboration helps to ensure that, for business history publications, the relevant business history literature is engaged with and used to motivate the study and the research questions. Similarly, the management literature should provide the relevant starting point and motivation when publishing historical papers in mainstream management journals. Methodological differences can influence the appropriate writing style and should also be borne in mind – for example the requirement to document archival evidence in business history research. Differences in methodological traditions suggest a certain need for caution for management researchers. In the end though, the objectives of both disciplines overlap, and are likely to increasingly converge, making for productive publication opportunities.

REFERENCES

Barney, J. (1991). 'Firm resources and sustained competitive advantage', *Journal of Management*, **17** (1), 99–120.

Bucheli, M., J. Mahoney and P. Vaaler (2010). 'Chandler's living history: *The Visible Hand* of vertical integration in 19th century America viewed under a 21st century transaction costs economics lens', *Journal of Management Studies*, **47**, 859–883.

Casson, M. and C. Casson (2014). 'The history of entrepreneurship: Medieval origins of a modern phenomenon', *Business History*, **56** (8), 1223–1242.

Chandler, A.D. (1977). *The Visible Hand*, Cambridge, MA: Harvard University Press.

Chandler, A.D. (1990). *Scale and Scope: The Dynamics of Industrial Competition*, Cambridge, MA: Harvard Business School.

Clark, P. and M. Rowlinson (2004). 'The treatment of history in organisation studies: Towards an "historic turn"?', *Business History*, **46** (3), 331–352.

De Jong, A. and D.M. Higgins (2015). 'New business history?', *Business History*, **57** (1), 1–4.

Edwards, R. (2011). 'Divisional train control and the emergence of dynamic capabilities: The experience of the London, Midland and Scottish Railway, c. 1923–c. 1939', *Management and Organizational History*, **6** (4), 391–410.

Filatotchev, I. and S. Toms (2003). 'Corporate governance, strategy and survival in a declining industry: A study of UK cotton textile companies', *Journal of Management Studies*, **40** (4), 895–920.

Filatotchev, I. and S. Toms (2006). 'Corporate governance and financial constraints on strategic turnarounds', *Journal of Management Studies*, **43** (3), 407–433.

Gunn, S. and L. Faire (eds) (2012). *Research Methods for History*, Edinburgh: Edinburgh University Press.

Hannah, L. (1983). 'New issues in British business history', *Business History Review*, **57** (2), 165–174.

Jacobides, M. (2015). 'What drove the financial crisis? Structuring our historical understanding of a predictable evolutionary disaster', *Business History*, **57** (7), 716–735.

Jenkins, M. (2010). 'Technological discontinuities and competitive advantage: A historical perspective on Formula 1 motor racing, 1950–2006', *Journal of Management Studies*, **47**, 884–910.

Kipping, M. and B. Üsdiken (2008). 'Business history and management studies', in G. Jones and J. Zeitlin (eds), *The Oxford Handbook of Business History*, Oxford: Oxford University Press, pp. 96–119.

Lamoreaux, N.R., D.M.G. Raff and P. Temin (2008). 'Economic theory and business history', in G. Jones and J. Zeitlin (eds), *The Oxford Handbook of Business History*, Oxford: Oxford University Press, pp. 37–66.

Lazonick, W. (2005). 'The innovative firm', in J. Fagerberg, D.C. Mowery and R.R. Nelson (eds), *The Oxford Handbook of Innovation*, Oxford: Oxford University Press, pp. 29–55.

Nelson, R. (2015). 'Evolutionary economics and the recounting of business history', *Business History*, **57** (7), 769–772.

Nelson, R. and S. Winter (1982). *An Evolutionary Theory of Economic Growth*, Cambridge, MA: Belknap Press.

O'Sullivan, M. and M.B. Graham (2010). 'Guest Editors' Introduction', *Journal of Management Studies*, **47** (5), 775–790.

Pfeffer, J. and G.R. Salancik (2003). *The External Control of Organizations: A Resource Dependence Perspective*, Stanford, CA: Stanford University Press.

Reveley, J. and S. Ville (2010). 'Enhancing industry association theory: A comparative business history contribution', *Journal of Management Studies*, **47** (5), 837–858.

Robbins, D.K. and J.A. Pearce (1992). 'Turnaround: Retrenchment and recovery', *Strategic Management Journal*, **13** (4), 287–309.

Rowlinson, M., J. Hassard and S. Decker (2014). 'Research strategies for organizational history: A dialogue between historical theory and organization theory', *Academy of Management Review*, **39** (3), 250–274.

Supple, B. (1977). 'Introduction: Approaches to business history', in B. Supple (ed.), *Essays in British Business History*, Oxford: Clarendon, pp. 1–8.

Teece, D. (2010). 'Alfred Chandler and "capabilities" theories of strategy and management', *Industrial and Corporate Change*, **19**, 297–316.

Toms, S. and J.F. Wilson (2003). 'Scale, scope and accountability: Towards a new paradigm of British business history', *Business History*, **45** (4), 1–23.

Toms, S., N. Wilson and M. Wright (2015). 'The evolution of private equity: Corporate restructuring in the UK, 1945–2010', *Business History*, **57** (5), 736–768.

Toms, S. and M. Wright, (2002). 'Corporate governance, strategy and structure in British business history, 1950–2000', *Business History*, **44** (3), 91–124.

Toms, S. and M. Wright (2005). 'Divergence and convergence within Anglo-American corporate governance systems: Evidence from the US and UK, 1950–2000', *Business History*, **47** (2), 267–295.

Umemura, M. (2014). 'Crisis and change in the system of innovation: The Japanese pharmaceutical industry during the Lost Decades, 1990–2010', *Business History*, **56** (5), 816–844.

Üsdiken, B. and A. Kieser (2004). 'Introduction: History in organisation studies', *Business History*, **46** (3), 321–330.

Williamson, O.E. (1981). 'The economics of organization: The transaction cost approach', *American Journal of Sociology*, **87** (3), 548–577.

30. Publishing human resource management research in different kinds of journals

Bill Harley

INTRODUCTION

A number of authors, me included, have suggested that Human Resource Management (HRM) research – and certainly that published in 'top' journals – appears to be dominated by a particular approach which emphasizes positivist methodology, a managerialist frame of reference and reliance on theory drawn from social psychology (Harley and Hardy, 2004; Kaufman, 2012; Godard, 2014). Nonetheless, academic HRM is a broad church, with scholars from a range of disciplinary backgrounds publishing quantitative and qualitative research informed by a range of theoretical traditions. This diversity may reflect the changing nature of universities, with many scholars who would previously have worked in discipline-based departments finding themselves in business schools as the former shrink and the latter grow. Particularly in the UK, Australia and Europe, there is a strong tradition of critique from scholars who work in business schools but who question much of the theoretical and practical foundation of contemporary HRM.

Reflecting the nature of the field, work on HRM is published in a wide range of journals. First, there are the general management journals such as *Academy of Management Journal, Journal of Management* and *Journal of Management Studies*, which publish papers on HRM along-side papers from the other major management areas. Second, there are discipline-based journals in psychology (e.g., *Journal of Applied Psychology* and *Personnel Psychology*), sociology (e.g., *Work Employment and Society*) and economics (e.g., *Labor Economics*) which publish work on HRM. Third, there are subject-based journals, including some dedicated to HRM such as *Human Resource Management* and *Human Resource Management Journal*, and journals such as *Industrial Relations* and *British Journal of Industrial Relations*, which publish a good deal of HRM material as well as more traditional industrial relations papers.

There are other dimensions on which the relevant journals vary, notably the extent to which they emphasize practice vs research, the extent to which they tend to favour either 'US' or 'European' style research (see Üsdiken, 2014), their openness to overtly critical research and the prestige they hold within different scholarly communities. There are, therefore, many potential outlets for research on HRM and a potentially confusing set of choices, particularly for early-career scholars. My aim in this chapter is to reflect on my own experiences and approach in a way which I hope will be useful to others, while noting that there is no single recipe for success in HRM publishing.

MY BACKGROUND AND PERSPECTIVE

Before turning to specific examples of publications in different kinds of journals, it may be useful to outline my own disciplinary background, career and general approach to publishing. Our backgrounds and career trajectories both shape and reflect our approach to research and publication. Thus, the material which I present about publishing in different kinds of journals is likely to make more sense if it is placed in context.

I completed a PhD in 1994 in a political science department, supervised by an academic with a background in economics and sociology. My topic linked macro-level changes in industrial relations policy in Australia to micro-level changes in workplace practices and outcomes. My particular concern was with how national-level policy changes had an impact on employees and their experiences of work. My research drew on theoretical resources from political science, sociology and industrial relations literatures and was informed by a critical sensibility. It was primarily based on secondary analysis of large-scale national survey data, augmented with qualitative studies of two industry sectors. While my doctoral research was clearly relevant to the field of HRM, it was not framed with reference to mainstream HRM work.

At the time that I graduated, there was a massive growth of job opportunities in business schools and a corresponding decline in job opportunities in traditional social science departments. My first job as a lecturer was in a business school, teaching some industrial relations, but predominantly HRM, and my appointments since that time have all been in business schools. My publishing, however, reflecting my background and interests, has not been primarily in 'mainstream' HRM journals. My approach has always been to target the journals which I find interesting and stimulating and in which I have judged my work most likely to have an impact. I have not pursued a strategy of choosing journals on the basis of their rankings alone and then framing my work to fit in. Indeed, I feel a certain discomfort with the emphasis that is currently placed on targeting 'big hits' at all costs. My approach has led me to target different journals with different kinds of papers at different times, although I cannot say that the 'quality' of journals as captured by the impact factor has not been among my considerations. In the next part of the chapter, I will reflect on a few of these publications and what they might tell others about positioning HRM research for different kinds of journals. My reflections are informed not only by my experience as an author, but also as an editor of *Journal of Management Studies* from 2010 to 2015 and a reviewer for numerous general management, discipline-based and subject-based journals.

GENERAL MANAGEMENT JOURNALS

By definition, general management journals publish across a range of different management-related topics and disciplines and hope to attract a broad readership, although the extent to which they are open to 'critical' work varies considerably. The challenge for authors publishing in such journals is that they must submit papers which seek to meet two, possibly competing, aims. First, they must have something to say which has implications beyond their own field and which appeals to readers from a range of fields within management. Second, at the same time they must seek to make a serious contribution to their own discipline and retain credibility within it. While this can be a challenge, there is some comfort in the fact that virtually all management scholars work within a sub-discipline of management, so we are all in the same boat when it comes to submitting to general management outlets.

My experience of publishing in general management journals is limited, simply because I have made a choice to focus on discipline- and subject-based journals, but I have published some papers in such outlets. An example which illustrates the points above is Harley and Hardy (2004). This paper was published in a special issue of *Journal of Management Studies* which celebrated the career of a long-time editor, Karen Legge, who was herself a scholar of HRM. Our aim in this paper was threefold – to reflect on Legge's work, to make a contribution to the field of HRM and also to contribute to broader methodological debates within management. In an attempt to balance these aims, we wrote a paper which used discourse analysis in an attempt to make sense of why

Legge's work had been less apparently 'impactful' than that of David Guest, as measured by citations. This allowed us to engage with a methodological debate within HRM, which could be summarized as 'positivism vs social constructionism' and in which Legge was a key participant, at the same time as contributing to broader methodological debates in management studies.

A paragraph from the introduction of this paper summarizes the way in which we sought to achieve our aims:

> This paper makes a number of contributions. First, by using discourse analysis to examine a selection of texts that is indicative of a larger corpus of texts on HRM, we are better placed to understand how academic HRM discourse has developed and how academic knowledge is produced. Second, we provide an understanding of some of the challenges confronting critical researchers as a result of the discursive context in which they work. A third contribution is the identification of some of the ways that critical researchers might engage in discursive work to meet these challenges. Finally, we make a methodological contribution by developing a systematic approach to discourse analysis. (Harley and Hardy, 2004: 378)

So, while the paper was squarely focused on research on HRM, at the same time it sought to make a contribution to broader debates about methodology and about academic practice within the management field.

DISCIPLINE-BASED JOURNALS

Here there is a similar challenge to that faced by HRM scholars publishing in general management journals, in the sense that authors must say something relevant to those working within the core discipline of the journal – sociology, psychology, economics and so on – while simultaneously making a contribution to HRM scholarship. Of course, the extent to which those twin aims present a challenge depends in part on how broad or narrow the disciplinary focus of the journal is.

Some of the issues can be illustrated by considering my experience with one discipline-based journal. I have published a number of papers in *Work, Employment and Society* (*WES*), which is the British Sociological Association's journal dedicated to the sociology of work and employment. Because the journal focuses on work and employment, it is a more natural home for HRM research than a broad sociology journal would be, but at the same time the types of HRM papers published reflect the preferences of the readership (and editors and reviewers). These are typically characterized by some foundation in sociological theory, but also by an orientation which is explicitly critical of mainstream HRM research and which commonly focuses on issues of power, domination and exploitation in the labour market and the labour process. Given my own disciplinary background and interests, *WES* might be seen as a natural home for my research, but positioning papers appropriately nonetheless presents challenges.

This can be illustrated by the example of Harley, Sargent and Allen (2010). This paper addresses a staple of mainstream HRM research – the apparent links between 'high performance work systems' practices (hereafter HPWS) and employee attitudes to work – and seeks to explain why such practices appear to be received positively by employees. The notion that HRM is universally 'good' for employees and that 'good HRM' can generate gains for both employees and organizational performance has been challenged vigorously by critical sociologists. The challenge for this paper was to try to explain how such practices might generate gains for employees, but by using critical sociological theory, and simultaneously offer an alternative explanation to mainstream unitarist approaches and some of the more simplistic critical approaches.

How did we do this? The paper started with a review of the empirical research on employee responses to HPWS to establish the lack of consistency in findings and to suggest that the prior debates had reached an impasse because they were couched in terms of HPWS being universally 'good' or 'bad'. This provided the motivation for an alternative approach. The paper then suggested that the failure to bring sociological theory to bear on understanding HPWS and employee responses had limited our understanding.

> This article seeks to develop a research agenda which draws on social and political understandings of the workplace and explicitly considers the role of interests in shaping outcomes. The agenda is informed by labour process theory (LPT), which underlies many of the critical analyses of HPWS (see Ramsay et al., 2000). While there are divergent views within LPT, at its heart is an understanding of workplace relations as shaped by the structure of capitalism and involving relations between capital and labour, rather than simply between human actors. (Harley et al., 2010: 742–743)

The paper then utilized Edwards, Collinson and Rees' (1998) 'disciplined worker thesis' to propose that HPWS were favourably received by employees when they enhanced order and predictability in work processes. Statistical analysis of survey data was then used to assess the extent to which a scale capturing order and predictability mediated associations between HPWS and positive employee outcomes. This provided an empirical basis to argue for the value of sociological theory for explaining outcomes which had previously been explained almost exclusively by psychological theory.

To summarize how we positioned this paper, we took a well-recognized finding – that HPWS are in at least some cases associated with positive employee outcomes – then problematized both the universality of this finding and the dominant explanations, thereby providing a critique of prevailing understandings. We then demonstrated, bolstered by statistical analysis, that positive outcomes could be explained by critical sociological theory, thereby producing knowledge with a strong empirical basis and a critical sociological orientation which fitted with the orientation of the journal.

SUBJECT-BASED JOURNALS

By subject-based journals, I mean those that focus on HRM, but which are cross-disciplinary in the sense that they do not publish papers exclusively within a particular base discipline. For example, the *British Journal of Industrial Relations* (*BJIR*), which I will discuss below, focuses on industrial relations and HRM, but publishes papers informed by a number of base disciplines, notably sociology and economics. Researchers working on the subject which is the concern of subject-based journals have the luxury of being able to write for an audience which is likely to be quite familiar with the specialist knowledge and language within that subject area, and prospective authors do not have to write for as broad an audience as they would if they were targeting a general management or a discipline-based journal. Subject-based journals in HRM tend to publish relatively high proportions of quantitative work, reflecting the disciplinary foundations of HRM scholarship in economics and organizational behaviour.

While some subject-based journals are quite broad and inclusive, it would be fair to say that others are quite narrow in their focus, both in terms of the topics covered and the range of perspectives which are welcomed. I have not often targeted 'mainstream' HRM journals, because of the orientation of my research towards critical perspectives. I have, however, published papers in the aforementioned *BJIR*, and consideration of this experience provides some potentially useful insights for HRM scholars targeting subject-based journals. In Harley, Allen and Sargent (2007), my co-authors and I presented research on associations between HPWS and employee experiences of work, which sought to explore the moderating effect of occupation on the outcomes for employees. The aim was to examine the extent to which the structure of labour markets within the service sector appeared to shape the outcomes of HPWS, by asking whether lower-skilled workers were denied the apparent benefits of such practices. In this way, we engaged squarely with debates within the HRM literature, while at the same time bringing in concerns likely to be relevant to industrial relations scholars informed by sociology and economics.

Because we were writing for an audience which was familiar with the HPWS literature, we could deal quickly with this and then turn very quickly to debates about working arrangements in the service sector and the role of employee skills – both staples of HRM and industrial relations literature. We thereby positioned the paper around streams of literature current in the subject area. In doing so, we were able to use language specific to the subject area, for example:

> The theoretical arguments made against the general applicability of HPWS in the service sector are based on the segmentation of employment in services. The logic of the argument is that markets for services are very clearly divided into low-value and high-value segments with the result that employment in service organizations is correspondingly segmented. According to this argument, in the low-value/low-skill segments of the sector, where work can be standardized to deliver a standard product, work will be characterized by Taylorist or neo-Taylorist practices, while in the high-value/high-skill segments, workers may enjoy more humanistic HR practices. (Harley et al. 2007: 610)

We could safely assume that readers were familiar with these debates and this language, in a way which we could not have if we had been targeting a general management or discipline-based journal.

Since *BJIR* is read by many scholars with backgrounds in economics and typically publishes a good number of statistical papers, we presented numerous figures and tables summarizing statistical analysis and assumed knowledge about technical terminology. In common with some general management journals but generally not discipline-based journals, the subject-based HRM journals tend to emphasize practical implications. Thus, we concluded the paper with, inter alia, some consideration of practice:

> In practical terms, [the findings] suggest that workers can benefit from HPWS in the service sector. This is not to say that workers and unions should rush forth and embrace HPWS. Rather, it is to caution against the assumption that they should necessarily resist such practices. The challenge for researchers who wish to inform practice is to build on existing research and to identify the conditions under which HPWS is beneficial for workers. (Harley et al. 2007: 623–624)

DISCUSSION AND CONCLUSIONS

In the final part of this discussion, I will briefly recap what seem to me the important lessons I have learnt from over twenty years as an author, reviewer and more recently as an editor. Most importantly, while it is crucial in terms of credibility and professional satisfaction to publish in journals which one finds interesting and credible, there is a range of such journals available to HRM scholars. This dictates that thought be given to how best to position papers when submitting to different kinds of journals. In general management journals, the key success factors appear to be appealing to a broad audience, while also speaking to HRM scholars, and to make a contribution to broader debates. In discipline-based journals, one needs to say something relevant to scholars working in that discipline – notably by framing one's work in theory drawn from that discipline – as well as to HRM specialists. When seeking to publish in subject-based journals, one has the luxury of 'preaching to the converted', but there is often an emphasis on practice. I do not pretend that this brief chapter covers everything which might be considered by HRM scholars when developing their publishing careers, but I hope that some of these insights are valuable.

REFERENCES

Edwards, P., M. Collinson and C. Rees (1998). 'The Determinants of Employee Responses to Total Quality Management: Six Case Studies', *Organization Studies*, **19** (3), 449–475.
Godard, J. (2014). 'The Psychologisation of Employment Relations?', *Human Resource Management Journal*, **24** (1), 1–18.
Harley, B., B. Allen and L. Sargent (2007). 'High Performance Work Systems and Employee Experience of Work in the Service Sector: The Case of Aged Care', *British Journal of Industrial Relations*, **45** (3), 607–633.
Harley, B. and C. Hardy (2004). 'Firing Blanks? An Analysis of Discursive Struggle in HRM', *Journal of Management Studies*, **41** (3), 377–400.
Harley, B., L. Sargent and B. Allen (2010). 'Employee Responses to "High Performance Work Systems" Practices: An Empirical Test of the "Disciplined Worker Thesis"', *Work, Employment and Society*, **24** (4), 740–760.
Kaufman, B. (2012). 'Strategic Human Resource Management Research in the USA: A Failing Grade after 30 Years?', *Academy of Management Perspectives*, **26** (2), 12–36.
Ramsay, H., D. Scholarios and B. Harley (2000). 'Employees and High Performance Work Systems: Testing Inside the Black Box', *British Journal of Industrial Relations*, **38** (4), 501–531.

Üsdiken, B. (2014). 'Centres and Peripheries: Research Styles and Publication Patterns in "Top" US Journals and Their European Alternatives, 1960–2010', *Journal of Management Studies*, **51** (5), 764–789.

31. Publishing in top international business and management journals

Stephen Tallman and Torben Pedersen

INTRODUCTION

Publishing in top international business and international management (IB/IM) journals generally follows the same paths with many of the same expectations and requirements as presented for top general management journals. There is, however, one major exception. That is the absolute need to follow the journal's guidance in defining what makes the content of an article international in scope. We will develop a discussion and provide some examples of this in the next section of this chapter. We also believe that expectations relating to topics, relevant literature, data collection, methods, and presentation tend to be a bit different in the IB/IM literature from general management. These, though, are matters of degree or focus or preference, while the demand that a paper be "international," whatever is meant by any particular journal in using that word, is essential.

INTERNATIONALISM – THE DEFINING CHARACTERISTIC

IB/IM involve the study of cross-border activities of economic agents, or the strategies and governance of firms engaged in such activity. International scope obviously is comprised of many parts as one could claim that very few economic activities do not have an international dimension. It is certainly true that more and more economic activities are becoming more international and global, so the context for studying economic activities will often be international, where the objects of study are different cross-border activities.

However, in IB/IM the key is not just to use the international dimension as the context of study, but to make the international dimension a key part of the study. The basic claim in IB/IM is that the international dimension is not just a matter of degree, but it changes the nature of many of the issues we scrutinize. When compared with domestic activities, international activities entail more risks, uncertainty, psychic distance, cultural distance, institutional distance and so on, but also more opportunities that come from diversity in knowledge, resources, and user preferences. These fundamental differences in conducting business domestically and internationally get to the core of IB/IM studies.

Therefore, all the key journals in IB and IM stress that the international dimension needs to be a primary focus of attention. Often, in fact, it is a make or break criterion for publishing in the top IB/IM journals. Box 31.1 offers short abstracts of the editorial policies of three major IB/IM journals (*Journal of International Business Studies (JIBS)*, *Journal of World Business (JWB)* and *Global Strategy Journal (GSJ)*), as described in their web pages, that are all very explicit about the key importance of the international dimension. The text that addresses this issue is highlighted in italics.

BOX 31.1   ABSTRACTS FROM WEBPAGES OF EDITORIAL
POLICIES FOR *JIBS*, *JWB*, AND *GSJ*

Journal of International Business Studies (JIBS)

"JIBS seeks to publish manuscripts with cutting-edge research that breaks new ground, rather than merely making an incremental contribution to international business studies. Manuscripts should address real-world phenomena, problems or puzzles; recognize that their contributions stand on the shoulders of prior researchers to highlight what is interesting and different; and include a clear statement of what it is they contribute to international business research. Theories whose *central propositions are distinctively international are encouraged*, as are theories where both dependent and independent variables are international.

"The major theme of a JIBS paper should highlight the insights that can be derived for the *international aspects of business activity* as such. Papers in which international business is in the background, or in which international business issues are secondary or peripheral to the main argument being developed, are not suitable for JIBS. Hence, a paper is applicable for JIBS *when the core argument developed and examined is inherently international in character*, which is not judged by the nature of the data used as such in any accompanying empirical investigation."

Journal of World Business (JWB)

"JWB publishes cutting-edge research that reflects important developments in the global business environment and advances new theoretical directions and ways of thinking about global phenomena. Although JWB's primary readers are scholars and researchers, the journal values contributions that explore and explicate implications for global enterprises and their managers, as well as consequences for public policy and the broader role of business in society.

"While manuscripts may focus on a single country or small group of countries, *all submissions should reflect some cross-border or comparative dimensions*, or explore and advance other *issues affecting international business*, consistent with the global scope of the journal."

Global Strategy Journal (GSJ)

"The domain of GSJ, as implied by the journal name, will be the study of any and all aspects of the environment, organizations, institutions, systems, individuals, actions, and decisions that are a part of or impinge on the practice or study of strategy and strategic management of business and non-business organizations in the global context. By global, we explicitly mean any cross-border activities described as international, global, transnational, multinational, multi-regional or by any other term that substantially implies that the activities take place in multiple countries and/or are integrated across borders.

"The journal will be defined clearly by its *focus on international and global organizational strategic management, rather than a universalistic approach to the study of strategy.*"

The obvious next question is then: What does it more precisely mean to say that the international aspect is at the center of the study? This implies that the theoretical part of the paper includes discussions of the international aspects and their implications for the theories and phenomena under investigation. Typically this should also be reflected in propositions or hypotheses that might well include some contextual variables evolving from the international setting – such as organizational complexity, institutional or cultural distance – that are affecting (e.g., main effect, moderating, or mediating) or being affected by other variables. As the current editors of *GSJ* (Tallman and Pedersen, 2011: 2), we say that the journal is "... primarily concerned with strategy in context or with the moderating effects of geographical, cultural, and institutional differences on strategic management ... ," and further that it is not interested in "... universal or context-free approach[es] to the study of strategy ..." Thus, the idea that international business or management studies should be explicitly focused on the international context and its effects on the discipline under consideration, strategy in the case of *GSJ*, is vital to IB/IM scholarship.

More especially this implies that a study that uses a multi-country dataset to test whether a theory of some aspect of business already established in a domestic context can be applied globally, while controlling for country effects (sources of international heterogeneity or variation), might not qualify as appropriate. For example, a study of how the use of performance appraisals affects firm performance would not be appropriate – even if the data used to test this was collected in multiple countries and possibly even if the study controlled for country differences. However, if the same data was used to study how the cultural context moderated the relationship between performance appraisal and firm performance, so that the theory and hypotheses focused on this interaction between the local culture and the tool of performance appraisal (i.e., how it might be perceived differently in different contexts), then it typically would meet the criteria of being inherently international in character.

A single-country study of a question such as "are MNEs more risk-averse than purely domestic firms?" would also qualify as an IB/IM study if the theoretical discussion centers on how the international or multinational dimension might determine behavioral differences between multinational enterprises (MNEs) and purely domestic firms. Likewise, a comparative study of business or management practices and consequences in multiple countries or regions is typically seen as an international study, presuming that the comparison is made both conceptually and empirically. A single-country study in which all observations are domestic, but in which explicit comparison is made to similar studies set in other countries and in which differences in national context are salient, may be considered international in scope in some journals, but perhaps not in others.

The main point highlighted here is that what makes an IB/IM study is not the multi-country nature of the applied data, but rather the theoretical and conceptual insights on the implications of conducting cross-national activities that the study brings to the table. That this conception of "What is international?" is both relevant and poorly understood is supported by a desk rejection rate of well over 50 percent of articles submitted to *JIBS*, according to its editors – the significantly increased rate over the 40–50 percent typical of top journals is due mostly to rejection of submissions of single-country, non-U.S. based studies as not being international research, and therefore inappropriate for the journal. *GSJ*, as a new journal, has a lower desk rejection rate overall and a less-rigorous definition of "single-country study," but perhaps a third of desk rejections are for a non-international perspective.

WHY SINGLE COUNTRY STUDIES ARE NOT CONSIDERED INTERNATIONAL

The majority of IB/IM journals, and all of the major journals in these fields, while mostly published in the U.S.A. or Europe, take an explicitly global perspective on their research domain. Thus, while *GSJ* is largely edited in the U.S.A. and Europe and published by Wiley in the U.K., it does not consider itself to be a U.S.- or industrial- world-centric outlet. Therefore, the idea that anything published about the actions or operations of companies, industries, or economies taking place in locations outside the U.S.A. is automatically international is not an accurate reflection of editorial policy. Rather, these are treated as domestic studies based in countries other than the U.S.A. or U.K. Thus, a study of local business responses to corruption in the legal system of a West African nation would be just as single-nation domestic in scope as a study of local business responses to boycotts in an American city based on local police shootings. Not the firms involved, the activities monitored, the conceptual relationships, nor the data offer any insight on doing business across borders, the activities of MNEs in or from the country, or comparisons between business actions in multiple countries. On the other hand, if the same studies proposed that and tested whether multinational firms operating in the same local market would respond differently than locally based firms, due to home country cultural or institutional distance from the host, we would have a study in which international issues affect theory, models, data, and resulting conclusions, and which would indeed be eligible for top IB/IM journals.

COMPARATIVE MANAGEMENT

The majority of papers published in IB/IM journals address the activities of multinational firms or activities such as foreign trade that implicitly involve cross-border transactions. However, for scholars of international business and management, comparative studies of business or management topics as they are pursued in different countries clearly are relevant to these journals. In the past, comparative management studies were relatively popular, as scholars grappled with differences in national settings. Comparative studies are also relatively popular in studies of the effects of cultural differences and national institutions, perhaps less so in the study of international strategies. However, there is much to be learned from comparisons of business or management processes and outcomes, whether at the individual, firm, or industry level, as they are manifested in different national contexts.

From the IB/IM perspective, the effects of national context are clarified in such studies. From a business or management studies perspective, such comparative studies are most useful in differentiating the universal aspects of the concepts from the international setting as a significant part of the modeling, not just some international data applied to a generic management framework. In some journals, a comparative study will be expected to compare management in two or more countries directly, using the same instruments and analytical tools. In others, a single-country study that pursues concepts that have been developed previously in other countries and benchmarks results explicitly (taking a theoretical concept well-developed empirically in the U.S. setting and developing comparable data and methods to compare responses in China, and to then extend the theory to be more general, for instance) may be accepted as international in scope despite the single-country nature of the original empirical work.

CONCEPTUAL SECTIONS

Literature reviews for IB/IM articles are likely to be somewhat more extensive and complex than for non-international research. Particularly in the top journals, the disciplinary literature (economics, strategy, organizational behavior, consumer behavior, etc.) will usually be brought into play, but the relevant international literature (trade theory, global strategy, cultural effects, institutional distance, etc.) also must be represented. In strongly empirical papers in a well-developed part of the field, most references may be other international business research, but more conceptual pieces will generally address the question of how general theories must be adapted to different contexts through the addition of moderating or mediating effects.

General business and management journals often focus on theory testing, using some specific setting as a source of data and to infer specific outcomes that should be able to support or deny the expectations of the theory or theories in question. IB/IM articles may be set up as a test of theory, particularly of moderating and mediating hypotheses that the strong contextual effects of an international setting are likely to highlight. However, with so many differences from place to place, phenomenological studies are very common in IB/IM. In such studies, the primary focus of the paper is to describe the actions of companies or other organizations or their members. Theories are brought into play to build and organize expectations of how the organizations, markets, or consumers in one country might respond to particular conditions and stimuli. Such papers are also found in top field journals, but the rich environment of international business makes such studies perhaps more common, but also of greater importance to scholarly researchers. Top journals still expect to see business/management theory being used to explain what is happening and why, but offering insights into investment into emerging market countries, for instance, is seen as equally important as whether tests on emerging market data tend to support or not to support current management theory. This is true in all management studies, but is much more apparent in IB/IM studies.

As discussed above, IB studies typically include some consideration of the setting or context, whether as the main topic, the setting of the study, or a source of potential moderating effects. Characteristics of the international business environment, location-specific or "distance" effects of the specific national/regional setting, the role of non-business actors such as international organizations (European Union, World Trade Organization, United Nations), nongovernmental organizations, or social networks are all considerations that are important in IB transactions. These contextual or locational considerations should be an explicit and apparent part of the conceptual development of the paper. They should be shown or predicted to affect, through moderating or mediating relationships, the relationships between the actions and outcomes of the business and managerial phenomena in question. They should also be an explicit part of the application of any business or management theories that are brought to bear on the study. Including IB/IM concepts in the conceptual development of the research is the key to making the paper inherently international in scope, as discussed above.

In building a conceptual framework for the research, we find that most business and management theories have some relevance to most locational settings and have been used in international business at one time or another. However, the manifestations of these theories – that is, the exact mechanisms by which they operate and the relative importance of the various organizational and competitive factors that impact their operations – are likely to vary from location to location, driven by differences in cultures, institutions, economic development, and infrastructure across borders. Thus, the resource-based view, institutional theory, real options, and other macro theories still apply, but the issue of varying contextual settings means that the organizational variables may interact with locational variables extensively – context is hard to avoid. In more micro studies, aspects of human psychology or social interaction may be fundamental to our species, but the exact decisions and actions undertaken by individuals are likely to be heavily influenced by cultural expectations and institutional constraints.

In creating testable frameworks of hypotheses and developing causal diagrams to outline empirical tests in IB/IM research, scholars should include explicitly international variables as explanatory variables, perhaps as the fundamental inputs to a structural equation model; as moderating variables, suggesting perhaps that the effect of company resources on performance may be moderated by their cultural appropriateness; or as control variables – but control variables with explicit effects, so that perhaps state ownership might need to be controlled for in a study of the effect of technology on human resource policies. If an author does not see a role for location-based variables in her model, whether purely theoretical or for empirical testing, she should expect a high probability of desk rejection by an IB/IM journal.

VARIABLES

Dependent Variables

Dependent variables in IB/IM studies are qualitatively much like those in any business or management research, whether measuring some organizational outcome or performance in the market or another external context. Thus, choice of acquisition or alliance in an expansion, profitability resulting from a strategic decision, or retention of employees might all be outcomes in any business or management research. In international business studies, though, contextual aspects may shift the exact terms of the dependent variable. For instance, an expansion may be across borders, so governance decisions focus on specific markets. Profitability might be for the entire corporation, but is often focused on national or regional units, and employee retention considerations might result in a comparison of home and host country nationals' retention rates. Many IB/IM studies do not use explicitly international dependent variables at the firm level, but when international or cross-border considerations are explicitly part of the dependent variable, establishing the study as international in nature is relatively straightforward.

Explanatory Variables

Again, the organizational variables that drive the dependent variable are often quite typical in quality, but may reflect geographical or locational considerations that do not appear in domestic studies. Thus, international diversification is much like product/market diversification in any study insofar as its anticipated mechanisms and effects, but at the same time explicitly incorporates considerations of differences across locations. Other possible independent variables such as cultural or institutional distance are often critical to an IB/IM study, but are essentially irrelevant or meaningless in a domestic setting. If variables measure stocks and flows of resources, products, ideas, or capital across borders or differences among national units or specific location-tied characteristics, this is often an indicator of an international study.

Moderating Variables

As discussed above, international or cross-border considerations often are where international context comes into empirical estimations, as organizational variables are predicted to have differential effects under different location-tied contextual conditions. When incorporated into the conceptual framework and modeled explicitly with measured variables, country-specific moderating variables are perhaps the most typical way for international effects to appear explicitly in organization or industry-level studies. As well as establishing a clear international provenance, however, the importance of context to the actual operationalization of many business and management concepts is demonstrated by the moderating effect of national differences. This, then, is often how the benefits of international studies to understanding the nuances of larger theoretical and conceptual models of business management are demonstrated. Where a domestic study may appear to support the expectations of a universalistic theory, an international study using appropriate variables and interactions can go far toward establishing the boundary conditions, limitations, and relevance of such theories.

Control Variables

International management studies typically offer multiple location-based control variables. Place matters, and we often see dummy variables for countries, but specific controls for cultural differences; levels of economic development; legal, political, and regulatory standards and requirements; geographical differences; and other aspects of location that might affect markets or organizations are also common. In general, IB/IM studies will use all the controls for organizational types typical of equivalent work in the discipline, then add a variety of controls related to international markets and/or the specific home and host markets.

DATA

Firm-level data is often not categorically different from that used in any related discipline-focused research, but may well be much more complex to collect and organize. Even secondary data on financial variables is inconsistent across legal jurisdictions. Cultural and institutional differences might mean that management and organizational measures are very different in scope, even in their meaning. Some of these issues are gradually being resolved by converging accounting standards and generally increasing transparency for publicly traded firms. One item of note, though, is that the relative importance to their local economies of state-owned, family-owned, and other firm types whose shares are not traded on public exchanges means that even when data is accessible, the importance of the observed organizations may vary widely across countries.

Data collection is often much more difficult. Gaining access to secondary data may be difficult for foreign-based researchers, so local collaborators are often necessary. The trustworthiness of data collected in emerging markets with less secure legal institutions may well be less than in industrial market economies. In addition, databases are typically expressed in the local language, often requiring translation, and again emphasizing the value of local collaborators. Likewise, collecting first-hand data through surveys or interviews requires more than a little additional effort, and often a multi national research team. Translation and back translation are essential. Careful pre-testing on individuals from the test country is needed. Variables may have different meanings to managers in different places and descriptive phrases may not translate directly and meaningfully. It is essential to follow procedures precisely and to maintain control of collection efforts when the validity of the data and the collection effort are likely to be queried (Chang et al., 2010). That is, the problems of single method, single instrument, single respondent research when using surveys are always at issue, but especially in emerging markets limits on communication and travel may make reliable data collection a real issue with a limited array of solutions. For instance, poor telephone service may limit the possibilities for phone surveys, unreliable mail may make mailed surveys uncertain, and cultural responses to intrusive questions in a setting where guarantees of confidentiality are seen as dubious may require person-to-person interviews even to administer closed-ended surveys (and these are difficult to schedule, particularly for foreigners). Also, the lack of reliable secondary data may eliminate complementary sources of some measures. Reviewers are typically hyper-alert to these issues in international research.

Multi-country data is generally expected in international business and management studies to avoid single-country studies, but as we have said it is not necessarily the case that multi-country data always makes for an international business study. If the conceptual aspect of a study is completely driven by disciplinary theory and the modeling does not include contextual controls or moderators, simply using non-U.S. or even multi-country data does not necessarily offer the necessary focus on international business to pass the "desk reject as inappropriate" test. At the same time, although data from only one country may pass muster in a study with a strong explicit comparison to previous work based in other countries in some journals, the general expectation is that multi-country data will be used to test these explicitly international models.

CONCLUSION

Typically, phenomenon-focused international studies may primarily offer opportunities to develop concepts and ideas about understanding what is happening in international or foreign markets or among foreign suppliers, customers, or partners. A challenge for authors focused on top international IB/IM journals is to move beyond this focus on what is happening in the world to understanding how and why it is happening, which generally means applying business and management theoretical concepts to the phenomenon in order to understand how the international context is or is not different from previously studied domestic contexts. And, in order to clearly model the impact of the international or multi-country context, the setting must be explicitly included in the specification of the theoretical and empirical frameworks. Early papers addressing an important new phenomenon may survive with little effort to build explicitly international models, but any novelty quickly fades, and theoretical inputs and consequences again take precedence.

Such issues can be seen, for example, in early studies of market entry into China – this was so new that any rigorous paper with seemingly reliable data could be published in virtually any journal. Within a short time, though, studies in top journals were expected to apply, test, and extend management theory in the Chinese setting, and IB/IM journals began to require a focus on the character of the multinational partner, the role of contextual distance in explaining differences across markets, and the development of new theoretical constructs for investment in emerging markets – just having reliable Chinese data was no longer sufficient.

In pushing for a focus on theory-related (applying, testing, proposing, extending) papers in the top journals, we also suggest that while theory-based papers must be able to address conceptual concerns in the IB disciplines (international management, international strategy, etc.), they will be stronger if they also have something to say about theory development in their primary disciplines. As discussed above, opportunities to propose boundary or moderating conditions for the relevance or application of the primary theory(ies) are common, but frequently overlooked, in IB/IM studies. As the top journals in the international business and management area are constantly concerned with becoming and remaining part of the larger business management conversation, explicit consideration of the potential impact of their published research on the underlying disciplines is very attractive. While the impact of cultural difference on the choice between contractual and equity alliances for market entry may be publishable, a study that considers cultural distance as a way of measuring uncertainty and bounded rationality for corporate decision makers, who then choose entry modes as much for behavioral as for rational economic reasons, is even more likely to attract interest among the top journals. Essentially, the higher ranking (or aiming) the journal, the more an explicit effort of theory building in both international and primary disciplines will help in justifying a supportive editing and review process.

As at the start of this chapter, we want to emphasize how much top IB/IM journals are like any top field journals in business and management. They look toward the theoretical impact of articles, whether to explicate the mechanisms of phenomena in their field, to test existing theory, to extend this theory, or to build new theory. The main difference is that they are interested in both disciplinary and internationally focused theory, and especially the intersection of the two. The international context offers excellent opportunity to build understanding of the boundaries and limits of business and management theory, and taking advantage of these opportunities is the focus of the top journals. In the end, though, the first and most fundamental characteristic of IB/IM research at all internationally oriented journals is that it is international in its intellectual scope, not just in its data or its setting, but in its conceptual development.

REFERENCES

Chang, S.-J., A. van Witteloostuijn, and L. Eden (2010). 'From the editors: Common method variance in international business research', *Journal of International Business Studies*, **41**, 178–184.

Tallman, S. and T. Pedersen (2011). 'The launch of *Global Strategy Journal*: Comments from the co-editors', *Global Strategy Journal*, **1** (1–2), 1–5.

32. Publishing at the interfaces of psychology and strategic management

Gerard P. Hodgkinson

INTRODUCTION

Every leading journal has a clear mission and attendant set of foci. Manuscripts falling across the desks of busy editors and reviewers are evaluated first and foremost in terms of the extent to which they fall within the thematic purview of the target journal. The craft of addressing messages to appropriately targeted audiences is thus an essential skill cultivated by all successful academic writers. Drawing on a range of examples, in this short chapter I offer my personal reflections on how in practice I have implemented this advice in positioning my own work and, in so doing, anticipated the likely reactions of potentially critical reviewers.

In a highly insightful book, Huff (1999) introduced the metaphor of 'conversation' as a means of analysing the all-important question of how to position scholarly journal articles for particular audiences. It is a metaphor that I have found to be rather helpful when reflecting on the relative successes and failures of my own work. Over the course of an academic career now entering its fourth decade, for the past thirty years the bulk of my scholarly research activity has centred on three major inter-related themes:

1. The construction and psychometric evaluation of instruments for the assessment of work-related individual differences (e.g. Gill and Hodgkinson, 1992, 1993, 2007; Hodgkinson and Sadler-Smith, 2003; Hodgkinson, Sadler-Smith, Sinclair and Ashkanasy, 2009);

2.   Cognition in the workplace (e.g. Healey, Vuori and Hodgkinson, 2015; Hodgkinson and Healey, 2008a), encompassing the psychological analysis of strategic management processes (e.g. Hodgkinson, 1997a, 1997b; Hodgkinson and Johnson, 1994) and the development and evaluation of tools and wider practices for intervening in such processes (e.g. Hodgkinson et al., 1999, 2002; Hodgkinson, Maule and Bown, 2004; Hodgkinson and Healey, 2008b; Healey, Hodgkinson, Whittington and Johnson, 2015);

3.   The significance of scholarly management and organizational research for academia and wider publics (e.g. Anderson, Herriot and Hodgkinson, 2001; Hodgkinson, Herriot and Anderson, 2001; Hodgkinson, 2006; Hodgkinson and Rousseau, 2009; Hodgkinson and Starkey, 2011; Romme et al., 2015).

Given the diversity of my interests, not surprisingly, my work has appeared in a wide array of scholarly outlets, spanning both general and subject specific journals, both in the management and organization sciences, and the wider social and behavioural sciences. Without exception, the journals in which my work has appeared have been chosen because the messages I wanted to convey had the potential either to: (1) start a conversation of likely significance among a recognized community of scholars within the relevant focal body of literature whose work I was looking to influence in some way; or (2) contribute in significant ways to an ongoing conversation among a recognized community of scholars, again with a view to influencing the future direction of their work and hence the focal body of literature at hand.

Adopting Huff's (1999) conversation metaphor, in order to initiate successfully a fresh conversation, or to contribute meaningfully to an ongoing one, it is essential that writers first clarify with whom (i.e. the audience) and on what subject matter (i.e. the content) they wish to converse. The breadth of the target audience and the content of the conversation will, of course, each vary enormously, from one context to another. In this chapter, therefore, I compare and contrast several of the strategies I have adopted variously across a range of disciplinary and interdisciplinary contexts, demonstrating how in each case the respective process adopted resulted in one or more 'successful' publications; that is, publications that were acceptable to editors and/or reviewers and that have attracted subsequently the attention of scholars within the focal body of literature thus targeted, and in some cases extending well beyond it.

The chapter is structured in five sections. Following this introduction, the second, third, and fourth sections offer my reflections on each of three strategies I have adopted over the years in relation to the framing of my work depending on the nature of the target audience and content. The final section offers my reflections more generally on the significance of these strategies as a means of ensuring a more suitably focused and coherent contribution to the body of literature thus targeted.

FOSTERING CONVERSATIONS WITH MORE SPECIALIST AUDIENCES AND RESTRICTIVE CONTENT

This strategy is perhaps best illustrated by the work I have published that falls within my first stream of work. The audiences to whom I have addressed my various articles on the development and validation of instruments for the assessment of personality and related individual differences (e.g. Gill and Hodgkinson, 2007; Hodgkinson, 1992, 1993; Hodgkinson and Sadler-Smith, 2003; Hodgkinson, Sadler-Smith, Sinclair and Ashkanasy, 2009) have been relatively narrow, in comparison with the more generalist audiences I have targeted either directly or indirectly within the second and third streams of my work. Furthermore, the articles I have published within this first stream have set out to achieve relatively modest scientific objectives. These pieces, which reported the application of well-established concepts and statistical procedures pertaining to psychometric theory, with a view to ascertaining the reliability and validity of the instruments concerned, were aimed primarily, although by no means exclusively, at a group of researchers with a focus on applied psychological measurement.

Given this comparatively restrictive focus, each of these papers was framed at a level of granularity that would appeal to researchers and practitioners looking to use instruments for the purposes of assessing work-related individual differences. Illustrating this more general approach, consider the paper reporting the 'Development and validation of the five-factor model questionnaire (FFMQ)' (Gill and Hodgkinson, 2007). In this article, the primary focus was on establishing to a predominantly technical audience why (yet another) personality assessment instrument for the assessment of the 'big-five' personality traits (i.e. neuroticism, extraversion, agreeableness, openness and conscientiousness) in the workplace was required at this critical juncture. The article then set about reporting the development and validation of the new instrument in question, which entailed a total of five methodological studies.

The front-end framing of this paper first establishes the ubiquity of the big-five and the related five-factor model of personality underpinning this particular collection of traits. The introductory section then problematizes the wide range of extant big-five instruments, noting that they have been devised primarily for general usage or more particularly clinical usage, as opposed to being work-related assessment tools. It then highlights the fact that the bulk of instruments presently available are targeted predominantly at well-educated, North American respondents. One further issue of note raised that an important motivation for the work reported in this paper is the fact that the individual questions used to assess the big-five are typically composed of statement-based items, whereas simpler, adjectival-based items, of the sort adopted in the FFMQ, are often more desirable.

The fact that this paper was published in *Personnel Psychology*, one of the world's leading technical journals devoted to personnel selection and assessment issues, illustrates how through such careful conversational targeting it is possible to 'sell' the importance of establishing the psychometric efficacy of an instrument devised primarily for use outside the US context to an audience composed largely, although by no means exclusively, of US readers: 'The development process for the FFMQ had the clear objective of producing a valid and reliable set of adjective-based measures of the Big Five for use in work-related settings. The resulting instrument is simple to administer, rapidly completed, and easily interpreted' (Gill and Hodgkinson, 2007, p. 736). Highlighting the limitations of the dominant US instruments and demonstrating the broader applicability of the newly constructed alternative resulted in a publication in one of the world's leading (US-based) field journals. Although this article went through several rounds of revisions, the overall journey from initial submission to final acceptance was a relatively smooth one. I believe the high degree of careful framing and preparatory work in designing and then reporting the constituent studies, so as to ensure that they contributed cumulatively, in a logical and coherent fashion to the overall goal of the paper, as encapsulated in the above quotation, was the most crucial factor that led to this relatively pain-free and successful outcome.

FOSTERING CONVERSATIONS WITH BROADER AUDIENCES AND LESS RESTRICTIVE CONTENT

The relatively narrower approach to framing the various personality and individual differences pieces outlined in the previous section stands in marked contrast to the approaches I have adopted in the framing of the various articles I have published under my second stream of work, falling under the broader theme of cognition in the workplace. Several of the latter pieces have targeted much broader/less restrictive content at wider audiences. Illustrating this alternative approach more generally, two of my relatively recent pieces – 'Intuition: A fundamental bridging concept in the behavioural sciences' (Hodgkinson, Langan-Fox and Sadler-Smith, 2008) and 'Cognition in organizations' (Hodgkinson and Healey, 2008a) – were targeted very broadly, with the intention in each case of initiating a series of conversations that would cut across specialist subfields, with a view to fostering more highly innovative theory and research.

The Hodgkinson, Langan-Fox and Sadler-Smith (2008) article was intended to provoke scholars working within the various specialist areas of academic psychology (e.g. cognitive psychology, social cognitive neuroscience, personality psychology) and its main applied areas (e.g. educational psychology, occupational/industrial–organizational psychology) to recognize the many parallel and complementary developments occurring across their respective scholarly domains that pointed toward the possibility that intuition (and more precisely dual-processing accounts of cognitive processes) might serve as a scientific foundation for greater cooperation across the psychology field as a whole. The *British Journal of Psychology*, which publishes research on all aspects of the discipline, was thus a natural home for this piece, in which we evaluated critically work published in selected mainstream journals in the various subfields and domains of application encompassed by our review.

The Hodgkinson (2008a) *Annual Review of Psychology* article was predicated on a similar logic of seeking to initiate a series of conversations among scholars who would not otherwise typically engage with one another. In this case, however, the focus was centred more narrowly on the subfield of occupational and organizational/industrial psychology. Intentionally wider-ranging in its reach, this article commences by outlining the history of theory and research on cognition in organizations, from its inception in World War II up to the early 2000s, and then offers an integrative review across ten major areas of industrial–organizational psychology, with a view to identifying points of convergence and divergence in theory advancement, empirical endeavour, and the development of new methods. The article seeks to deepen a conversation between scholarly researchers falling variously in the 'human factors tradition' and the 'organizations tradition' and highlights opportunities for greater collaboration across those traditions. In so doing, it advances a cross-cutting agenda across the ten substantive domain areas surveyed, covering the period 2000–2007.

Although highly ambitious and wide-ranging in scope, again I believe the key factor that led to the acceptance of these particular pieces was the careful groundwork undertaken beforehand, thus ensuring that in each case the constituent subfields/topic areas addressed were covered in just sufficient depth to enable my co-authors and I to lay suitable foundations for subsequent engagement on the part of the scholarly communities thus targeted, avoiding the twin pitfalls of superficiality and unnecessary detail. Relative to my other publications, these two particular pieces have amassed high citation counts over a short space of time, and they have done so across a wide range of disciplinary subfields and topic areas, suggesting that our fundamental goal of seeking to attain significant cross-disciplinary and cross-topic reach across our targeted areas has at least succeed in part. It is still too early, however, to discern whether the cross-fertilization of ideas, through interdisciplinary and cross-functional team working, has occurred on the scale we were ultimately hoping to achieve.

FOSTERING BROADER CONVERSATIONS WITH MORE SPECIALIST AUDIENCES

This third framing strategy is perhaps best illustrated with a couple of papers I have published that fall respectively within the second and third of my research streams. The first example, 'The practitioner–researcher divide in industrial, work and organizational (IWO) psychology: Where are we now and where do we go from here?' appeared in a special issue of the *Journal of Occupational and Organizational Psychology* that celebrated 100 years of the field's achievements at the turn of the 21st century (Anderson et al., 2001). Unlike the other contributors to this particular volume – whose papers offered state-of-the-art reviews of the literature pertaining to some of the field's central topics such as personnel selection and assessment (Robertson and Smith, 2001), performance appraisal and management (Fletcher, 2001), and well-being and occupational health (Sparks, Faragher and Cooper, 2001) – our own paper was intentionally framed more broadly, in an attempt to stimulate a wider-ranging conversation across the IWO psychology community as a whole regarding what we argued was a growing divide between research and practice, with a view to encouraging a re-strengthening of the scientist–practitioner model, arguably the bedrock of the field (Anderson, Herriot and Hodgkinson, 2001). Deliberately provocative, our goal was to engender feelings of discomfort among our readers, with a view countering what we saw as some unfortunate consequences of the effort–reward mechanisms in play among the academic and practitioner wings of the profession. Contrasting research that is highly rigorous but largely irrelevant to practice (Pedantic Science) with research that is seemingly highly relevant but of poor scientific quality (Popularist Science), and research that is both irrelevant to practice and of poor scientific quality (Puerile Science), we argued that researchers should be encouraged to advance the cause of research that sought to achieve the highest possible standards of scientific excellence, but with a focus on the more difficult and enduring problems of concern to the practitioner wing of the profession (Pragmatic Science). Needless to say, our thesis, as intended, stimulated a rich and highly diverse debate that rapidly spilled over into many other fields and subfields, well beyond the confines of the specialist IWO psychology audience to which it was initially directed!

Once again, I believe it was the judgement calls we made in respect of the front-end framing of this particular piece for the constituent audience of the target journal that led to its ultimate success. In this particular case, the call for papers accompanying the special issue reflecting on a century's achievements provided us with a suitable platform on which we were able to build on a series of conversations which we had held informally with journal editors, and fellow researchers and practitioners, through attendance at the main professional and academic conferences over many years. I believe that the enduring success of this article is in no small part due to the fact the basic framework and embryonic concepts we articulated captured the growing sense throughout the IWO psychology community that all was not well among its academic and practitioner wings, an analysis that seems to have resonated with several other branches of the psychology field and the wider social and behavioural sciences, evidenced by the breadth of citations it has attracted.

Further illustrating the efficacy of this third framing strategy of fostering broader conversations with more specialist audiences, I turn now to consider finally one of my relatively recent papers on the psychological foundations of strategic management (Hodgkinson and Healey, 2011). From the outset of my career, the bulk of my work on this topic (see, e.g. Hodgkinson, 1997a, 1997b; Hodgkinson and Johnson, 1994; Hodgkinson et al., 1999), like much of the behavioural strategy literature in general, has centred on the analysis of cognitive processes in strategy formulation and implementation (for a recent overview, see Powell, Lovallo and Fox, 2011). Drawing on the insights of state-of-the-art-advances that have taken place in the affective sciences over the past two decades, our goal in the Hodgkinson and Healey (2011) paper, which appeared in a special issue of *Strategic Management Journal* devoted to the 'Psychological foundations of strategic management' (Fox, Lovallo and Powell, 2011), was to move along the conversation on cognition and strategy away from an affect-free conception of strategists as cognitive misers (and sensemakers), toward a 'hot' cognition alternative, one that recognizes that strategists are ultimately, 'governed by thoughts and feelings: always boundedly rational, but manifestly driven by emotion' (Hodgkinson and Healey, 2011, p. 1512). Using the much-cited dynamic capabilities paper of Teece (2007) as an overarching framework, our analysis demonstrated systematically how each of the psychological foundations underpinning Teece's (2007) framework are predicated on psychological conceptions that are outmoded when viewed in the light of more recent advances in social cognitive neuroscience (e.g. Lieberman, 2007) and neuroeconomics (e.g. Loewenstein, Rick and Cohen, 2008), in turn rendering his prescriptions for fostering dynamic capabilities (through increased efforts to engage in systematic and disciplined reasoning and analysis) highly problematic. Our analysis highlights instead the central role of meta-cognitive awareness and emotion regulation as essential psychological foundations of strategic adaptation. Once more, in framing this particular paper, the occasion of a special issue provided a useful enabling context to raise questions that ran against the grain of the mainstream alternatives dominating the literature, in ways that have begun to move the conversation on the role of cognition in strategy formulation and implementation in new and highly innovative directions: the primary goal of the special issue guest editors.

CONCLUDING REMARKS

Over the course of an academic career now entering its fourth decade, I have been privileged to work with some of the world's brightest and most distinguished scholars in the business and management research community. Their generous friendship and mentoring has nurtured my ability and given me the confidence to submit and ultimately publish my work in some of the best North American (e.g. Gill and Hodgkinson, 2007; Healey, Vuori and Hodgkinson, 2015; Hodgkinson et al., 1999; Hodgkinson and Healey, 2008a, 2011) and European (e.g. Hodgkinson, 1997a, 1997b; Hodgkinson and Healey, 2008b; Hodgkinson and Johnson, 1994) journals and other distinguished outlets (e.g. Hodgkinson and Starbuck, 2008). In this chapter I have offered my reflections, albeit all too briefly, on the important question of how, as an interdisciplinary researcher situated primarily at the interfaces of psychology and strategic management, I have positioned variously my journal articles to particular audiences.

Returning to Huff's (1999) conversation metaphor, I have identified three distinctive types of audience–content combination across a range of disciplinary and interdisciplinary contexts, demonstrating how in each case the essential messages were anchored to current debates in the focal literature I was seeking to influence. My paper reporting the development and validation of the FFMQ (Gill and Hodgkinson, 2007), for instance, was positioned within a growing stream of literature that has debated how to enhance the validity of big-five assessment practices in the workplace (see e.g., Salgado, 2003). Similarly, my more recent piece arguing the case for re-theorizing strategic adaptation as a 'hot' cognitive process (Hodgkinson and Healey, 2011) used Teece's (2007) well-known dynamic capabilities framework as the entry point and key foundation for organizing the contribution as a whole, thus ensuring that our arguments would appeal to a wide-ranging audience of strategy scholars.

Arguably, the single most valuable lesson I have learned, both as an editor and a writer in my own right, is that almost invariably, the authors of successful journal articles render abundantly clear their intended contribution within the first three–four sentences. Known as the 'hook', it is these early passages that explain the significance of an article to its intended audience, thus addressing the 'so what?' question at the outset.

Irrespective of the (inter-)disciplinary field or subject matter, the abstract/summary and opening paragraphs of the main body of text and concluding discussion sections of any academic paper are arguably its three most important elements. Confronted by a myriad of manuscripts to consider for potential publication, when new submissions arrive electronically in their in-boxes or land physically on their desks, hard-pressed editors-in-chief and their teams of action editors and reviewers typically first scan the abstract and then read the first few sentences of the main body of text to gain an overall sense of what the author(s) are claiming to have contributed to the literature pertaining to the focal topic at hand. Next, they typically move to the concluding discussion and similarly read the first few sentences, to ascertain the extent to which the promise of the manuscript's opening claims are revisited systematically as the author(s) bring(s) their contribution to a close. In an empirical contribution, they then typically jump finally to skim read the methods and results sections to ascertain the extent to which the research design and results are appropriate for the conclusions thus presented.

The actions I have just described in the preceding paragraph constitute the essential features of what is commonly known in scholarly editorial circles as 'the coherence test'. A manuscript is coherent to the extent that the fundamental contribution stated at the outset is supported, consistently, throughout. All seasoned editors and reviewers adopt this test as standard practice. Any manuscript failing the coherence test, which takes only a matter of minutes to complete, is in serious trouble. The majority of such manuscripts are desk rejected routinely by the world's leading journals. If, however, an editor or action editor in receipt of such a manuscript decides to err on the side of generosity, the odds of it surviving the next stage, the first-round double-blind peer review process are, at best, extremely low.

The three strategies I have enumerated in the previous sections of this chapter illustrate some of the ways in which I have striven to ensure that my own work passes this essential test. Devising a hook that is compelling for the target audience and ensuring it is used intelligently to anchor the remainder of the manuscript content is, I believe, the essence of my success, both in stimulating new conversations and contributing to ongoing ones. Although taking the time and trouble to reflect on how best to align the content of an article with the needs of its target audience may seem like a rather obvious piece of advice, surprisingly, based on my many years of experience as a journal editor and reviewer, it is a piece of advice that all too often I have found even the most seasoned of authors neglect to their cost.

REFERENCES

Anderson, N., P. Herriot and G.P. Hodgkinson (2001). 'The practitioner–researcher divide in industrial, work and organizational (IWO) psychology: Where are we now and where do we go from here?', *Journal of Occupational and Organizational Psychology*, **74**, 391–411.

Fletcher, C. (2001). 'Performance appraisal and management: The developing research agenda', *Journal of Occupational and Organizational Psychology*, **74**, 473–487.

Fox, C.R., D. Lovallo and T.C. Powell (2011). 'Psychological foundations of strategic management', *Strategic Management Journal*, **32** (Special Issue), 1369–1523.

Gill, C. and G.P. Hodgkinson (2007). 'Development and validation of the five-factor model questionnaire (FFMQ): An adjectival-based personality inventory for use in occupational settings', *Personnel Psychology*, **60**, 731–766.

Healey, M.P., G.P. Hodgkinson, R. Whittington and G. Johnson (2015). 'Off to plan or out to lunch? Relationships between strategy workshop design characteristics and outcomes', *British Journal of Management*, **26**, 507–528.

Healey, M.P., T. Vuori and G.P. Hodgkinson (2015). 'When teams agree while disagreeing: Reflexion and reflection in shared cognition', *Academy of Management Review*, **40**, 399–422.

Hodgkinson, G.P. (1992). 'Development and validation of the Strategic Locus of Control Scale', *Strategic Management Journal*, **13**, 311–317.

Hodgkinson, G.P. (1993). 'Doubts about the conceptual and empirical Status of context-free and firm-specific control expectancies: A reply to Boone and De Brabander', *Strategic Management Journal*, **14**, 627–631.

Hodgkinson, G.P. (1997a). 'The cognitive analysis of competitive structures: A review and critique', *Human Relations*, **50**, 625–654.

Hodgkinson, G.P. (1997b). 'Cognitive inertia in a turbulent market: The case of UK residential estate agents', *Journal of Management Studies*, **34**, 921–945.

Hodgkinson, G.P. (2006). 'The role of JOOP (and other scientific journals) in bridging the practitioner–researcher divide in industrial, work and organizational (IWO) psychology', *Journal of Occupational and Organizational Psychology*, **79**, 173–178.

Hodgkinson, G.P., N.J. Bown, A.J. Maule, K.W. Glaister and A.D. Pearman (1999). 'Breaking the frame: An analysis of strategic cognition and decision making under uncertainty', *Strategic Management Journal*, **20**, 977–985.

Hodgkinson, G.P. and M.P. Healey (2008a). 'Cognition in organizations', *Annual Review of Psychology*, **59**, 387–417.

Hodgkinson, G.P. and M.P. Healey (2008b). 'Toward a (pragmatic) science of strategic intervention: Design propositions for scenario planning', *Organization Studies*, **29**, 435–457.

Hodgkinson, G.P. and M.P. Healey (2011). 'Psychological foundations of dynamic capabilities: Reflexion and reflection in strategic management', *Strategic Management Journal*, **32**, 1500–1516.

Hodgkinson, G.P., P. Herriot and N. Anderson (2001). 'Re-aligning the stakeholders in management research: Lessons from industrial, work and organizational psychology', *British Journal of Management*, **12** (Special Issue), S41–S48.

Hodgkinson, G.P. and G. Johnson (1994). 'Exploring the mental models of competitive strategists: The case for a processual approach', *Journal of Management Studies*, **31**, 525–551.

Hodgkinson, G.P., J. Langan-Fox and E. Sadler-Smith (2008). 'Intuition: A fundamental bridging construct in the behavioural sciences', *British Journal of Psychology*, **99**, 1–27.

Hodgkinson, G.P., A.J. Maule and N.J. Bown (2004). 'Causal cognitive mapping in the organizational strategy field: A comparison of alternative elicitation procedures', *Organizational Research Methods*, **7**, 3–26.

Hodgkinson, G.P., A.J. Maule, N.J. Bown, A.D. Pearman and K.W. Glaister (2002). 'Further reflections on the elimination of framing bias in strategic decision making', *Strategic Management Journal*, **23**, 1069–1076.

Hodgkinson, G.P. and D.M. Rousseau (2009). 'Bridging the rigour–relevance gap in management research: It's already happening!', *Journal of Management Studies*, **46**, 534–546.

Hodgkinson, G.P. and E. Sadler-Smith (2003). 'Complex or unitary? A critique and empirical re-assessment of the Allinson-Hayes Cognitive Style Index', *Journal of Occupational and Organizational Psychology*, **76**, 243–268.

Hodgkinson, G.P., E. Sadler-Smith, M. Sinclair and N.M. Ashkanasy (2009). 'More than meets the eye? Intuition and analysis revisited', *Personality and Individual Differences*, **47**, 342–346.

Hodgkinson, G.P. and W.H. Starbuck (eds) (2008). *The Oxford Handbook of Organizational Decision Making*, Oxford: Oxford University Press.

Hodgkinson, G.P. and K. Starkey (2011). 'Not simply returning to the same answer over and over again: Reframing relevance', *British Journal of Management*, **22**, 355–369.

Huff, A.S. (1999). *Writing for Scholarly Publication*, Thousand Oaks, CA: Sage.

Lieberman, M.D. (2007). 'Social cognitive neuroscience: A review of core processes', *Annual Review of Psychology*, **58**, 259–289.

Loewenstein, G., S. Rick and J.D. Cohen (2008). 'Neuroeconomics', *Annual Review of Psychology*, **59**, 647–672.

Patterson, F. (2001). 'Developments in work psychology: Emerging issues and future trends', *Journal of Occupational and Organizational Psychology*, **74**, 381–390.

Powell, T.C., D. Lovallo and C.R. Fox (2011). 'Behavioral strategy', *Strategic Management Journal*, **32** (Special Issue), 1369–1386.

Robertson, I.T. and M. Smith (2001). 'Personnel selection', *Journal of Occupational and Organizational Psychology*, **74**, 441–472.

Romme, A.G.L., M.J. Avenier, D. Denyer, G.P. Hodgkinson, K. Pandza, K. Starkey and N. Worren (2015). 'Towards common ground and trading zones in management research and practice', *British Journal of Management*, **26**, 544–559.

Salgado, J.F. (2003). 'Predicting job performance using FFM and non-FFM personality measures', *Journal of Occupational and Organizational Psychology*, **76**, 323–346.

Sparks, K., B. Faragher and C.L. Cooper (2001). 'Well-being and occupational health in the 21st century workplace', *Journal of Occupational and Organizational Psychology*, **74**, 489–509.

Teece, D.J. (2007). 'Explicating dynamic capabilities: The nature and micro-foundations of (sustainable) enterprise performance', *Strategic Management Journal*, **28** (13), 1319–1350.

Index

family capitalism
  business and management 245
family firm contribution 182
family firm research paper
  conflict among family members 184
family firms, negatives 66
feedback from colleagues 123
feedback on journal ranking 173
fictitious names for authors 4
finance
  leading journals 211–12
  management and entrepreneurship
    217
  versus entrepreneurship/management
    journals publishing 211–36
financial leverage, peer review 100
Financial Times
  top 200 MBA programmes 59
Financial Times 45 major journals list
  173, 183, 239
firm-level data 271
firm performance (DV)
  entrepreneurs in an industry 132
five-factor model questionnaire 277–8
'flexibility' 14, 20
focused commitment 14
  approaches to business model
    development 11
  versus simultaneous experimentation
    21–22
footnotes in business history journals
  data sources indication 249
foreign trade, cross-border transactions
  266
Fortune 500, 140
Franklin, Benjamin
  'an ounce of prevention, worth a
    pound of cure' 136

gender and fraud topic, paper 214
general management journal 24, 182
German university professor,
  self-plagiarism 35
gift authorship 37–8
global business transactions 77
Global Economic Crisis 2008
  'Varieties of Asian Capitalism' 76
Global Strategy Journal (GSJ) 263

'good citizen' 219
good research 164
Google Scholar hits 189
Gottinger, Hans Werner
  misappropriation of work of others as
    his own 33
governance in multinational
    corporations 2011
  Point-CounterPoint Section (PCP) 57
governmental bodies
  for publications career 59
guest editing special issues 58

Harvard Business Review, top
    executives 168
Harvard Law Review 216
heterogeneous portfolio for sustained
    career 56
'high performance work systems'
    (HPWS) 257
  employee skills 259
  service sector 259
high-quality research 191
historical papers
  in management journals 245–50
'home bias', strong in finance 213–14
hospital executives, sample
  strategic planning processes 140
Human Relations 241
  academic journal 70
Human Resource Management (HRM)
  industrial relations 70
  research 253–60
  teaching in business schools 245, 254
hypotheses 164
  management journals 226
  management research 138
  stated or unstated 91
Hypothesizing After the Results are
    Known (1988)
  HARKing 36–7

IB/IM studies 263
IB *see* International Business
identification of problems 114–15
illustration of sustaining publication
    output 51–3
IM *see* International Management